WHEN

GLOBALIZATION

FAILS

WHEN

GLOBALIZATION

FAILS

THE RISE AND FALL OF PAX AMERICANA

JAMES MACDONALD

FARRAR, STRAUS AND GIROUX   NEW YORK

Farrar, Straus and Giroux
18 West 18th Street, New York 10011

Printed in the United States of America
First edition, 2015

Library of Congress Cataloging-in-Publication Data
Macdonald, James, 1951–
    When globalization fails : the rise and fall of Pax Americana / James
Macdonald. — First edition.
        pages   cm
    Includes bibliographical references and index.
    ISBN 978-0-374-22963-4 (hardcover) — ISBN 978-0-374-71294-5 (ebook)
    1. International economic relations—History—20th century.   2. United
States—Foreign economic relations.   3. United States—Foreign relations.
4. Balance of power.   5. World politics.   I. Title.

HF1359 .M326 2015
337.73—dc23

                                                                    2014016963

Designed by Abby Kagan

Farrar, Straus and Giroux books may be purchased for educational, business, or promotional
use. For information on bulk purchases, please contact the Macmillan Corporate and
Premium Sales Department at 1-800-221-7945, extension 5442,
or write to specialmarkets@macmillan.com.

www.fsgbooks.com
www.twitter.com/fsgbooks • www.facebook.com/fsgbooks

1   3   5   7   9   10   8   6   4   2

For my family

CONTENTS

WHEN

GLOBALIZATION

FAILS

INTRODUCTION

How stable is the era of peace and prosperity that the world has enjoyed since 1945? Such a question may sound complacent given the more than ten million deaths that have occurred in localized conflicts over the past decades. But what has been avoided is the extraordinary carnage of the period from 1914 to 1945, when the Great Powers fought each other and the better part of one hundred million people lost their lives.[1] The question is all the more compelling because the outbreak of war in 1914 shattered a long period, like the postwar era, of extraordinary progress and rising prosperity. Moreover, it was precisely the most industrialized countries that went to war—raising the issue of whether something in the process of industrialization made them prone to self-destructive violence. If this is the case, a number of further questions need to be answered: Are the same underlying tensions that led to war a century ago still present? If so, what restraints held them in abeyance for the last seventy years? And are these restraints still as powerful as before, or are they threatened in any way?

This book attempts to answer these questions by looking at the history of war, peace, and trade over the past two centuries. In the mid-nineteenth century it seemed clear to progressive thinkers, as it does to many commentators today, that the way to perpetuate peace was through international trade. Free trade would not only foster economic growth, but the bonds of commerce would break down the barriers between nations and, by interconnecting their economies, would make war unlikely, if not impossible. Richard Cobden campaigned for a world in which free trade would be "drawing men together, thrusting aside the antagonism of race, and creed, and language, and uniting us in the bonds of eternal peace."[2] The philosopher John Stuart Mill was even more optimistic, declaring that the expansion of commerce was "rapidly rendering war obsolete."

On the surface it looks as if the connection between trade and peace held good in the nineteenth century. The period from 1815 to 1914 has been described as both the "long peace" and the "first era of globalization." International trade expanded at an unprecedented rate, with total imports and exports growing from 2 percent to 17 percent of world GDP over the course of the century.[3] And yet the rising tide of commerce could not prevent the outbreak of Great Power conflict. In 1914, Germany went to war with Britain and Russia in spite of the fact that they were its leading trade partners. What happened to the ideas and hopes of the free-trade liberals?

As the nineteenth century progressed, the connection became clouded. Countries started to turn away from free trade, and tariff barriers, which had fallen progressively in the middle of the century, started to rise. There were two reasons for this change. The first was a rival economic doctrine that argued that free trade merely cemented the advantages of the most highly industrialized countries at the expense of their competitors. A more insidious development grew out of a concern that is one of the central themes of this book: the anxiety that industrialization makes countries vulnerable even as it makes them wealthy. Before the Industrial Revolution, countries had been largely self-sufficient; now they depended on imports of raw materials and on export markets for their manufactured goods.

In the later nineteenth century, the common response to dependence on trade was to attempt to reestablish self-sufficiency by creating colonial empires that would provide the materials and markets that were lacking at home. The process of decolonization that had characterized the beginning of the century went into reverse, and the Great Powers scrambled to take over those parts of the world that still appeared to be up for grabs. Empires were of little use without navies to protect the sea trade that connected them, and the Great Powers, some of which had hitherto possessed minuscule maritime forces, now rushed to build the most modern fleets in an arms race that quadrupled the size of their navies in the twenty-five years before 1914. Yet rising military spending increased rather than diminished their sense of insecurity.

Was there any way to mitigate these tensions? After the First World War, people looked back at the prosperity of the nineteenth century and talked of Pax Britannica—the time when Britain ruled the waves and presided over the peaceful growth of the international economy. However, Pax Britannica, insofar as it ever existed, had become threadbare by the end of the century. British industrial supremacy was a thing of the past. The Royal Navy may still have been the largest naval force in the world, but Britain had no power to limit the growth of dangerous military rivals or to keep the peace. Moreover, in the eyes of Britain's rivals, the Royal Navy appeared a threat, not a comfort. In a multipolar world only cooperation could alleviate international friction. The Great Powers sometimes convened conferences to mediate international tensions, but these meetings could occur, not to mention succeed, only if countries agreed to participate—and in July 1914 they did not.

When war came, it broke out not over some distant colony but over an obscure landlocked part of the Balkans with no known raw materials worth fighting for. However, the devastating impact of the assassination in Sarajevo was possible only in a context where the Great Powers lived with a combination of fears and ambitions that led them to risk a global war.

The First World War fulfilled the worst fears of those who had worried about the unintended consequences of industrialization. It was not just that the enormous productive powers generated by the Industrial Revolution now unleashed warfare of a hitherto unimagined destructiveness. It was also that the combatants set about exploiting their rivals' growing dependence on imports by attempting to starve them into submission through naval blockades. The war came to a close amid rioting soldiers and civilians demanding "peace and bread."

After the war, there was an attempt to put the genie back in the bottle. But the peace settlement was a near-complete failure. The insecurities of trade dependence were supposed to be relieved by a reaffirmation of unfettered international commerce and by the creation of a supranational body, the League of Nations, to act as global police force. But in practice, trade was less free than before the war; and the league proved an ineffective peacekeeper, not least because the United States, by now the most powerful country on earth, refused to take part.

Moreover, very little was done to resolve the issue of colonial rivalries—except that the losers lost their empires, leaving the winners in complete possession of the field. The result was that the world now appeared more than ever to be divided into those countries that controlled the resources necessary for survival and those that did not. When the tentative steps toward the restoration of world trade in the 1920s turned into outright protectionism in the 1930s in the wake of the Depression, it was scarcely surprising that "have-not" countries started to demand a redistribution of the world's resources so that they too could become self-sufficient. Before 1914, the underlying tensions between free trade and economic security had bubbled below the surface of an era where trade was still largely free. By the 1930s, the debate about control of raw materials was naked and vociferous.

The result was a dramatic turnaround: The ideas of the nineteenth-century liberals were increasingly turned on their head. Trade and economic interdependence were now seen by many as leading only to conflict. Economic self-sufficiency was claimed to be the path to peace. This idea was put forward not only by Germany and Japan as justification for their territorial claims and ambitions, it also found surprising converts among liberals themselves, most notably John Maynard Keynes.

But in the end, the drive for autarky led not to peace but to war. When the overlay of racial barbarity is removed from the Second World War, what remains is a struggle for resources—especially the oil fields of Russia and the Dutch East Indies upon which Germany and Japan's dreams of self-sufficient empires hinged. As before, each side tried to exploit the vulnerabilities of the other by economic strangulation. This time air power extended the reach of navies and made the economic war more lethal than ever.

In 1945, there was a second chance to clear away the web of economic ambitions and fears that had led to so much devastation. This time, fortunately, the United States had rethought its position. Before 1914, America had taken the benefits of the first era of globalization for granted while maintaining the highest trade barriers of any state. After the war, the country retreated into isolationism and increased its tariffs in spite of its emergence as the most powerful economy in the world. However, the awful history of the period from 1918 to 1945 persuaded the country's leaders that it could not afford to do so again. They now understood that the multipolar world of the first era of globalization was inherently unstable. The enjoyment of free access to raw materials and markets had proved illusory. The inexorable growth of Great Power rivalry threatened it, and finally destroyed it. The only way to ensure a world free from the perils of economic nationalism was to reintroduce the free trade that had been promised, but never delivered, in 1919, and for America to take a leading role in policing the world.

The main architect of the new American foreign policy was Cordell Hull, Roosevelt's secretary of state. He took the classic liberal view that international trade not only promoted peace but was its sine qua non. "Without expansion of international trade," he argued, "there can be no stability and security either within or among nations."[4] In June 1941, the United States and Britain published the Atlantic Charter as a vision for a postwar world. The fourth of its nine provisions directly addressed the economic insecurities that had propelled Germany and Japan toward war. The allied countries now committed themselves "to further the enjoyment of all States, great or small, victor or vanquished, of access, on equal terms, to the trade and raw materials which are needed for their economic prosperity."

The result was a second shot at establishing world peace. The Bretton Woods Agreement was designed to prevent currency wars by tying countries to fixed exchange rates. The General Agreement on Tariffs and Trade (GATT) was designed to lower trade barriers. Underlying the economic settlement was the new world police force: the United Nations, and in particular its Security Council—the peacetime continuation of the wartime alliance against Germany and Japan, with the United States as its leading member.

Whether this new regulator of global order would prove any more effective than its predecessors was never put to the test. In practice, the Cold War prevented the Security Council from fulfilling its role because it was permanently gridlocked. However, the Cold War turned out to be a blessing in disguise. It forced the United States to assume the role of benign hegemon—one that would not use its power to deprive others of their right to prosper—and it forced other Western countries to accept American leadership. Instead of a UN-led peace, as originally intended, the world ended up with Pax Americana.

Like the Pax Britannica of the nineteenth century, this arrangement was entirely informal, but it was more solidly based because of America's unparalleled economic and military predominance, which far exceeded that enjoyed by Britain. Moreover, it was cemented by fear of the Soviet Union, whereas there was no such bogeyman in the late nineteenth century to mute the rivalries of the Great Powers.

Pax Americana would have been of little use if the tensions that had led to war in the first half of the century had been replaced by an equally destabilizing economic competition between the two rival superpowers. Fortunately, this was not the case. Although Soviet Russia was a serious threat militarily and ideologically, it did not pose a direct threat to Western economic security. Thanks to its vast endowment of natural resources and the instinctive communist preference for self-sufficiency, it did not participate in the international economy and therefore did not compete for raw materials and markets. To preserve the basis of postwar Western prosperity, it was necessary to keep the Soviet bloc contained and ensure that no more of the globe fell into what was, from an economic perspective, a black hole.

Yet the economic containment of the Soviet Union was made more difficult by the dissolution of the Western empires. During the war, the United States had been a strong advocate of decolonization—as was appropriate if imperial rivalries were seen as an underlying cause of world wars. In a world of true free trade, empires should not be needed. But communism complicated the issue, not just because of the risk of ex-colonies falling into the Soviet bloc but also because socialist doctrine portrayed the economic relationship between industrialized and nonindustrialized countries as one of unjust exploitation and advocated economic self-sufficiency and protectionism as an alternative economic model.

In practice, third-world economic nationalism turned out to be less of a threat to world prosperity than it had appeared at first sight, largely because the countries that possessed the most important resources (in particular, oil) were keen to keep up their incomes, whatever their political or economic philosophies might suggest. The only time that this new type of economic nationalism posed a serious threat for world peace and prosperity was when it coalesced with the Arab-Israeli conflict, leading to the oil embargoes of 1967 and 1973–1974. Yet, paradoxically, the oil crises of the 1970s led not to a retreat into economic isolationism but to an expansion of world trade, further cementing the postwar economic order.

Under the American umbrella, the noncommunist world flourished just as the creators of the postwar order hoped. It was no longer necessary for Germany and Japan to demand empires and navies in order to enjoy their place in the sun. The other ex-imperial countries of Europe found that they too could prosper without their colonial appendages.

The end of the Cold War and the discredit of Soviet and Mao-ist economic doctrines appeared to represent the triumph of the Western model. For a time, it seemed possible that the world might be policed as originally intended in 1945, by a United Na-tions freed from Cold War gridlock. Or, if that was too optimis-tic, then the informal Pax Americana, which had protected the noncommunist world, might now be extended to the whole planet. But it turned out to be more complex than that. The fall of communism brought major players into the global economy who owed no allegiance to the Western postwar order. China, whose total foreign trade represented less than 6 percent of its GDP in 1970, has turned itself into the world's largest exporter; its foreign trade now amounts to close to 50 percent of GDP. Economically, China has followed the recipe for rapid growth first set out by Japan and then copied by other Asian economies: export-led growth stimulated by high domestic savings and an undervalued exchange rate. Politically and militarily, however, it does not feel the same obligation to adhere to principles of the American-led postwar order. As a communist country, it was not just outside the umbrella but also militarily hostile to the United States. Moreover, China's sheer size means that, unlike the other Asian tigers, it is in a position to challenge American preemi-nence. Since the fall of the Soviet Union, Russia has also become more integrated into the world economy than at any time in the country's history. Its foreign trade has grown to over 40 percent of GDP from only 7.5 percent in 1970. But it does not accept Western rules of global governance. The growth of historically nonaligned India to Great Power status is likely to further com-plicate the global power balance.

The result is that, as in the late nineteenth century, we are now living in a world where the existing geopolitical order is being called into question by the rise of new powers. The question is: Can this process take place without a rerun of the tensions that led to end of the first era of globalization?

In the 1990s, Russia's relations with the West were by historical standards relatively amicable. But since the turn of the century, relations have progressively soured to the verge of outright hostility. Russia has started to use its veto power in the United Nations with almost the same fervor as the old Soviet Union, and has also shown itself willing to use all the means in its power to overturn what it sees as the avoidable and regrettable collapse of the Soviet empire at the end of the Cold War. In other words, Russia's view of the global order has become overtly revisionist.

By contrast, the official Chinese position is that its rise will never be anything but peaceful and that it is not a threat to the existing order. However, there are a number of reasons not to take such statements at face value. The first is that insofar as the existing world order is provided by Pax Americana, China's position is one of outright rejection. The second is the rapid rise of China's military budget to a point where it is second only to America's and vastly exceeds those of its neighbors. Moreover, the nature of this military buildup suggests that its main objective is to deny access to the western Pacific by the US Navy, which has controlled the area since the Second World War, providing vital sea-lane security to trade-dependent countries such as Japan that have hitherto accepted Pax Americana as an alternative to empire. This would be less dangerous if China did not view control of the seas as a method of getting control of raw materials at the expense of its neighbors. A dangerous struggle is under way in the Far East as China and other nations contest possession of tiny uninhabited islands so that they can enlarge the areas in which they can drill for oil and gas. Moreover, China's rejection of Pax Americana has the perverse effect of making it anxious about its own economic security, since its dependence on sea trade through the narrow Straits of Malacca makes it potentially vulnerable to blockade. In the meantime, other countries in the area are building up their own navies in response to what they see as a potential Chinese security threat. The Far East, in other words, shows dangerous signs of reverting to a pre-1914 mind-set.

On the other hand, it is argued, China and Russia are now closely integrated into the world economy. They can have no interest in damaging the system that forms the basis of their prosperity. According to this argument, globalization protects itself by interconnecting the economies of its participants so that they could not want to go to war. A good example of this line of thinking is Thomas L. Friedman's "Dell Theory of Conflict Prevention" put forward in his book *The World Is Flat*: "The Dell Theory stipulates: No two countries that are both part of a major global supply chain, like Dell's, will ever fight a war against each other as long as they are both part of the same global supply chain. Because people embedded in major global supply chains don't want to fight old-time wars anymore."[5] In other words, it is "the great extent and rapid increase of international trade [that is] the principal guarantee of the peace of the world." But that, of course, is what they said in the nineteenth century.

Friedman, like the nineteenth-century liberals, views militarism and violence as atavistic throwbacks. This book makes an argument that is in many ways more disturbing: In a multipolar world, militarism grows out of globalization itself. The Industrial Revolution created a new source of tension among countries. Rising wealth was accompanied by a growing dependence on trade, and with it a growing sense of strategic vulnerability. The hope of the liberals was that economic interdependence would remove incentives for fighting while making war so costly that no rational government would willingly risk one. It turned out that this hope was in vain. Economic interdependence in a multipolar world led not to disarmament but to an arms race, with war as the almost inevitable outcome.

The answer, it seemed to many people, was to restore the economic self-sufficiency that industrialization had eroded. But the search for self-sufficiency was not a solution because economic independence could not be achieved for more than a tiny minority of countries given the global distribution of raw materials. Economic security for one country could come only at the expense of others. The result was as dangerous for peace as economic interdependence.

The only solution was a return to global free trade, but this time backed up by a police force with sufficient power that the insecurities of wealth could be forgotten. An attempt was made to create exactly this combination after the First World War, but it fell at the first hurdle. After the Second World War, a second attempt was made. This time it succeeded, but not in the way that was anticipated. It was always assumed that the role of global police should be performed by a multinational body. Nobody planned that the role should be taken over by a single country. And yet, for a while at least, the paradox of wealth was solved by the dominance of the United States.

The issue remains whether there is any solution for the insecurity that comes with economic interdependence other than benign hegemony. The hope that an intergovernmental body uniting all nations could police the world and prevent wars holds little promise. Countries are not willing to surrender to an international body the kind of power that is needed to enforce the peace; and the most powerful among them have always insisted on maintaining a veto on its decisions. This book uses the history of the twentieth century to argue that our return to a multipolar world is fraught with danger. If the world's great and rising powers are going to avoid conflict, it will require a determined effort to avoid the pitfalls of history.

1

THE FIRST ERA OF GLOBALIZATION

It is commerce which is rapidly rendering war obsolete . . . [and] it may be said without exaggeration that the great extent and rapid increase of international trade, in being the principal guarantee of the peace of the world, is the great permanent security for the uninterrupted progress of the ideas, the institutions, and the character of the human race.

—JOHN STUART MILL,
Principles of Political Economy, 1848

THE ERA OF PEACE AND FREE TRADE

It all seemed so simple around the middle of the nineteenth century. The world that Mill described seemed to be coming into existence. After more than a century of nonstop fighting, armed conflict had been replaced by trade. There had been no European wars since the final defeat of Napoleon in 1815.

From one point of view, the postwar peace was due to the Congress of Vienna. The victories of Napoleon's armies had been the result of a combination of revolutionary nationalism and traditional dynastic imperialism. The peacemakers in Vienna had sought to put both genies back in the bottle. The restoration of legitimate (prerevolutionary) regimes was to put an end to popular revolutions. The reestablishment of a stable balance of power was to ensure that no country could again seek to dominate the others. The Great Powers, acting in concert, would forestall any further threats to the peace of the continent.

But liberals such as Mill sought the underpinnings of peace elsewhere. It was not democratic nationalism that led to warfare. Once the peoples of Europe were freed from the rule of alien autocracies and allowed to control their own fates, harmony would reign among them, or so it was claimed. As for the balance of power, it was derided by the English radical John Bright as no more than "a gigantic system of outdoor relief for the aristocracy of Great Britain,"[1] whose members could indulge their preference for military office rather than productive work by pretending that they were maintaining the peace.

Moreover, liberals questioned the very idea that wars could be economically productive. How wrong it was to think that the mercantilist-driven struggle for empire had achieved, or could ever have achieved, its objectives. In 1824, the economist John Ramsay McCulloch declared such warfare to be economically futile: "The greater part of the wars of the last century . . . were waged for the purpose of preserving or acquiring some exclusive commercial advantage. But does any one suppose that these contests could have been carried on, at such infinite expence of blood and treasure, had the mass of the people known that their object was utterly unattainable?"[2]

What was truly needed to preserve peace was free trade. It was the development of commercial intercourse between nations that would prevent the recurrence of the wars that had blighted the previous two centuries. This message was affirmed in the strongest terms by its most vocal advocate, Richard Cobden.

Free Trade! What is it? Why, breaking down the barriers that separate nations; those barriers, behind which nestle the feelings of pride, revenge, hatred, and jealousy, which every now and then burst their bonds, and deluge whole countries with blood; those feelings which nourish the poison of war and conquest, which assert that without conquest we can have no trade, which foster that lust for conquest and dominion which sends forth your warrior chiefs to sanction devastation through other lands . . ."[3]

When Cobden spoke, the battle for free trade was in full swing. He was addressing a meeting in Covent Garden advocating the repeal of the Corn Laws, which had protected British agriculture from foreign imports since the end of the Napoleonic Wars. The debate between Britain's free traders and protectionists was waged with growing intensity over the following decades. A major first step was taken in 1820 when Parliament declared that future legislation should be framed with the advancement of free trade in mind. The outcome of the struggle was decided with the repeal of the Corn Laws in 1846, and three years later of the Navigation Acts, which had for centuries protected British shipping. The repeal of the Corn Laws, in particular, gave rise to a violent political battle that split the Conservative Party and led to the fall of the government. The immediate cause of the repeal was the Irish potato famine, which created a desperate need for cheap imported grain. However, there was a broader economic trend that led to the defeat of protectionism.

The Industrial Revolution led to mass migration from the country to the new manufacturing towns. Although industrialization was accompanied by an agricultural revolution that constantly increased food output, there was a growing shortfall between what the countryside could produce and the needs of the growing urban population. At the same time, the factories were turning out a quantity of manufactured goods that was greater than could be easily absorbed within the country and for which overseas markets were required. The solution to both these problems was free trade, which would open Britain to imports of cheap food, and foreign countries to exports of British manufactures. It is no surprise that the school of thought most closely connected with this belief was to be found in Manchester, the most dynamic of the new manufacturing centers. In many ways, the victory of free trade in 1846 can be characterized as a victory of the town over the country, of merchants and factory workers over landlords and farmers. It was also a victory for the liberal association of trade with peace. Napoleon had banned all trade with Britain during the wars. The Corn Laws had been enacted because the return of peace made possible the importation of cheap European wheat, threatening to put domestic farmers out of business and leaving the country dangerously dependent on foreign supplies in the event of another conflict. Free trade, by rendering war obsolete, would make such concerns redundant—or so it was hoped.

The following twenty years witnessed not only a rapid growth in trade but also the fastest increase of real wages of the entire nineteenth century, justifying the hopes of the Manchester liberals. The British conversion to the cause of free trade was mirrored elsewhere. Perhaps the most important moment was the signing in 1860 of the Cobden-Chevalier Treaty between Britain and France, appropriately named after two of free trade's most vocal advocates. In the wake of the treaty, which led to the doubling of trade between the long-term rivals, the Prussian ambassador was moved to remark that war between the two countries had now become "impossible."[4] Until the 1870s, the trend was for the reduction of tariffs and trade barriers throughout Europe. In 1855, a Belgian association for customs reform was set up, inspired by the example of Britain "where, since the introduction of Sir Robert Peel's reforms, agriculture, navigation and industry, far from declining, have flourished in force and energy in the most unexpected way."[5] In 1862, Germany* and France lowered duties on many goods by as much as 80 percent, and in the following years a number of intra-European trade treaties were set up with clauses

* Germany was not yet politically united, but it had created a customs union (*Zollverein*) as a first step toward union in 1834.

that guaranteed the signatories tariffs no higher than those prevailing with either country's "most-favored nation." This encouraged reciprocity and the ratcheting down of barriers throughout the continent.

The move toward free trade was one of several trends that favored the rapid advance of commerce in the nineteenth century. Among these was what can be described as the first era of decolonization. The footprint of the European empires had reached an apex in the mid-eighteenth century with the expansion of British and French claims to territory on top of the older Spanish and Portuguese dominions. By the 1820s, however, the vast majority of the Americas had been decolonized. The first to achieve independence were Britain's thirteen American colonies in 1783. Then, in 1803, the French territories in North America were sold to the United States by Napoleon. In 1801, the colony of Saint-Domingue, the jewel of the French empire in the Caribbean, rebelled and by 1804 had achieved independence as the republic of Haiti. Spain's mainland colonies were liberated in a series of wars between 1811 and 1825, although its Caribbean empire lingered until the end of the century. Brazil achieved de facto autonomy in 1808 and formal independence in 1822.

To the Manchester liberals, this was as it should be. In a world of peaceful free trade, empires were an unnecessary burden. Richard Cobden argued that "the desire and the motive for large and mighty empires; for gigantic armies and great navies . . . will die away; I believe that such things will cease to be necessary."[6]

Decolonization boosted international trade because the early European empires had operated as closed shops in which trade with the colonies was monopolized by the mother country. The dissolution of the Spanish and Portuguese empires led to the end of their restrictive trade controls, and while the newly independent countries of Latin America set up their own tariff barriers on imported goods, these were less of an impediment to trade than the restrictions they replaced. At the same time, the two Northern European empires were moving away from mercantilist controls and toward trade liberalization. The Dutch East India Company was dissolved in 1808. The English East India Company lost its monopoly of Indian trade in 1813. After 1822, British colonies were allowed to trade with each other as well as with the mother country, and in 1825 customs duties on non-British goods were lowered sharply. After the 1840s, tariffs were either small or nonexistent in most colonies, and the preferential rates that had favored trade with Britain disappeared.

As important as the reduction of barriers to trade was the reduction of transport costs. Road surfaces were progressively improved using the techniques pioneered by John McAdam in the late eighteenth century. These advances were accompanied by the creation of alternative and more cost-effective forms of land-based transport: canals and then railways. By the 1850s, 7,000 miles of railway track had been built in Britain alone; Germany was not far behind, with 5,000 miles. The rate of building in the United States, especially in the second half of the century, was astonishing, as befitted the vast expanses that had to be covered. The first transcontinental line was completed in 1869, and by 1890 America had 130,000 miles of railroad track, of which nearly half were in the West. The railway revolution was not by any means confined to the industrialized world. The British built tracks all over their empire and elsewhere, and by 1913 India had the fourth-largest network in the world.

Steam power also transformed sea trade. When oceangoing steamships were introduced in the 1830s, they were so expensive that they largely carried passengers and high-value goods, like present-day aircraft. However, by the end of the century they were carrying bulk commodities as well, and sail ships had all but disappeared. The cost reduction effected by steamships was cumulative rather than instant, but they have been calculated to have reduced shipping costs by 1.6 percent per year over the second half of the century. When canal-building techniques were applied to sea trade, the result was an immediate reduction in transit times, as with the opening of the Suez Canal in 1869.

The combined effect of these innovations was remarkable. The cost of transporting wheat from America to Britain fell by two-thirds from 1860 to 1910, while the cost of shipping coal from Britain to Italy fell by more than three-quarters. As a result, the prices of goods in different countries started to equalize, even those separated by vast continents and oceans. Between 1870 and 1913, the premium on American bacon in Britain fell from over 90 percent to a mere 18 percent.[7]

Moreover, after 1915, importers and exporters could operate in a world of stable monetary conditions. The French Revolution had set off a period of monetary instability throughout Europe, but after the war matters rapidly stabilized. In 1821, Britain restored the convertibility of sterling into gold at the prewar exchange rate, and thereafter sterling was the primary anchor of the international financial system. The French franc, which remained stable through a string of political upheavals, provided a secondary international currency, especially within Europe. The unifications of Italy and Germany simplified the monetary map of Europe by creating single currencies within their boundaries. In 1865, France, Italy, Belgium, and Switzerland formed the Latin Monetary Union, which unified their currencies and created interchangeable coins based on the franc. The monetary unification of the world was furthered by the spread of the gold standard, whereby currencies were fixed in relation to a single precious metal. Britain had been on a de facto gold standard since 1821. Other countries joined it from the 1870s onward. By the first decade of the twentieth century, not only were all European countries on the gold standard but also the United States, Canada, Mexico, Argentina, Australia, New Zealand, and Japan. In addition, the currencies of many other parts of the world were fixed to the major European centers through their empires. There was probably never a time in which global monetary arrangements were simpler than the late nineteenth century.

Spurred by these favorable tailwinds, the nineteenth century experienced an unprecedented growth in international trade. Between 1815 and 1914, the volume of European trade rose almost forty times, compared to only two or three times in the eighteenth century. In 1815, exports had amounted to around 3 percent of European GDP. By 1914, they represented 14 percent.

THE LIMITS OF PAX BRITANNICA AND PAX EUROPAEA

The nineteenth century has been described as the first era of globalization. Certainly, with its combination of rising international trade, falling communication costs, and freedom of exchange, the century would seem to fit this description. It has also been referred to as the era of Pax Britannica—when the world economy experienced an unprecedented economic expansion and military conflict was minimal compared to both the prior and the following centuries. But how much did this peaceful expansion owe to the fact that Britannia ruled the waves?

The position of Britain in the middle of the century was certainly remarkable. Victory in the Napoleonic Wars had left it with no global competitors. The remnants of the French colonial empire had disappeared through sale to the United States or annexation by Britain. The Spanish and Portuguese colonies in the Americas gained independence in the 1820s. The British Empire, by contrast, even without its thirteen American colonies, remained formidable. It still possessed extensive territories in the Americas as well as in the Indian subcontinent and Australasia. Although Britain showed little interest in further territorial expansion in the following decades, a series of judicious acquisitions of strategic bases such as Cape Town, Aden, Singapore, and Hong Kong helped to consolidate the empire's global footprint. The empire was protected by the Royal Navy, which by the end of the Napoleonic Wars disposed of forces equivalent to all other navies combined. Even though the navy was scaled back after the war, it remained in a dominant position for the rest of the century, and Britain was able to maintain a "two-power standard"— the principle that the Royal Navy should be as large as the next two forces combined—right up to the outbreak of the First World War.

In addition to its navy and its empire, Britain held an unassailed lead in industrial development. Its dominance reached a peak by the middle of the century, with one study showing that in 1860 Britain had 35 percent of total world manufacturing capacity and was three times as industrialized per capita as its nearest rivals.[8] One of the bases of this industrial precociousness was Britain's plentiful supply of coal and iron ore, the two key raw materials of the Industrial Revolution. Coal provided fuel for transport and industry, and together with iron ore it provided the base for the all-important iron and steel industry. In 1850, Britain produced half the world's iron and steel and two-thirds of the world's coal. Abundant coal not only fueled Britain's domestic industry, it also allowed the country to become the main world exporter of this crucial commodity. Coal also helped underpin Britain's continued dominance of shipbuilding and shipping as steam replaced sail. In 1880, British steam-powered merchant tonnage was two and a half times greater than that of the rest of the world combined.

To complement these strengths, Britain was the world's financial powerhouse. The Napoleonic era had destroyed the credit of most of Europe so that after 1815 the British public debt was the only security that could be said to enjoy investment-grade status. Over the course of the century, the interest rates paid by other countries declined, but until the 1880s Britain's borrowing costs were typically 1 percent to 1.5 percent lower than any other Great Power. The Bank of England was central to the operation of the international gold standard, and London was the major source of capital for international investment. Britain's overseas investments rose by leaps and bounds in the second half of the century, and by

1914 amounted to almost 150 percent of the country's GDP. These investments not only gave the country extensive influence around the world but also provided a substantial financial buffer that could be tapped in time of need.

Britain, in other words, disposed of a remarkable set of assets in the nineteenth century. But did it fill the role of a benign hegemon—a global policeman who kept the peace and enhanced the growth of the world economy? It is easier to support the second part of this statement than the first. The progressive reduction of tariffs and other barriers at home and throughout the empire was certainly in part responsible for the expansion of world trade during the century. Equally important was the role of the Royal Navy in protecting the sea-lanes from piracy. And if the word "benign" is to mean anything, a mention should be made of the navy's role in suppressing the slave trade—even if it could be argued that this was one sort of commerce that British action reduced rather than encouraged.

But whether Britain kept world peace is a more difficult proposition to maintain. Those who deployed the term "Pax Britannica" were generally not looking at the question of peace among the Great Powers of Europe. More often than not it was a reference to the Pax Romana—the peace maintained by Rome *within* the borders of its empire. Imperial eulogists liked to emphasize the advantages of British rule for its subjects: bringing the rule of law and the benefits of civilization where there had been perpetual conflict or anarchy. In 1913, Lord Milner summed up the concept with the classic self-certainty of an imperial ruling class at its apogee: "The British race has become responsible for the peace and order and the just and humane government of three or four hundred millions of people who . . . do not possess the gift of maintaining peace and order for themselves . . . The *Pax Britannica* is essential to the maintenance of civilised conditions of existence among one-fifth of the human race."[9] Few imperial apologists thought that Pax Britannica held much sway outside the confines of the British Empire—any more than Pax Romana had applied outside the Roman Empire.

It is true that there was no Great Power conflict for almost forty years after Waterloo. But the lull in rivalry was only partly the result of British preeminence. Thanks to British sea power, the other great imperial powers of prior centuries had been reduced to shadows of their former selves, making conflict outside Europe unlikely. Within Europe, however, British naval power meant little. Instead of Pax Britannica there was a Pax Europaea, a "Concert of Europe" policed by the five Great Powers that had sought to establish a durable peace at the Congress of Vienna in 1815. Instead of relying on shifting alliances as in the past, the Great Powers agreed to act in concert whenever developments that might threaten the peace of the continent occurred. The system proved successful in the 1830s, when it averted war over the future of Belgium by guaranteeing Belgium's independence and neutrality. However, the Concert of Europe depended on the cooperation of its members, and it proved incapable of preventing conflict if any of them had other ideas.

In 1854, the long peace was broken when Britain and France went to war to block Russian expansion around the Black Sea. This area was not, strictly speaking, covered by the Congress of Vienna. However, as a military conflict between three of the five members of the Concert of Europe, the Crimean War demonstrated the fragility of the idea of Great Power cooperation. A conference called in Vienna in 1853 had failed to avert the conflict. The Crimean War also demonstrated the limits of Pax Britannica. Russia's ambition to get control of the Turkish Straits and thereby access to the Mediterranean was a direct threat to Britain's control of sea routes (routes that would become even more important with the opening of the Suez Canal). Yet even at the height of its relative power, Britain was not strong enough to impose its will in a matter of strategic importance without resorting to force, and even then it needed allies to succeed.

THE EMERGENCE OF RIVALS

The Crimean War showcased the revival of France as a significant force under Napoleon III. It was unlikely that a nephew of Napoleon Bonaparte would be content with France's hobbled position after 1815, and even though the new emperor hastened to reassure Europe that "*l'Empire, c'est la paix*" (the Empire means peace), his actions spoke otherwise. In the wake of the war, Napoleon showed that onetime allies could easily become rivals by ordering a naval modernization program (including the early adoption of ironclad hulls, propeller power, and explosive shells) that for a time threatened the invulnerability of the Royal Navy and led to a brief British invasion scare in 1859. French imperial ambitions were revived with the start of its colonial presence in Indochina and with the attempt to bring Mexico under French control by imposing the rule of Austria's Archduke Maximilian.

More significant than any of these overseas ventures was Napoleon's foolhardy decision to encourage the overthrow of the post-1815 settlement in Europe. His support of the kingdom of Piedmont in its attempt to put an end to Austrian rule in northern Italy led to war in 1859 and to the subsequent unification of the whole peninsula under a Piedmontese dynasty. The sudden establishment of a new power in the south altered the balance of power not just in the Mediterranean but potentially throughout Europe as well. Austria, the ultimate conservator of the old order, was weakened, and in the wake of Piedmont's example, Prussia was emboldened to seek the unification of Germany under its own royal house. The stunning successes of the Prussian armies against Austria in 1866 and against France in 1870 led to the installation of William I as the first kaiser of a German empire that stretched from Metz (now in France) to Tilsit (now in Russia), and that became, overnight, the largest state in Europe apart from Russia. This was to have even more far-reaching effects than the unification of Italy—not least the collapse of Napoleon's rule and the terminal weakening of France's position in Europe.

The rise of new powers within the European heartland was complemented by developments beyond its borders. Russian ambitions in the Black Sea were dealt only a temporary blow by the Crimean War, and Russia's eastward expansion was unaffected. By 1860, it had reached the Pacific. Moreover, Alexander II's reforms, designed to modernize the nation in the wake of its Crimean defeat, helped inaugurate a period of industrialization and railway building that culminated with the completion of the Trans-Siberian Railway at the beginning of the twentieth century. A similar process was taking place in the United States, where the end of the Civil War in 1865 allowed the country to refocus its energies on completing the domestication of the West. The first transcontinental railroad was completed in 1869, to be followed by four other routes in the 1880s. By 1890, the West was almost entirely colonized. As in the case of Russia, it was likely that the energies that had hitherto concentrated on creating these enormous continental giants would be felt with increasing intensity beyond their borders.

The arrival of new powers on the international stage might have meant less if Britain had retained its industrial supremacy. But after 1870, Britain's lead over other countries shrank to the point where it was threatened or surpassed. Nowhere was the change more apparent than in iron and steelmaking, the industry that more than any other defined economic and, ultimately, military potential. In 1870, Britain still had around 48 percent of the world's iron- and steelmaking capacity, four times more than either America or Germany. By 1913, however, Britain's share had shrunk to under 12 percent, while Germany's had advanced to 24 percent and America's to over 40 percent.[10] If Britain could not impose its will on its rivals even during its heyday, it was increasingly unlikely that it would be able to do so in this far more competitive world.

With Pax Britannica ever less credible, peace among the Great Powers depended on the residual hope that cooperation would avert conflict. In reality, the Concert of Europe had died by 1871. The unification of Italy and Germany had been brought about by wars that broke out without any international attempt to stop them. Yet the hope that the Great Powers might cooperate to keep the peace lingered. Conferences were called in Berlin in 1878 and in London in 1912–1913 to settle the recurring problem of the Balkans. But after the wars of 1854–1871, it was clear that the Great Powers would cooperate only as and when they chose. In July 1914, Britain attempted to convene a conference to settle the crisis in Bosnia, but Germany and Austria-Hungary refused to take part.

The arrival of a multipolar world might not have mattered if the Great Powers had agreed with Cobden's vision of peaceful free trade without empires. However, such a vision looked increasingly remote after the 1870s. The movement toward free trade was reversed and protectionism regained ground. There were a number of interwoven causes in this reversal. First was the challenge to the doctrine of free trade posed by an alternative philosophy that argued for protection as a way to foster industrial development. The most powerful voice of this idea was Friedrich List, whose seminal work, *The National System of Political Economy* (1841), took issue with Adam Smith. Nations did not rise to preeminence through free trade, as Smith claimed, but rather by protecting and fostering their commerce and industry. This was particularly true of England, which in the Middle Ages had been a simple supplier of wool for the textile industry of Europe. "Had the English left everything to itself—'Laissé faire et laissé aller,' as the popular economical school recommends—the [north German] merchants . . . would be still carrying on their trade in London, the Belgians would be still manufacturing cloth for the English, England would have still continued to be the sheep-farm of the Hansards."[11]

As for Smith's theory of competitive advantage, this would merely condemn nonindustrialized countries to remain as suppliers of raw materials and prevent them from rising to the wealth and power that only manufacturing provided. As a result of generations of protective policies, England had risen to a position of commercial preeminence that allowed it to pursue free trade from a position of advantage. Its economic relations with Europe were reversed from their medieval pattern, and it was happy to keep them this way: "It is therefore no exaggeration if we maintain that the tendency of the English proposals aims at nothing less than the overthrow of the entire German protective system, in order to reduce Germany to the position of an English agricultural colony."[12]

List was before his time. He died in 1846, just as the tide of free trade was in full swell, but he raised issues that still resonate today. As other forces turned countries toward protection in the 1870s and '80s, his views came more sharply into focus. Germany was among the first to return to a set of policies that had more than a passing resemblance to the supposedly discredited mercantilism of the seventeenth and eighteenth centuries. Industries were protected by a rising barrier of tariffs and by the creation of monopolistic cartels to protect them from the whims of free-market competition. Right-minded opinion in Britain was outraged, *The Times* declaring in 1877 that "the growth of a strong protectionist party in Germany has been one of the most unsatisfactory signs of the limited political training of that country."[13] Only Britain and the Netherlands retained their commitment to free trade in the period before the war. Elsewhere in Europe, tariffs were on the increase. By 1913, typical duties on manufactured goods had risen to 13 percent in Germany, 18 percent in Italy and Austria, and 20 percent in France.

Across the Atlantic, the United States witnessed its own battle between the opposing forces of commercial freedom and protectionism. The agrarian areas of the South and the West, with their highly competitive production of cotton and foodstuffs, had always favored free trade. Other voices, starting with Alexander Hamilton in the 1790s, favored protecting American industry to ensure the country's transformation into a manufacturing power. Henry Clay, the senator from Kentucky, anticipated many of Friedrich List's points in the 1820s and '30s, arguing that nations that cultivate the "manufacturing arts . . . will excel in strength, and maintain a superiority."[14] Confronted with Andrew Jackson's reversal of the protectionist tariffs of the 1820s, he declared that the Democrats misunderstood the implications of free trade: "It is not free trade that they are recommending to our acceptance. It is, in effect, the British colonial system that we are being invited to adopt; and if their policy prevails, it will lead substantially to the recolonization of these states, under the commercial dominion of Great Britain."[15] Until the Civil War, the battle between the two forces was relatively evenly waged. But in the wake of the defeat of the South in 1865, the tide turned sharply toward protectionism. In 1868, duties on imported European manufactures were raised to around 50 percent, far higher than any tariffs within Europe, and they remained in that region until 1913, in spite of the attempts of Grover Cleveland, the only Democratic president between 1860 and 1912, to lower them.

The urge to foster industrialization was not the only reason for the resurgence of protectionism. The financial crash of 1873 ushered in an economic depression in Europe that discredited the principle of free trade. Even when recovery got under way, the European economies found their traditional agricultural production undermined by the opening up of the vast potential of the Great Plains of the American West, which by the late 1870s had begun to flood European markets with cheap grain. In January 1879, a leading businessman complained to Bismarck's personal assistant about the sixfold increase in American exports of grain, flour, and meat: "For German agriculture, there must be a grain, flour and meat tariff as an unconditional necessity if we are not to expose it to the same fluctuations as industry."[16] As with Britain's Corn Laws, import duties were justified not just as a way of protecting agriculture from competition but also as a way of ensuring adequate domestic food supplies in wartime.

This turn toward protectionism should logically have damaged the growth of international trade, but curiously, this was not the case. In the forty years before the First World War, the volume of world trade trebled. There are several reasons for this outcome, which would appear to contradict the expectations of the liberals. First, Great Britain, the world's largest importer and exporter, did not join the general trend toward protection. Second, the rise in tariffs was offset by the fall in transport costs. Finally, outside tariffs, trade was hampered by few restrictions, and within the operations of the gold standard there was no such thing as currency manipulation or competitive devaluation.

The resurgence of protectionism was therefore, perhaps, less important in itself than as a sign of changing attitudes. It was accompanied by a dramatic return to the process of European empire building. With the exception of the French conquest of Algeria in the 1830s, the continent of Africa had remained largely immune to European expansion, apart from some scattered trading posts along the coastline and the Boer settlements in the south. Excitement at the possibilities of wider settlement was generated by travelers into the interior in the 1850s and '60s who brought back reports of vast unexploited mineral wealth. The trigger for what later became known as the "scramble for Africa" occurred in 1881–1882, when the French annexation of Tunis was followed by the British takeover of Egypt. At the same time, the first step toward colonizing the African interior was being taken by the explorer Arthur Stanley in the Congo at the behest of King Leopold of Belgium. In 1884, a conference was held in Berlin to set down some rules for what was likely to become a race. When huge gold deposits were discovered in Witwatersrand in South Africa in 1886, the stories of Africa's untold mineral wealth seemed to be confirmed. The scramble was now well and truly under way, and by 1913 the continent had been almost entirely divided among the European powers, with only Abyssinia (Ethiopia) and Liberia still under native rule. The lion's shares fell to Britain and France, the two Great Powers that already had a head start in this process, with smaller prizes going to Belgium, Germany, and Italy. The outcome was particularly galling to Germany, which felt that its late arrival on the imperial scene had left it with colonial assets that were not proportional to its industrial power, which had already outstripped France and was rapidly overtaking Britain.

After Africa, the most important remaining portion of the globe that appeared to be ready for colonization was East Asia. As the wave of imperial expansion got under way in the 1880s, Britain asserted control over Burma and the Malay Peninsula, while France expanded its presence on the Vietnamese coast to create a formal colony of French Indochina. The greatest prize of the East, however, was China, which had been attracting interest since the First Opium War in 1841. The calculations of how best to take advantage of this potential market of hundreds of millions were complicated not just by the size of the prize but also by the number of contestants. The scramble for Africa had involved two or three major players. The scramble for Asia drew in not only Britain and France but also Germany, Russia, the United States, and a surprising new entrant into the race: Japan.

Japan had maintained almost total isolation since the early seventeenth century, when it had reacted to the first inroads of European expansion by retreating from all contact with the outside world. Its opening up under the pressure of an American naval contingent in the 1850s should have been no different from the opening of the Chinese and Siamese markets through similar shows of force. However, a significant part of the Japanese ruling class was of the opinion that the only way to beat the foreign barbarians was at their own game. Within a year of Japan's first reluctant acceptance of a commercial treaty with the United States in 1854, it had acquired a modern propeller-driven warship from the Dutch—not in itself an adequate barrier against Western advances but a sign of things to come. After the Meiji Restoration of 1868 demolished feudal tradition, Japan followed a rigorous policy of modernization. A new constitution was adopted, together with a new military system, and a new legal code, a new educational system, and a new calendar—all based on Western models—and the government encouraged industrialization with single-minded determination.

By contrast, China floundered. The Second Opium War of 1856–1860 brought further concessions to foreign powers, with Britain, France, Russia, and the United States obtaining trading and diplomatic rights in a series of unequal treaties. Thereafter, China attempted to modernize under the "Self-Strengthening Movement," but the forces of tradition and corruption were too great an impediment. In 1895, the contrasting trajectories of China and Japan were laid bare by the Sino-Japanese War, which resulted in the shocking defeat of China by a neighbor historically considered very much its inferior. Japan now became an imperial power in its own right, gaining a colony in Formosa (Taiwan) and trading rights on the Chinese mainland comparable to those of the Western powers.

The second major disruption in the status quo in the Far East in the 1890s was the collapse of the remnants of the Spanish Empire, which was replaced by two new imperial contenders: the United States and Germany. The United States had started looking across the Pacific almost as soon as it had acquired California in 1848. William Seward, the future secretary of state under Lincoln, was the first to set out a vision of US involvement with the western Pacific. The United States "must command the empire of the seas, which alone is real empire," he told the Senate in 1850. The contest for empire was "not on the American lakes, nor on the Atlantic coast, nor on the Caribbean sea, nor on the Mediterranean, nor on the Baltic, nor on the Atlantic ocean, but on the Pacific ocean, and its islands and continents."[17] It was in pursuit of this vision that Commodore Perry sailed his ships into Yokohama harbor in 1854 to open Japan to the benefits of international commerce, and that the United States sided with Britain in the Second Opium War to do the same for China. However, American influence in the area remained relatively limited until 1898, when it leveraged its military intervention against Spain in support of Cuban independence to take over the Philippines. At the same time, Germany used Spain's discomfiture to acquire its smaller Pacific island chains: the Marianas and the Carolinas. The flock of new entrants into the race for Asian colonies and spheres of influence was such that by the time China attempted to throw the "foreign devils" off its soil in the Boxer uprising of 1900, it found itself opposed by an alliance of eight imperial powers that now included not just Britain and France but also America, Russia, Germany, Japan, Austria-Hungary, and Italy.

THE DYNAMICS OF IMPERIALISM

What drove this wave of imperial expansion? The colonial powers often liked to justify their empires by asserting that they were bringing the light of civilization to their backward subjects. At other times they scarcely appeared to know, acknowledging that the drive for colonies seemed to feed on itself. "*L'appétit vient en mangeant*" (Appetite comes with eating), as the British prime minister Lord Salisbury explained to the French ambassador as they discussed the reasons for the carve-up of Africa. The French advocate of imperial expansion, Jules Ferry, stated simply that "an irresistible movement is bearing the great nations of Europe towards the conquest of fresh territories. It is like a huge steeplechase into the unknown . . . whole continents are being annexed . . . especially that huge black continent so full of fierce mysteries and vague hopes."[18]

Behind such complacent attitudes lay a more complex set of views about the nature of power and prosperity that were simultaneously reassuring and unsettling. The Industrial Revolution had divided the world into manufacturing and raw-material-producing nations. It was clear that true wealth and power were to be found among the former, not the latter. Friedrich List put the case clearly in his outline of European economic history: "If we carefully consider the commercial policy of Venice, we see at a glance that that of modern commercial and manufacturing nations is but a copy of that of Venice, only on an enlarged (i.e. a national) scale . . . The maxim thus early held good that it was sound policy to import raw materials from other states and to export to them manufactured goods."[19] William Seward, the apostle of American overseas expansion, saw the world in similar terms: "The nation that draws the most materials and provisions from the earth, fabricates the most, and sells the most of productions and fabrics to foreign nations, must be, and will be, the great power of the earth."[20]

However, the rush to industrialize produced its own complications. As Britain had already discovered, the more developed an economy, the less it was self-sufficient and the more it depended on less-developed economies to complement and sustain its growth. It was inevitable that, in a world of empire, there would be a temptation to ensure that these less-developed areas were under the control of the industrial heartland. These colonies would fulfill three functions: as producers of raw materials, consumers of manufactured goods, and destinations for emigration from an increasingly densely populated mother country. As the French economist Paul Leroy-Beaulieu put it, "the most useful function which colonies perform . . . is to supply the mother country's trade with a ready-made market to get its industry going and maintain it, and to supply the inhabitants of the mother country— whether as industrialists, workers or consumers—with increased profits, wages or commodities."[21]

Leroy-Beaulieu was a liberal writing in the early 1870s. Although he advocated colonial expansion as a useful support for the domestic economy, he still favored an open-door policy whereby countries could trade freely with each other's empires, arguing that "the whole world will benefit from this, for there is no question of going back to the restrictions dating from the days of exclusive trading."[22] As time passed, however, the return of protectionism increased the sense that colonies were there to provide a competitive advantage for the mother country. In 1887, the Bordeaux Chamber of Commerce, once a bastion of free trade, argued that France needed colonies to find secure markets for its manufactures: "The revival of differential tariffs would seem justified at this stage by the need to strengthen the links, now too weak, which link France with her colonies. Experience has proved that France, whose overseas exports are held back by ever-increasing competition, must find in colonies inhabited by her own nationals guaranteed markets for her primary and industrial products."[23]

Other writers went further and argued that empires were a necessity for national survival. The German nationalist writer Friedrich von Bernhardi worried that industrial development without an empire put Germany in a dangerous position:

> There is, however, a reverse side to this picture of splendid development. We are absolutely dependent on foreign countries for the import of raw materials, and to a considerable extent also for the sale of our own manufactures. We even obtain a part of our necessaries of life from abroad . . . The livelihood of our working classes directly depends on the maintenance and expansion of our export trade. It is a question of life and death for us to keep open our overseas commerce . . . If the unfortunate course of our history has hitherto prevented us from building a colonial Empire, it is our duty to make up for lost time.[24]

Industrialization and empire building were increasingly seen as part of a zero-sum race for success, for it was not clear that there was room for more than a certain number of successful industrialized countries at the same time. The British writer Benjamin Kidd sought to explain the rush for colonies by the need to gain competitive advantage in a world where there were suddenly multiple industrial centers:

As the forces of industrial rivalry have . . . developed themselves . . . as transport and communication have become
cheaper and more rapid, and technical knowledge has been
more widely distributed and more easily conveyed, rival industries may be seen flourishing in different countries . . .
Competing nations in most cases possess but little advantage
one over the other.[25]

In such circumstances, the possession of a colonial empire that
provided resources and markets could make the difference between success and failure. The drive for empire was boosted by
the perception that, now that the great uncharted expanses of
America, Asia, and Africa had been mapped, the planet was finite. It was inevitable that a few powerful industrial nations with
global reach would come to dominate the world. Benjamin Kidd
wrote of the "the vast world-shaping rivalry . . . the struggle of the
Western races for the larger inheritance of the future."[26] Paul
Leroy-Beaulieu put France's choice in dramatic terms: "Colonization is for France a question of life and death,—either *France
must become a great African Power*, or she will be in a century or
two but a secondary European Power."[27] In Germany, the nationalist historian Heinrich von Treitschke spoke in similar terms:
"Every virile people has established colonial power . . . All great
nations in the fullness of their strength have desired to set their
mark upon barbarian lands and those who fail to participate in
the great rivalry will play a pitiable role in time to come."[28]

Even in Britain, with its vast possessions, there was anxiety
about the future. The geopolitical thinker Halford Mackinder
worried that the days of maritime empires like Britain's were
threatened by the advent of railways that allowed the uniting of
great continental "heartland" empires like Russia. "Is not the
pivot region of the world's politics that vast area of Euro-Asia
which is inaccessible to ships, but in antiquity lay open to the
horse-riding nomads, and is today about to be covered with a

network of railways?"[29] In response, Britain should not only prevent Russia from gaining access to the sea but also consolidate the empire behind a tariff wall to reinforce its economic and political coherence.

If empires were needed to ensure national success, so too were navies. In 1890, the American naval officer Alfred Mahan published the first of a series of highly influential books that argued that the race for commercial dominance had been won on the high seas. With the ever-growing importance of international trade, navies were not a luxury: They were essential for any country that aspired to power. Without a navy, a country's trade, its overseas possessions, and even its very survival were at the mercy of its rivals.

> If navies, as all agree, exist for the protection of commerce, it inevitably follows that in war they must aim at depriving their enemy of that great resource; nor is it easy to conceive what broad military use they can subserve that at all compares with the protection and destruction of trade . . . Great Britain's navy, in the French wars, not only protected her own commerce, but also annihilated that of the enemy; and both conditions—not one alone—were essential to her triumph.[30]

Mahan's work was taken to heart not just in his own country but in the capitals of all the Great Powers. The rush for empire was paralleled by a naval arms race, motivated, as with the drive for colonies, by a combination of ambition and insecurity. In 1880, the total tonnage of the warships of the Royal Navy was 650,000, a figure as great as the next three navies combined. Ten years later, after a decade of complacency, Britain became so alarmed by the erosion of its naval lead that the "two-power standard" was enshrined as a formal national policy. In Germany, 1897 was a wake-up call. Talk of intervention in support of the independent Boer republics in southern Africa against British aggression led to a stern warning to the country's ambassador in

London. Britain would if necessary go to war to protect its interests, and "a blockade of Hamburg and Bremen and the annihilation of German commerce on the high seas would be child's play for the English fleet."[31] The following year, Admiral Tirpitz introduced a bill in the Reichstag authorizing the rapid buildup of the German navy, arguing that "a state which has actively taken up trade, and has thereby become a considerable competitor in world markets, cannot exist without a certain measure of naval power or else it must go under."[32] Asked whether Hamburg could be held in the event of war, he replied that it was irrelevant since "war with Britain meant the extinction of colonies and trade . . . We could do nothing except make peace as quickly as possible."[33]

By 1914, Germany's navy had undergone an extraordinary transformation, growing from only 88,000 tons in 1880 to 1,305,000 tons and becoming the second-largest in the world. Hans Delbrück, the well-known historian of warfare, was arguing that its original defensive role was no longer sufficient: "It was true in the past that our fleet was created to protect our commerce. But today we can set ourselves a higher goal. The purpose of our fleet is not only to protect our overseas trade but also to bring us our fair share of that world domination which is allotted to civilized nations by the very nature of mankind and its higher destiny."[34]

Impressive though Germany's navy may have been, its growth had been nearly matched by a number of others. By 1914, France, Russia, the United States, and Japan all had navies larger than Britain's in 1880. The American fleet had grown from 169,000 tons in 1880 to 985,000 tons in 1914. The Japanese fleet grew from a tiny 15,000 tons to 700,000 tons.[35]

This international surge of naval building was viewed with considerable alarm in London. Since Britain had abolished the Corn Laws in 1846, it had depended more and more on food imports. Unlike Germany, Britain had not responded to the arrival of cheap American grain by raising tariff barriers to protect domestic agriculture. Its only insurance against wartime vulnerability was the Royal Navy. In 1902, the Liberal politician Richard Haldane made exactly this point in Parliament, arguing that "the commerce of this country was something approaching £1,000,000,000 and the [naval] Estimates only amounted to some 3 per cent on that. That was not an extravagant premium of insurance."[36] Given this dependence on control of the seas, the rapid growth of the foreign navies, especially Germany's, was seen as a major threat to British security.

In 1904, a royal commission was set up to examine the issue of wartime vulnerability. It considered the extent and flexibility of overseas supplies, the transport resources available, and the risks of losses in the light of modern naval technology. It concluded that there would undoubtedly be some "captures of British ships engaged in the carrying trade . . . But *with a strong fleet* we find no reason to fear such an interruption of our supplies as would lead to the starvation of our people" [italics added].[37]

The commission looked at the idea of stockpiling food but rejected the idea as too expensive and disruptive of the normal workings of the market. This left the Royal Navy bearing the entire responsibility of securing the nation's food supplies. Not surprisingly, the main outcome of its report was to reinforce the naval building program, which began in earnest in 1905. In that year, Admiral John Fisher, the head of the navy, commissioned HMS *Dreadnought*, a battleship whose large guns, heavy armor, and high speed rendered all previous big warships obsolete. The result was a further increase in the pace of the global naval arms race. Fisher demonstrated that Britannia meant to continue ruling the waves, not just by the revolutionary design of the ship but also by the astonishing speed with which it was built. *Dreadnought* was ready for action in only fifteen months. The rapid progress of technology meant that existing naval assets were liable to instant obsolescence, and this gave a potential advantage to a technological powerhouse like Germany, which might outweigh the far greater starting size of the British navy. However, even when fleets had to be rebuilt from scratch to keep up with technical advances, Britain retained an advantage because of the global dominance of its shipbuilding industry. For the time being it could simply outbuild any rival. By 1914, the Royal Navy had grown to 2,714,000 tons, and the two-power standard was still intact. But even so, Britain could no longer feel sure of its ability to deal with any combination of naval threats in any quarter of the globe at any time.

On the continent of Europe, the arms race was equally visible on land. People were only too aware that between 1859 and 1870 the map of Europe had been redrawn by military force. The effectiveness of the Prussian army, based on a system of compulsory military service, had impressed all observers, and other nations felt that they had to respond. France introduced conscription in 1872, and by the outbreak of the First World War every major continental nation had an army based on compulsory short-term military service. The numbers in the armed forces grew steadily in every country between 1880 and the outbreak of war, rising by 110 percent in Germany, 80 percent in Austria-Hungary, 71 percent in Russia, 68 percent in France, 60 percent in Italy, and 45 percent in Britain. By early 1914, France had 827,000 men under arms (compared to only 144,000 in 2011), Germany had 761,000, and Russia had 1,445,000.[38] And behind these figures for peacetime strengths were even larger numbers of military reservists who could be called up at short notice. Germany, for instance, could quickly mobilize an army of more than two million men if it decided to go to war.

This combination of rising protectionism, the drive for imperial expansion, and the inexorable increase in military spending was a terrible setback for the belief that trade should foster peace. Some liberal thinkers, like John A. Hobson, despaired:

> Cobden and his friends primarily conceived nations as bound together by the play of purely commercial interests. If we could have free trade established between the different parts of the world, then the material business interests of these different parts would bind together the world so closely and so

quickly that it would be impossible for war to be maintained in the future . . . Those who see to-day that the fiercest struggles between members of different nations are for the markets of the world smile scornfully on this dream of Richard Cobden.[39]

Trying to explain what had gone wrong, in 1902 Hobson published *Imperialism,* a book that was to become the basis of the standard socialist critique of empires for decades to come. Capitalism had a tendency to overproduce and increasingly found itself short of markets for its wares. The result was that competition among firms was replaced by competition among countries as they sought to acquire monopoly markets for their output, without which the profits of industry would fall. The resulting race for colonies was a threat to world peace. However, there was a simple solution: social reform and the redistribution of income so that industrial output could be consumed at home. "The struggle for markets . . . is the crowning proof of a false economy of distribution. Imperialism is the fruit of this false economy; 'social reform' is its remedy. The primary purpose of 'social reform' . . . is to raise the wholesome standard of private and public consumption for a nation, so as to enable the nation to live up to its highest standard of production."[40]

But there was an unresolved conundrum in this thesis. Hobson claimed that the ideas of the imperialists were based in part on a false analysis of trade patterns. The bulk of international trade was between industrialized countries, not within their empires, and this trade between the imperial rivals was growing faster than colonial trade. As Hobson put it caustically, "The greatest increase of our foreign trade is with that group of industrial nations whom we regard as our industrial enemies."[41] The largest level of intra-imperial trade was, not surprisingly given its scope, within the British Empire. But even there, only 37 percent of British exports went to the empire in 1913. Elsewhere the proportions were far lower. Only 13 percent of French exports went to its colonies, yet France had by far the largest empire after Britain. If Hobson had wanted to make a case about the evils of imperialism, he would have done better to focus on colonies as sources of raw materials rather than as markets for manufactured goods. France absorbed 50 percent of the exports of its colonies; the figure was 90 percent in the Belgian empire. But even here, the case was not very strong. The British colonies sold only 42 percent of their goods to Britain.[42]

Hobson was not unaware of the possible contradiction in his theory. If capitalists preferred to trade outside the empire, how was it possible to blame them for imperialism? To resolve this difficulty, he had a deus ex machina: the wicked financiers who looked for monopoly profits in their colonial investments. The problem with this idea was that the overseas investments of the imperial powers were, rather like their trade, largely outside the colonies. Even counting its massive investments in the autonomous dominions of Canada and Australia, less than half of British overseas assets were within the empire. The largest single destination of capital flows from London was the United States. The situation in France, the second-largest source of capital after Britain, was even more lopsided. Only 9 percent of French investments were in the French empire, compared to 25 percent in Russia and 13 percent in Latin America. Germans had more excuse for ignoring their relatively modest colonial possessions, investing 46 percent of their funds in Europe, 32 percent in the Americas, and 8 percent in Turkey.[43]

Hobson's critique was taken up by Marxists such as Hilferding, Bukharin, and Lenin. They agreed with his basic premises of the inherent tendency of capitalism to overproduce, the move from competition between companies to competition between states, and the pernicious role of finance. To Communists, especially once Lenin put his seal on the maxim that "imperialism is the highest stage of capitalism" in 1916, it was an orthodoxy that capitalism meant imperialism, and that imperialism meant war.

There were other voices, however. In 1909, the journalist

Norman Angell published his bestselling *The Great Illusion*, in which he reaffirmed the old beliefs of the Manchester free-trade liberals about the futility of war, but with two new arguments. He contended, not entirely convincingly, that wealth could not be annexed, and rather more credibly that financial interdependence had now been added to commercial interdependence to make conquest self-defeating. A German invasion of London would be futile, he declared. "Because of the internationalization and delicate interdependence of our credit-built finance and industry . . . German credit [would] collapse." In colorful language he continued:

> The German Generalissimo . . . would soon find the difference between himself and Attila. Attila, luckily for him, did not have to worry about a bank rate and such-like complications; but the German General, while trying to sack the Bank of England, would find that . . . the value of even the best of his investments dwindled as though by a miracle; and that for the sake of loot, amounting to a few sovereigns apiece among his soldiery, he would have sacrificed the greater part of his own personal fortune.[44]

Angell, like Hobson, had his supporters on the left. In 1911, August Bebel, the parliamentary leader of the German Socialists, disagreed with those who argued that international finance posed a threat to world peace. A war scare over a colonial dispute between Germany and France was setting off a financial panic, and Bebel told the Reichstag, "I say openly that the greatest guarantee for the preservation of world peace today is found in the international investments of capitalism. These investments make war so dangerous for both sides that it would be pure madness for any government to push things to the brink over Morocco."[45]

How were these two opinions of the effects of capitalism to be reconciled? One possible answer was that economics had nothing to do with imperialism at all. This was the theory proposed after the war by the political economist Joseph Schumpeter, who argued that the war had been caused not by capitalism but by the relics of feudalism in the upper echelons of governments and armed forces.[46] This is an idea with some plausibility, given that the decision to go to war in 1914 was taken by small coteries of men, especially in Germany, Austria, and Russia, who, with the exception of the German chancellor Bethmann-Hollweg, came almost exclusively from aristocratic-military backgrounds.

However, a better line of argument is that in a competitive multipolar world, governments were dealing with a "prisoner's dilemma" of whether they should cooperate or compete. It may have been fine for small countries to rely on the protection of the Royal Navy for their international trade. But was that a safe bet for countries like Germany that were sufficiently large to pose an economic and therefore geopolitical threat to Britain? Given its circumstances, it was logical for Germany to compete for colonies and to build up a navy. Yet the attempt to carve out safety for one country was potentially threatening for others, leading to a self-fulfilling prophecy.

The first person to suggest this paradox was one of the great liberal thinkers of the midcentury, the French political economist Frédéric Bastiat. One of the biggest reasons to protect domestic production, acquire colonies, or build up navies was to reestablish the self-sufficiency that industrialization had eroded—leading to potential vulnerability in time of war. And yet, as Bastiat pointed out, the search for self-sufficiency tended to make war more rather than less likely:

> A nation isolates itself looking forward to the possibility of war; but is not this very act of isolating itself the beginning of war? . . . Let countries be permanent markets for each other's produce; let their reciprocal relations be such that they cannot be broken without inflicting on each other the double suffering of privation and a glut of commodities; and they will no longer stand in need of naval armaments, which ruin them, and overgrown armies, which crush them.[47]

Curiously, the great apostle of naval power, Alfred Mahan, also perceived the outlines of this paradox. In 1907, he recognized the logic of Germany's naval buildup, while at the same time noting that the country's earlier defenselessness had been more conducive to the maintenance of peace: "In the development of her merchant shipping Germany, to use a threadbare phrase, has given a hostage to Fortune . . . Unless she equip a navy adequate to so great a task as protecting fully the carrying trade she has laboriously created . . . this trade is . . . a circumstance making for peace."[48]

THE DESCENT INTO WAR

The question is: Did the combination of colonial rivalry and military buildup lead inevitably to war? The causes of the descent into war in July–August 1914 are so hard to fit into a simple pattern that more than thirty thousand books and articles have been written on the subject without coming to a definitive conclusion. After the war, it was easy to blame the escalating prewar imperial rivalries of the belligerents for the conflict, and Communists worldwide, following Lenin's conclusive statement on the matter, never wavered in this belief. Yet this explanation has always encountered difficulties with the fact that war broke out not over some distant, resource-rich colony but over a landlocked province in the Balkans with no obvious raw materials or markets to quarrel about.

There were certainly plenty of moments in the years before 1914 when it looked as if war might break out over colonial rivalries. The first of these crises occurred when competing British and French plans to create empires that spanned Africa from one coast to another met in the middle. In 1898, a French expedition met a British force at Fashoda in southern Sudan, the unclaimed intersection of their territorial axes. A tense military standoff was finally resolved by French acceptance of British claims. In

1905 and again in 1911, France and Germany teetered on the brink of war about Morocco, on which they both had imperial designs.

On the surface, the peaceful resolution of the 1911 Moroccan Crisis seemed to reinforce the liberal view that commercial and financial interdependence was reducing the likelihood of war. The financial panic in Berlin was one of the reasons that Germany backed down and caused Bebel to suggest that international capitalism was becoming a force for peace.

However, Bebel's hopes were premature. The colonial crises, although resolved without resort to arms, had ramifications that made war in Europe more likely. The resolution of the Fashoda incident foreshadowed a fundamental realignment of European politics. Britain abandoned its policy of "splendid isolation" and aligned itself with France. In exchange for French acceptance of Britain's position in Egypt and Sudan, Britain tacitly agreed to accept French claims in Morocco. In 1905 and 1911, Britain came down decisively on the side of France, threatening military action if Germany did not withdraw its claims. From a British perspective, the thought of the German navy gaining bases on the Atlantic and Mediterranean coasts of Morocco was far too dangerous to contemplate. From a German viewpoint, however, the success of the Anglo-French front in 1905 and 1911 only encouraged the country to believe that it was surrounded by enemies intent on denying it its place in the sun and increased its determination to break out of its encirclement. At the same time, by challenging France in Morocco, Germany brought into question one of the unspoken bases of European peace since 1870. Bismarck had encouraged France to expand into Africa as a way of distracting it from its loss of Alsace and Lorraine. A dispute about colonies in Africa reawakened more dangerous antagonisms closer to home.

Moreover, the idea that imperial rivalries would not lead to war falls afoul of an obvious rejoinder: that what can be seen as the first skirmish of the First World War, the Russo-Japanese War of 1904–1905, had already occurred—and it was clearly about colonies.

In 1900, the Great Powers had cooperated in confronting the Boxer uprising in China. However, there were unresolved differences of opinion about how to divide the Qing empire between them. In the earlier part of the century, Britain had been content to establish a local trading base in Hong Kong and bargain for open access to the Chinese market. As competition heated up, the rival powers felt it was best to divide China into spheres of interest as a way of avoiding clashes between them—although the United States continued to argue for open access for everyone. In the north, however, the Russians and Japanese had other ideas and looked to lop bits off the old empire that they could control in a more formal way. Russia gained Outer Manchuria in the 1860s, and in 1895 Japan gained Taiwan.

What happened next confirmed the worst fears of those who believed that imperialism must lead to war. In 1905, the two rivals went to war over Inner Manchuria, which Russia considered vital because it gave it access to a warm-water port on the Pacific,* and to which Japan felt entitled after its victory in 1895, even if it had been forced to return the Chinese cession of the area in the face of the opposition of the Western powers. There had been colonial conflicts before the Russo-Japanese War, but they had always been one-sided events in which an imperial power confronted either some backward tribes or a declining empire like China or Spain. This was the first time that two of the rising contenders for empire had fought one another with the full might of modern military technology. The Russo-Japanese War was shocking not just for its outcome, which witnessed the victory of an Asiatic

---

* In 1860, Russia took over much of Outer Manchuria from China and established Vladivostok as its first port on the Pacific. However, Vladivostok was icebound for several months during the winter, and in 1897, Russia forced China to grant it control of the strategically placed Port Arthur (now in the Chinese city of Dalian) in southern Manchuria, over strong Japanese objections.

upstart over one of the traditional Great Powers of Europe, but also precisely because it showed that conflict over empire could not always be avoided.

Why was it that Russia and Japan failed to resolve their differences peacefully whereas the other powers in the area managed to do so? The answer is likely to be proximity. Russia and Japan were neighbors of China and therefore viewed the acquisition of its territory as an inexorable process of national expansion—particularly Russia, which had extended its empire across Asia by precisely this method. The annexation of contiguous land was not only easier to contemplate but also spilled over into questions of national security. For Japan, Russia was not just a colonial competitor but a long-term threat to its safety. For Britain, France, and Germany, by contrast, China was very remote—even more so than Africa.

The same dangers of proximity can be seen in the struggle over the other great crumbling imperium that had long been ripe for dismemberment: the Ottoman Empire. By the beginning of the twentieth century, the empire was already much reduced from its heyday. In Africa it had lost Algeria, Tunis, and Egypt; in Europe it had lost Serbia, Greece, Bulgaria, Montenegro, and its Romanian provinces. The Ottomans retained, however, a huge swath of territory from Turkey through the Middle East. This area was to be the scene of a struggle among the European powers that at times looked as if it might well endanger the peace. The project of a railway linking the Bosphorus to the Persian Gulf was perhaps the most important and certainly most contentious of all the major railway projects of the late prewar period. Germany, which obtained the concession in 1899, aimed to become the major power in the area and to gain access to its vast agricultural and mineral riches (including, people now started to speculate, petroleum). The advantages of the railway went beyond access to resources. It also had a geopolitical dimension. In alliance with Turkey, the railway would provide a method of projecting German military power into Asia where it could threaten the British

Empire. In 1903, the German writer Paul Rohrbach made the strategic implications clear:

> If it comes to war . . . all idea of invading England is purely chimerical . . . England can be attacked and mortally wounded by land . . . only in one place—Egypt. The loss of Egypt would mean for England not only the end of her dominion over the Suez Canal, and of her connexions with India and the Far East, but would probably entail also the loss of her possessions in Central and East Africa . . . Turkey, however, can never dream of recovering Egypt until she is mistress of a developed railway system in Asia Minor and Syria.[49]

Not surprisingly, Britain was deeply hostile to the project and responded by creating a protectorate in Kuwait to block access to the Persian Gulf, and then refused to allow any increase in Ottoman customs duties to finance the Mesopotamian stretches of the railway.* More than one observer saw the parallels with the tensions that led to the Russo-Japanese War:

> The trans-Mesopotamian Railway . . . will play in the Near East the same ominous part which the Trans-Siberian played in the Far East; with this important difference, however, that whilst the Far Eastern conflict involved only one European Power and one Asiatic Power, the Near Eastern conflict, if it breaks out, must needs involve all the European Powers, must force the whole Eastern Question to a crisis, and, once begun, cannot be terminated until the map of Europe and Asia shall be reconstructed.[50]

---

* In the wake of the Ottoman default in 1875, the empire's finances were controlled by its European creditors to assure the punctual service of the restructured debt. Each major European power had to approve any change in the taxes administered by the Ottoman Public Debt Administration.

Unlike Russia and Japan, Britain and Germany managed to resolve their differences without resorting to arms. They did so by the classic Great Power method of dividing the area into spheres of interest. In a series of agreements between 1911 and 1914, Britain agreed to lift its objections to the railway as long as it went no farther than Baghdad, leaving Britain with an unchallenged dominance in southern Mesopotamia and the Gulf. Germany was left with a preeminent position in Anatolia and northern Mesopotamia, while France and Russia were satisfied with Syria and Armenia respectively.

However, even if the quarrels over the Bagdad Railway could be settled peacefully, this did not mean that compromise would always rule the day closer to home. It was in the Ottoman Empire in Europe that the most intractable conflicts arose, and it was in the Balkans that the "long peace" from 1815 to 1914 finally came to an end, when the assassination of the heir to the Austro-Hungarian empire by a Bosnian Serb nationalist led to a war that sucked in all the Great Powers. How could such a disastrous outcome to an apparently localized crisis have come about?

In many ways, the descent into war was the result of a series of missteps in which the Great Powers sleepwalked to disaster.[51] Apart from Austria-Hungary, which actually wanted a war, the other powers were gambling in a high-stakes poker game in the expectation that the other side would be forced into a humiliating climb down. The risks were compounded by strict timetables for military mobilization, which gave the decision for war a use-it-or-lose-it quality reminiscent of the Cold War. However, it is also true that the powers would not have been playing poker if they had not had underlying strategic reasons to contemplate resorting to war, and if the Balkan crisis had not seemed an opportune moment to gamble.

The First World War was, like several previous European wars that had involved most of the continent, a series of different conflicts fought concurrently, each with its own causes. It is scarcely surprising that with so many participants it is impossible to disentangle a single cause. Moreover, the Great Powers endeavored to win domestic support for war by presenting their opponents as aggressors and themselves as innocent victims—thus making their words and actions in July 1914 harder to decipher.

For Austria-Hungary, the war was about survival. As a multiethnic empire whose minorities were already chafing at the bit of German and Hungarian domination, it was highly vulnerable. Serbian nationalism threatened more than its Bosnian and Croatian provinces, potentially provoking the complete disintegration of the empire. The lesson of the Spanish-American War was that, in a world now ruthlessly divided into rising and declining empires, being European was no guarantee against being dismembered by more successful rivals. The only solution to Austria-Hungary's existential crisis was to eliminate the Serbian threat once and for all. The assassination in Sarajevo gave it the opportunity to do so.

Russian motives were more complex. As the self-proclaimed protector of Orthodox Christian Slavs throughout Eastern Europe, it could not allow the destruction of its Serbian client without suffering a considerable loss of prestige and influence in the Balkans. But more important were its long-term strategic ambitions in the Black Sea. Russia had never given up on its plans to get control of the Turkish Straits so as to gain unfettered access to the Mediterranean. It had already fought wars to achieve this ambition in the 1850s and the 1870s. As Russia's foreign minister Sergey Sazonov told Tsar Nicholas in January 1914, "The state which possesses the Straits will hold in its hands not only the key of the Black Sea and Mediterranean, but also that of penetration into Asia Minor and the sure means of hegemony in the Balkans."[52] But the straits were not only a key to further imperial expansion; they also were a potential threat to Russia's survival. Whoever controlled them could block Russia's use of its only warm-water port in Europe and prevent the export of wheat, the country's major source of foreign exchange. In the Russo-Japanese

War, Russia's Black Sea fleet had been prevented from taking part in the campaign against Japan because of Turkey's long-standing prohibition of foreign warships passing through the straits. Now Russia's hope of gaining control of the straits was threatened by Turkey's pending acquisition of two dreadnought battleships that were due to be delivered before the end of 1914. These ships would render Russia's fleet obsolete overnight. Once that occurred, the Russian ambassador in Constantinople warned, "in the event of a crisis, . . . the Turkish fleet will be able to strike a decisive blow against us. This blow will not only be devastating to our Black Sea fleet, but to our entire position in the Near East."[53] Since Britain had consistently opposed any attempt by Russia to take over the straits (and was supplying the dreadnoughts to Turkey), Russia's only hope of resolving this conundrum was to attack Turkey as part of a wider war in which Britain was on Russia's side. The Balkan crisis offered such a possibility.

Germany's calculations were equally complex. Like Russia, it could not stomach the damage to its prestige of a climb down by a close ally—especially after Germany's recent humiliation during the second Moroccan Crisis. And also like Russia, Germany faced a narrowing window of opportunity to go to war before the military odds turned against it.

Since the accession of William II in 1890, Germany had succeeded in maneuvering itself into a military cul-de-sac. Bismarck, once he had succeeded in unifying the country, had shown no further desire for military adventures and was concerned only to avoid making enemies. While there could be no friendship with France after the annexation of Alsace-Lorraine, Germany could at least maintain amicable relations with the other Great Powers. It was Bismarck's diplomacy, as much as anything, that kept the European peace in the 1870s and '80s. William, however, was convinced that Germany should no longer be content with its position in the world. Bismarck was dismissed, and the new aggressive tone of German foreign policy alienated many of the country's previous friends. The key alliance with Russia, which had lasted in different forms since 1815, was allowed to lapse in 1890. France was now able to woo Russia into an alliance in 1892—ending the isolation so carefully orchestrated by Bismarck and threatening Germany with invasion on two fronts in the event of another war. The solution to Germany's military dilemma was the Schlieffen Plan, which counted on knocking France out of the war in a few weeks before the ponderous might of the Russian army could be thrown against it. But after 1913, Russia had embarked on a program to increase the size of its army and, more important, to upgrade and expand its railway system. When completed, Russia would be able to reduce the time for mobilization to just over two weeks, and the Schlieffen Plan would be rendered useless. For Germany, the ideal war was one that started in the Balkans and therefore included Austria-Hungary, which would provide vital assistance against Russia in the crucial early weeks of fighting. It was for this reason that Germany was willing to gamble on the possibility of war by giving the Austrians a blank check to take as firm a position as they wished against Serbia in July 1914.

However, the rulers of Germany did not see war purely in terms of preemptive defense. There was a strong feeling that the worldwide scramble for imperial possessions had left Germany without its due rewards. Africa and East Asia were already carved up (although Admiral Victor Valois of the German navy could declare publicly in 1912 that "the division of continental possessions among the European powers will not be accomplished by claims on territory and colonial treaties. These decisions will be made only on the great European battlefields of the future"[54]).

There remained Europe. An increasing number of Germans were convinced that the only way for the country to ensure its rightful place among the top world powers was through the economic and political domination of the continent—whether by peaceful or nonpeaceful means. This was the basis of the "September Program," which outlined German aims in the first weeks of the war when a rapid victory still seemed possible. Russia should be thrust back out of Eastern Europe, and its role there replaced by a Central European customs union that would be extended to include France, Belgium, Holland, Demark, and Italy. In theory the union would have little formal authority, but "in practice [it] will be under German leadership and must stabilize Germany's economic dominance over Central Europe [Mitteleuropa]."* As part of this plan, France would have to sign a commercial treaty that would make it "economically dependent on Germany [and secure] the French market for our exports." Holland, related to Germany through ethnic ties, should be brought into a close relationship with the German empire without any compulsion, but in a form that would leave it "independent in externals, but be made internally dependent on us."[55] Such phrases make for uncomfortable reading in light of recent events in the eurozone. If Germany had won the war, most of Europe would have become an informal Teutonic empire.

After the war, France liked to portray itself as the hapless victim of German aggression. But its role was less innocent than it appeared. As the Balkan crisis unfolded, the French president Raymond Poincaré visited St. Petersburg, where he encouraged Russia to take a hard line against any Austrian aggression against Serbia. Although it is likely that the leaders of both countries were planning on an Austrian climb down rather than war, the military option was clearly on the table. Russia started to mobilize in secret as soon as Poincaré left. The decisions made in St. Petersburg were as important as those made in Vienna and Berlin in the collapse of peace.

Behind France's gamble lay its long-term rivalry with Germany. The loss of Alsace and Lorraine in 1871 was not only a deep and continuing affront to national pride; it was also a matter

---

* Mitteleuropa, as understood at the time, included Germany, Austria-Hungary, and most of the countries of what, after 1945, would be referred to as Eastern Europe—including Poland, the Baltic States, Romania, and Bulgaria.

of geostrategic importance. Lorraine contained Europe's largest deposits of iron ore, without which Germany's dominance of steelmaking would never have occurred. Before 1870, the iron- and steelmaking capacity of the two countries had been more or less equal; but after Germany's victory, its steel industry had powered ahead until by 1914 its output was almost four times greater than France's. Yet German economic ascendancy depended on "French" iron ore. For the next forty years, the mines of Lorraine were to be at the center of the struggle for the fate of Europe. Although France had no immediate thought of going to war with Germany to reclaim its lost provinces in 1914, they were at the top of any list of potential war aims. The French were well aware that they would have no hope of overcoming their enemy single-handedly. They could hope to succeed only in a general war where Germany would have to fight multiple enemies at once. A war that started in Eastern Europe, and pulled in Russia first, would be to its advantage.

That left Britain. The country had less reason than any other to want war. It had settled its differences with Germany over the Bagdad Railway, and the naval arms race appeared to have cooled down, with Berlin accepting that Kaiserliche Marine would not achieve anything like local parity with the Royal Navy in the foreseeable future. Moreover, Britain's ententes with France and Russia did not oblige it to go to war. Knowing this, Germany attempted to keep Britain out of the war almost as hard as France attempted to pull it in. Yet in the end Britain went to war over a mere "slip of paper"—the treaty that guaranteed Belgium's neutrality—siding with France and Russia in an act that the kaiser condemned as "racial treachery."

However, Britain, like France, Germany, and Russia, had strategic reasons to go to war that went beyond its official justification. For centuries British foreign policy had focused on preventing the rise of a single dominant power in Europe for fear that it would jeopardize British security. There was no reason to abandon this policy now; and in some ways it was even more relevant in 1914 than in earlier centuries because of Britain's growing dependency on sea trade. Whatever Germany said about respecting the territorial integrity of Belgium, it was more than likely that a German victory would give it control of the Belgian seaports, posing a direct threat to British control of the Channel. As the foreign secretary Sir Edward Grey explained the position to the cabinet, there were three fundamental British interests that could not under any circumstances be abandoned: (1) the German fleet should not occupy, under Britain's neutrality, the North Sea and English Channel; (2) Germany should not seize and occupy the northwestern part of France opposite Britain; and (3) Germany should not violate the ultimate independence of Belgium and occupy Antwerp as a standing menace to Britain.[56]

The other British calculation was more circuitous yet no less important. According to Grey, had Britain not declared war, "We should have been isolated; we should have had no friend in the world; no one would have . . . thought our friendship worth having."[57] This sounds on the surface like a simple piece of postfactual moralizing. Yet it reflected an important strategic reality. Britain's ententes with France and Russia were skin-deep. Little more than ten years earlier they, not Germany, had been seen as Britain's chief imperial rivals. To abandon them would risk reactivating their anti-British imperial strategies, which, in the case of Russia in particular, were seen as extremely dangerous. As Sir George Buchanan, the British ambassador to Russia, wrote to the Foreign Office in April 1914, "Russia is rapidly becoming so powerful that we must retain her friendship at almost any cost. If she acquires the conviction that we are unreliable and useless as a friend, she may one day strike a bargain with Germany and resume her liberty of action on Turkey and Persia."[58] Allies, in an unstable multipolar world, were potentially as dangerous as enemies. In the end, Britain was forced to compromise its long-standing policy of keeping Russia away from the Mediterranean in order to keep Germany away from the Channel.

Trade featured prominently in the motives that drove Europe

to war in 1914. For Britain and Russia it was control of straits that in hostile hands threatened economic strangulation. For Germany it was the expansion of its commercial empire. But in a grotesque inversion of the hopes of the liberals, trade was no longer the keeper of peace between nations but was at the center of a fight to the death for survival.

What was certain was that the rising bonds of commercial interdependence had not made war "obsolete" or "impossible" as had been claimed. In 1913, Germany's foreign trade was dominated by three partners: Britain, Russia, and the United States, each of which was more important to it, commercially, than its ally Austria-Hungary. For Britain, Germany was its second-largest trade partner, behind the United States but ahead of India. For Russia, Germany was even more important, constituting a third of its total trade. If the liberals had been right, these countries should never have gone to war—yet they did.

2

ECONOMIC WARFARE, 1914–1918

"That is good news, M. Bloch," I replied; "but is it not somewhat of a paradox? Only last year we had the Spanish-American war; the year before, the war between Turkey and Greece. Since when has war become impossible?"

"Oh," replied M. Bloch, with vivacity, "I do not speak of such wars. It is not such frontier brawls, or punitive operations such as you in England, for instance, are perpetually engaging in on the frontiers of your extended empire, that I refer to when I say that war has become impossible . . . The war of the future, the war which has become impossible, is the war that has haunted the imagination of mankind for the last thirty years, the war in which great nations armed to the teeth were to fling themselves with all their resources into a struggle for life and death."

—IVAN S. BLOCH,
Is War Now Impossible?, 1899

In 1898, the Russian political economist Ivan Bloch made a very convincing case that war between the Great Powers had become impossible, not in the sense that it could never occur but because the military and economic devastation that would ensue would make it unsustainable. Most of the terrible effects of modern warfare that Bloch described would require time to take their toll. But in 1914, financial devastation arrived even before the war started.

One of the striking things about July 1914 is that while in some ways the Great Powers were well prepared for war, in other ways they were scarcely ready at all. Their great military machines were, unfortunately, only too well primed for action. Mobilization plans went into effect almost like clockwork. It took only three days after its declaration of war on August 1 for Germany to invade Belgium with an army of 1.5 million men. Within a few weeks, over 6 million men had been mobilized and thrown into battle.

However, in other ways, the combatants were scarcely prepared at all. Among the least ready were the financiers who were supposed to lie behind imperialist wars. Far from being warmongers, they panicked at the thought of conflict. Ivan Bloch had forecast that "the immediate consequence of war would be to send securities all round down from 25 to 50 per cent."[1] A similar argument about the effect of war on asset prices had been made by Norman Angell in 1909. It turned out, however, that Bloch and Angell had *underestimated* the vulnerability of the global financial system. As the July crisis looked as if it might drag in Russia, Germany, and France, a wave of selling forced the closure of stock markets, including London's, even before war was declared. Government bond prices collapsed as Bloch had predicted. But the crisis went deeper and wider than that, spreading with astonishing speed around the world. Stock markets closed all over Europe, the United States, Latin America, and the Far East. The London discount market, responsible for financing half of all world trade, collapsed, rendering almost all the great names of merchant banking potentially insolvent. By August 1, *The Economist* was reporting that the financial world was "staggering under a series of blows such as the delicate system of international credit has never before witnessed, or even imagined . . . Nothing so widespread and so world-wide has ever been known before."[2] The worldwide "dash for cash" led to bank closures, the suspension of convertibility, and to moratoria on debt repayments. Economic activity came to a virtual standstill. Unemployment surged, rising in Berlin from 6 percent to 20 percent of the workforce.[3]

The problem was that the financiers appeared to have digested Angell's warnings all too well. They had been lulled into a sense of false security by their awareness of the awful consequences of war between industrial powers, but they had too little influence in government to prevent it. Lord Rothschild, the head of the English branch of the banking house, invested all his energy in attempting to forestall the downward spiral toward war, encouraging his French cousins to use their influence in France and Russia, and intervening with *The Times* to tone down its prowar editorial stance—to no avail. In 1902, Hobson had argued that financiers like the Rothschilds controlled the destiny of Europe: "Does any one seriously suppose that a great war could be undertaken by any European State, or a great State loan subscribed, if the house of Rothschild and its connections set their face against it?"[4] How wrong he was.

Hobson may have been proved wrong, but so, it turned out, was Angell. The threat of war may have set off the financial crisis that he had foretold—indeed, the crisis was more severe than he had imagined—but it was not enough to forestall the conflict. Governments simply ignored the chaos and went to war anyway. Yet perhaps there was still a chance. Even if governments insisted on fighting, the speed of financial and economic collapse might be such that they would run out of money before too many people were killed.

Unfortunately even that hope was dashed by events. It turned out economies and financial systems could be adjusted to war conditions after all. The gold standard came to an end as countries refused to convert money into gold, even in Britain and the United States, which maintained the pretense that their currencies were still convertible. Once liberated from the need to back their notes by gold, central banks resolved the liquidity crisis by issuing more paper money. The sophisticated international financial system that had underwritten the first era of globalization was replaced by a single crude equation: The markets financed the government, and the government paid in cash. Bond markets settled after their initial falls, and governments were able to borrow enormous sums at rates of between 4.5 percent and 6 percent. These rates were around 2 percent higher than before the war, but they were not unaffordable. Where bond markets proved inadequate, central banks stepped into the breach. This did, in due course, lead to inflation, as Bloch had predicted, but not to financial collapse. The initial slump in economic activity was short-lived once unprecedented levels of government war spending started to act as a fiscal stimulus. Unemployment was replaced by labor shortages as conscription thinned the ranks of industrial workers. Industries had to adapt their output to the needs of war, but there was no shortage of demand for their goods. The speed with which the global financial system was put back on its feet and retooled for war is the reason why Richard Roberts, the author of the authoritative book on the subject, describes the episode as the "unknown financial crisis."[5]

But if the war dashed the hopes of those liberals who believed that economic interdependence would make war impossible, it confirmed the worst fears of their philosophical opponents who worried that dependence on trade rendered their countries vulnerable in time of war.

In 1914, there were many who hoped the war would be brief—if only because the alternative was too dire to contemplate. As a result, although every country had plans for a short war, almost none had prepared for the war of grinding attrition that actually ensued. By October, munitions were already running low among all the combatants. None of them had accumulated any stockpiles of food or strategic raw materials. Ivan Bloch, however, had forecast that a Great Power war, if it occurred, would be one of attrition, and he made one particular prediction about how it would be decided: "In reality the war of the future, if ever it takes place, will not be [ended by] fighting; it will be terminated by famine." He looked at the relative exposure of different countries to the interruption of their food supplies and noted that it was the most economically successful countries that were most at risk, precisely because they were the most industrialized and urbanized. Their strength was their weakness. "It cannot be too often repeated that the disastrous consequences of war will be especially felt in countries with highly developed industries—that is in Germany, France, and England."[6]

In particular he pointed to Britain as the most vulnerable country of all. Because its teeming industrial cities were confined within a small island, domestic production of wheat and other grains was no more than one-third of its needs. In Bloch's view, a few swift enemy cruisers roaming the seas could be enough to disrupt the country's food supply:

> The immense development of British industry is calculated upon access to the markets of the whole world, and relies upon the uninterrupted export of products. In England every cessation of export means a stoppage of work, involving the withdrawal of the means of subsistence from the greater part of her population. The production of wheat in that country . . . has . . . diminished to such an extent that the stoppage of the import of wheat into England would threaten the whole population with famine.[7]

British governments were well aware of the country's vulnerability. This was why they were determined to maintain its naval dominance at all costs. But they were equally aware that it was not only Britain that was vulnerable. Germany had a growing dependence on seaborne trade as well. As long as the Royal Navy commanded the seas, Germany could be blockaded into submission. In 1906, Admiral Fisher had mused,

> It is so very peculiar that Providence has arranged England as a sort of huge breakwater against German commerce, which must all come either one side of the breakwater through the

Straits of Dover, or the other side of the breakwater the north of Scotland. It's a unique position of advantage that we possess, and such is our naval superiority that on the day of war we "mop up" 800 German merchant steamers. Fancy the "knockdown" blow to German trade and finance![8]

Before the war, some British strategists had hoped that the mere threat of such a British blockade would act as a deterrent. In 1912, Lord Esher, an influential Liberal politician, argued that Great Britain possessed "the means of exercising such enormous and fatal pressure upon Germany, by putting every obstacle in the way of commercial intercourse . . . that I . . . can hardly conceive that Germany, except by an act of madness, would embark upon a war under such conditions."[9] By August 1914, such apparently rational hopes were proved to have been in vain. Germany ignored the threat of blockade, just as it ignored the financial crisis. Yet there remained the hope that a blockade, if executed with sufficient determination, might bring the war to a close without too much loss of life. While the continental powers prepared for a land war conducted by armies, Britain prepared for an economic war conducted at sea. The bulk of the fleet was moved to Scapa Flow in the Orkneys, where it could control the sea-lanes between Scotland and Norway. A smaller contingent was left to control the narrow Straits of Dover. The British "navalist" strategy contemplated at most a small expeditionary land force to support France in its battle with the German army until the sea blockade would bring the war to an end. In the cabinet meeting of August 1, Winston Churchill, the First Lord of the Admiralty, argued that a naval war would cost no more than £25 million.

Such hopes of a quick and relatively painless outcome also proved in vain. Although the British blockade did turn out to be a powerful weapon, it took years, not weeks, to make an impact. The initial effect of the war was to bring all trade with Europe to a halt, even without the formal declaration of a blockade. The Royal Navy cleared the seas of German merchant ships, and no others dared to put to sea. However, it was soon found that a total stoppage of trade, although undoubtedly damaging to the German economy, was not sustainable. Economic warfare on this scale harmed not only Germany but also the highly trade-dependent British economy, compounding the effects of the barely contained financial crisis.[10] More important, it ran afoul of international political realities. What was to happen to trade with neutral countries? In the Napoleonic War, Britain had seized neutral ships that it suspected of trading with France, and this had led to war with the United States in 1812. One hundred years later, the United States had grown into an economic behemoth, armed with a powerful navy and a determination to uphold the rights of neutral states in wartime. Britain could not afford to alienate a country on whose goods and credit it would increasingly rely, let alone risk another War of 1812.

The most immediate issue between Washington and London was the fate of the American cotton crop. Cotton was important not only for making clothes; it was vital for making explosives. Moreover, in 1914, cotton was still substantially the largest American export, producing around $550 million in foreign exchange annually compared to only $200 million from wheat exports. The collapse of international trade in August 1914 threatened not only economic ruin in the Southern states but also the loss of foreign exchange and the consequent threat of America being forced off the gold standard. Against the strong opposition of the Royal Navy, the British government bowed to pressure from Washington to remove cotton from the list of contraband materials in October. The result was that American exports of cotton to Holland and Scandinavia rose from 21,000 tons in 1913 to 330,000 tons in the first year of the war, almost all of the additional tonnage destined for Germany.[11]

The navy argued that a huge opportunity to bring the war to an end had been wasted through the interference of politicians. But even though the blockade was not as lethal as originally hoped, it was not ineffective. Ways were found progressively to tighten its grip, most importantly by making agreements with neutral countries to limit their imports to prewar levels. Germany's imports could not be stopped entirely, but in 1915 they were more than 40 percent below prewar levels, while its exports fell by more than 70 percent.[12] The most important impact of the blockade was on food supply. Before the war, Germany had imported approximately 19 percent of its total calories. This was a considerably lower level of dependence on overseas supply than Britain's, but it was made possible only by the intensive use of fertilizer to obtain very high agricultural yields at home. Before the war, Germany managed to feed seventy to seventy-five people per one hundred acres of farmland, compared to forty-five to fifty people in Britain. The most important items in the British list of contraband, therefore, were not so much foodstuffs themselves, but fertilizers. The amounts allowed to neutral countries were severely curtailed to ensure than none filtered through to Germany. As a result, the country had to cope not just with the shutting off of food imports but also with lower harvests at home. By 1917, the tonnage of rye, the basic cereal in the German diet, was down to 57 percent of its prewar level, and wheat and barley were as low as 50 percent. In an attempt to keep up cereal production, meat production was reduced to a bare minimum so that it provided no more than 12 percent of prewar dietary levels. But even cereal consumption was reduced by 50 percent, and overall calorie intake was probably as low as 30 percent of prewar levels.[13]

Germany had no clear answer to a British blockade, even though it had understood the risk before the war. Like Britain, it rejected the idea of precautionary stockpiles as too expensive and impractical. Tirpitz's strategy of building a powerful battleship fleet to rival the Royal Navy turned out to be a waste of money, creating a "show fleet" that did little or nothing to alter the balance of power. Not only had Britain won the naval arms race, but by making strategic alliances with other countries, Britain had been able to redeploy the large majority of its fleet to the North Sea. There remained the hope that the Royal Navy would attempt a close blockade of the German coast following tactics used in previous wars. By deploying the new asymmetric technologies of mines, torpedo boats, and submarines, Germany would be able to weaken the British forces to the point where a showdown between the mighty dreadnoughts could take place on favorable terms, producing a decisive victory that would overturn British control of the seas.

The problem with this plan was that Britain did not take the bait. It merely stationed its fleet at Scapa Flow in the Orkney Islands where it could block any attempt of German warships to break out into the Atlantic to disrupt British sea trade. Instead of a close blockade, Britain instituted a "distant blockade." This was nearly impossible to counter by military means short of a direct confrontation with the British fleet, which the German navy did not wish to face. Much historical attention has been focused on the Battle of Jutland in May 1916, when the two fleets finally met in the largest combat between armored battleships in history. The outcome, somewhat to the chagrin of the Royal Navy, which expected a repeat of Trafalgar, was an indecisive series of encounters after which the German fleet retreated back to base while claiming victory on the basis of sinking a few more ships than it lost. In reality, however, no outcome other than an overwhelming German victory at small cost would have affected the shape of the war, and such an outcome was never in the cards since the German strategy was only to ambush and destroy a small part of the British fleet in the hopes of slowly tilting the overall naval odds in its favor. Finding itself instead lured into a battle with the whole British fleet, it retreated as fast as possible rather than face destruction, never again venturing out into the high seas for the remainder of the war. The North Sea stayed firmly in British hands, and the blockade remained intact.

A far more plausible strategy was to concentrate on British weakness. After all, Britain was even more dependent on sea trade than Germany, importing around two-thirds of its food supplies. Given the dominance of the Royal Navy, a full-scale blockade of the British coast was impossible, but attacks on British trade by fast cruisers around the world might create such a panic that the country would be forced to the negotiating table. Under Tirpitz's influence, Germany's prewar planning was always focused on the main battle fleet, but preparations were also made for commerce warfare. In 1911, the head of the German cruiser fleet, Vice Admiral von Krosigk, argued that not only would commerce raiding throw the British economy into crisis; it also would force the Royal Navy to disperse its forces away from the North Sea, giving the German fleet the opportunity of battle on favorable terms.[14] Germany's problem in implementing this strategy was that compared to Britain, it had very few overseas bases from which its cruisers could operate. The best placed of these was at Tsingtao in Germany's Chinese concession, where its East Asia cruiser squadron was deployed. However, as part of its strategic realignment at the beginning of the century, Britain had allied itself with Japan. At the start of the war, it encouraged Japan to declare war on Germany and take over its poorly protected East Asian empire—an invitation the Japanese, unsurprisingly, found easy to accept. Once the Japanese navy blockaded Tsingtao, the East Asia squadron was deprived of its base, and while attempting to return to Germany, it was destroyed en route at the Battle of the Falklands. One lone member of the squadron, the *Emden*, conducted a whirlwind campaign against British shipping in the Indian Ocean before being put out of action by an Australian warship in November 1914.

Commerce warfare conducted by cruisers was therefore a nonstarter. The alternative lay with a completely new form of naval technology. Submarines had come into service after 1900, and although largely untested, their ability to attack unseen raised alarm throughout naval and political circles. During the late nineteenth century, at the same time as advances in military technology were making possible slaughter on a hitherto unimaginable scale, the nations of the "civilized world" had been attempting to put limits on the horrors of war. The International Red Cross was founded in 1863, and under its auspices the Geneva Conventions of 1864 and 1906 laid down standards for dealing with sick and wounded enemy soldiers. At the same time, the Hague Conventions of 1899 and 1907 attempted to set limits for the use of force. The 1907 convention made a particular attempt to come to grips with the issues surrounding naval blockades. Among these was the treatment of intercepted merchant ships. A code of practice was established that demanded that ships suspected of carrying contraband should be notified, then searched. If a ship could not be seized and taken to port, the safety of its crew had to be ensured before it was sunk.

There were two problems with the Declaration of London— the agreement produced by the 1907 convention. The first was that it was never fully ratified, even though all countries started out the war as if its terms were in effect. The second, and more significant, defect of the Hague Conventions was that technology was rendering them redundant even as they were being negotiated. In the light of subsequent history, the 1899 convention's ban on the dropping of bombs from balloons appears quixotic. The 1907 convention simply ignored the possible use of submarines in commerce warfare. Clearly they did not have crews large enough to take over merchant ships, nor did they have enough space to take merchant crews on board before sinking their prizes. By the terms of the Declaration of London they were effectively barred from taking part in blockades and were restricted to use against warships.

Yet even at the time, some were aware that the civilized codes of conduct embodied in the declaration might not be worth the paper they were written on. Admiral Fisher, for one, was skeptical that anyone would play by the rules when it came to war. "Did anyone say one word when Admiral Togo, in cold blood, and before the declaration of war [in 1895], sank an English steamer with 2,000 Chinese troops on board, and only picked up the British crew?" he asked rhetorically in a memorandum in early 1914 to Winston Churchill—who responded with understandable indignation but complete failure to foresee what was in store: "I do not believe this would ever be done by a civilised power."[15]

German hopes of a quick defeat of France were destroyed at the Battle of the Marne in September 1914, and by the end of the year it was clear that defenders armed with machine guns and protected by trenches and barbed-wire fields were almost impossible for attackers to overcome. The war of attrition, so much feared, had arrived. The British blockade was starting to tighten its grip, and the German fleet was impotent to stop it. A new strategy was needed, and German naval command came to the conclusion that the only solution was submarine warfare. That this would mean tearing up the Hague Convention was clear, and the risks to Germany were enormous. It might not matter too much to sink British merchant ships without warning, since the countries were at war anyway. But British supplies might be carried in neutral ships, or on British passenger ships that might also be carrying the citizens of neutral countries. For the German blockade to be successful, all ships would have to be sunk. Britain could perhaps afford irritating the United States by progressively extending the scope of its blockade, since this involved only property. Germany's resort to unrestricted submarine warfare would surely end up killing American citizens, and this could easily provoke the United States into casting aside its neutrality and joining Germany's enemies. In February 1915, after much debate, the kaiser gave permission for unrestricted submarine warfare around the British Isles, and in May the British liner *Lusitania* was sunk with the loss of 129 American lives among 1,198 total deaths. The public was outraged, and the United States very nearly entered the war at that point. To avoid this outcome, which would inevitably lead to defeat, Germany was forced to scale back its submarine war against merchant shipping in the Atlantic, and then cancel it altogether in September. The U-boat campaign remained in force elsewhere, taking a continuous toll of shipping in the Mediterranean. But without a blockade of the Atlantic sea-lanes it was never going to bring Britain to its knees.

Although naval blockades and counterblockades were the most visible part of the war of resources, there were other equally important battlefronts elsewhere. The Industrial Revolution was based, more than anything else, on two fundamental inputs: coal and iron ore. Without the two, steel could not be manufactured and modern warfare would be impossible.

In 1914, the world steel industry had three major centers, each one connected with an area where both coal and iron ore were found in abundance. The first to be developed was in Britain, which nature had endowed with plentiful supplies of both resources connected first by canals and later by railways. By 1914, the greatest steelmaking area of all was in the United States, where the Great Lakes provided a cheap way of linking the iron ore deposits of Minnesota with the coalfields of Pennsylvania and Ohio. Continental Europe also had an abundance of the two materials within convenient transport range. However, as a result of the tortuous turns of European history, they were spread over three countries. Coal was found in a sweep from Westphalia in Germany, through Belgium and into northeastern France, with the largest deposits located in the Ruhr Valley. The great iron ore basin of Lorraine provided the other necessary raw material, with transport between the two regions provided by the Rhine and its numerous tributaries.

The most cost-effective arrangement was for the steel mills to be located close to coal deposits, where they could easily supply the manufacturers of steel products who also depended on coal for their power. This explained why Pittsburgh, Pennsylvania, was the great American steel town, not Duluth, Minnesota. The logic of transport suggested that the largest concentration of steelworks in continental Europe would be in the Ruhr Valley.

These geopolitical facts were well understood by politicians and military planners. In 1870, Germany's steelmaking industry was in its infancy, but it was already recognized that the country lacked iron ore, and that ample supplies were to be found just over the border in France. The presence of German-speaking populations in Alsace and Lorraine was a convenient excuse for their annexation after the Franco-Prussian War. In the late nineteenth century, the iron ore of Lorraine became essential to Germany's rise to dominance of European steel manufacture. But the German part of Lorraine was not sufficient for German needs. The French had discovered even larger reserves in the residual French part of the province, and by the early twentieth century these ores had become a crucial resource for both German and French steelmaking. It was abundantly clear that Lorraine was a major economic prize, and the temptation for both countries to shift the border in their favor was enormous. The annexation of the French part of the iron ore basin became a central part of Germany's war aims, just as the return of its lost provinces was the central feature of France's.

After the war, France published a captured document as evidence of the lust for power and conquest that had driven Germany's war strategy:

> Our mining base enlarged by the addition of Briey and Longwy [in French Lorraine] would insure for a century the future of our iron industry, and would hence insure also our retention of the place which . . . we have conquered during the last ten years among the iron-making countries of the world, at the cost of hard struggles with Great Britain . . . All of Lorraine in the hands of Germany would constitute not only a war indemnity and a support for the German fatherland, but also a guarantee of a lasting peace and a gauge for the security of the empire . . . If this opportunity be neglected, the German people will in a future war be doomed to ruin.[16]

When the document was written, Germany was sitting pretty in terms of essential industrial resources. Its initial thrust into France through Belgium, even if unsuccessful in its objective of knocking France out of the war, had left Germany in possession of not only France's iron ore but also 60 percent of its iron- and steel-manufacturing capacity. Moreover, its conquest of Belgium and northeastern France had given it control of coalfields that provided half of France's coal and all of Belgium's. In August 1914, the steelmaking capacity of the rival alliances had been almost equal at around twenty-two million tons each. By the end of the year, the balance had tilted strongly in favor of the Central Powers by the transfer of around six million tons of capacity from France and Belgium to Germany.[17]

But even with Lorraine in its pocket, German steelmaking was not entirely self-sufficient. Before the war, both British and German steelmakers depended on imported high-grade iron ore to supplement the relatively low-grade output of British and Lorraine mines. The main sources were Sweden and Spain. As long as it kept the sea-lanes open, Britain could import iron ore from wherever it liked during the war. But for Germany it was another matter. Spain was effectively closed as a result of the British blockade. Sweden was the only possible source of supply. The country was impossible for Britain to blockade with surface ships because the German navy dominated the Baltic (this at least was a positive outcome of the German naval buildup). Britain managed to deploy a squadron of submarines to the area, but their operational success was limited by their adherence to the gentlemanly rules of the Declaration of London.

There remained coal, Europe's essential fuel. Before the war, Britain was not only Europe's largest coal producer but also, and more importantly, its predominant exporter, accounting for 60 percent of total world exports. Among its customers was Sweden, a fact that should have provided the necessary leverage to keep its iron ore out of German hands. But Germany's conquest of French and Belgian coal mines in 1914 brought its output closer to the level of Britain's, so that it was now able to wield the coal weapon almost as effectively as its rival. In 1915, a confidential memorandum to Bethmann-Hollweg noted, "Today coal is the most decisive means of influence. The neutral states are obliged to obey the commands of that one of the belligerents who can supply them with coal."[18] Britain's hoped-for leverage with Sweden was greatly reduced once Germany was able to offer an alternative source of fuel.

The major concern of British coal strategy was supplying its allies, especially once the territorial losses of 1914 made France heavily dependent on imports. The problem was aggravated by falling British production as a result of conscription. Before the war, France and Italy had taken 30 percent of British coal exports. By 1916, this had risen to 60 percent. The Italian supply route was particularly hazardous since German U-boats continued to attack at will in the Mediterranean, unconcerned about American opinion. By 1916, coal prices in Italy had risen to six times their prewar level. However, the German blockade was never able to reduce French or Italian overall wartime imports, which rose throughout the war while Germany's declined. By 1917, France's total imports were 80 percent higher in real terms than in 1913, while Germany's were more than 60 percent lower.[19]

Against Russia, however, the German naval blockade was more effective. Although Russia had substantial coal mines in the Donbass region in southeastern Ukraine, it remained partially dependent on British coal for its industrial base near the Baltic. The outbreak of war meant an instant closing of the Baltic supply route, leaving the Black Sea route via the Turkish Straits more vital than ever. In August 1914, at the behest of Russia, Britain canceled its pending delivery of two dreadnoughts to Turkey. This left an opportunity for Germany to fill the British void. The German Mediterranean squadron, consisting of the modern battle cruiser *Goeben* and the light cruiser *Breslau*, managed to evade the British and French fleets in a dramatic game of cat and mouse as it made a dash for the Dardanelles. There the two warships handed themselves over to Turkey and were immediately reflagged as Turkish even while the Ottoman Empire was still neutral. Two months later, the *Goeben*, now renamed the *Yavuz* but still with its German crew, was instrumental in bringing Turkey into the war on the German side by bombarding Sevastopol without authorization.

Russia's prewar fears about Turkish possession of a modern battleship proved correct. The *Goeben* outgunned anything the Russians possessed, and the Turkish Straits were closed to Russia for the duration of the war, preventing exports of grain or imports of coal or war matériel. The unsuccessful British campaign at Gallipoli in 1915 was designed to reopen the Black Sea supply route by capturing Constantinople. Its failure left Russia dependent on supplies from the distant ports of Vladivostok and Murmansk. This, and the constant need to transport coal to the north, exacerbated the strains on the backward Russian railway system. Russia's increasing inability to keep supplies moving was one of the factors in the economic collapse that led to the demise of the regime and Russia's withdrawal from the war.

The war of iron and coal was largely a stalemate, with the advantage tilting toward Germany. But there was another fuel whose presence was beginning to make itself felt where there was a somewhat greater chance of Allied success. At the start of the war, coal was almost the only fuel of any military significance. It was coal that powered the trains that carried soldiers and munitions to the front. Beyond the railheads, transport was provided largely by horses, as had been the case before the Industrial Revolution. The German army mobilized 700,000 horses in the first weeks of the war. However, the rapid wartime technological changes brought petroleum into the picture. Motorized transport became increasingly important, and by the end of the war the British army had 57,000 motor vehicles. In the meantime, the stalemate on the Western Front was being broken by two oil-powered inventions: tanks and aircraft. At the beginning of the war, air forces did not even exist, yet by the end of the war France had produced 68,000 military aircraft, Germany 48,000, and Britain 55,000. At sea, the battle of the blockades was being radically altered by diesel-powered submarines. Moreover, in 1912,

Britain was the first to start converting its surface fleet to oil in the interests of increased speed and range. By 1918, nearly half the ships in the Royal Navy were (or could be, since many were dual-fuel) powered by oil.

The potential Allied advantage in the oil war derived, paradoxically, from the fact that unlike coal, relatively little oil was to be found in Europe. World production before the war was dominated by the United States, with 65 percent of the total. Russia had another 16 percent, and there were smaller quantities in Mexico, Romania, Galicia (in Poland), and the Dutch East Indies. The only supplies in the British Empire were in Burma, but there was increasing interest in the possibilities of the Middle East. In 1901, the British entrepreneur William Knox D'Arcy had obtained a concession to prospect in Iran, which in 1909 became the basis for the Anglo-Persian Oil Company (later BP). The safety of British oil interests in the Persian Gulf, as well as the prospect of major finds in Mesopotamia, was one of the issues that lay beneath the surface of the Anglo-German disputes over the Bagdad Railway before the war. In June 1914, in order to establish secure oil supplies for the navy, the British government bought a 51 percent interest in Anglo-Persian. After Turkey entered the war, there were worries that it would mount an attack on the company's refinery on the island of Abadan at the top of the Persian Gulf. This, as much as anything else, prompted the British invasion of Mesopotamia in late 1914. Although Anglo-Persian's production rose rapidly during the war, it was able to satisfy only 20 percent of the navy's increasing appetite for oil. But Britain had other ample sources of supply, not least from the United States—as long as the sea-lanes remained open.

Germany's position was far more difficult. Before the war, it had depended on oil from Galicia, Romania, and above all the United States. During the war, American oil was cut off, Galicia was a battleground in 1915, and Romania declared war on Germany in 1916. As German petroleum needs escalated to cope with the increasing demands of its submarines, aircraft, and motor transports, it was forced to develop substitutes based on coal tar. But its most important objective was to capture the Romanian oil fields in which German consortia had invested so much before the war. A combined German and Austro-Hungarian offensive looked set to take the fields in late 1916, but a last-ditch demolition was carried out under the direction of a team sent from Britain, which was well aware of the stakes. German engineers worked around the clock to repair the damage, but production in 1917 was only 30 percent of its old level. Throughout the war, Germany suffered from a chronic shortage of oil, and its ability to conduct mechanized land warfare was always constricted. Moreover, in 1917, priority had to be given to the needs of the navy.

It was on the seas that Germany would make its greatest gamble of the war. The Royal Navy ruled the waves, but German submarines moved largely unchallenged below. The desire to turn the tables on the British blockade had never left the German navy, and it continued to lobby for a return to unrestricted submarine warfare. Studies by German economists showed that British wheat supplies were sufficient for six to seventeen weeks. If the U-boats could sink an average of 600,000 tons of shipping per month, Britain would have to sue for peace within six months. It would not matter if the Americans declared war: The outcome would be decided before they could mobilize their resources. In January 1917, the die was cast, and Germany announced the resumption of unrestricted submarine warfare around the British Isles at the beginning of February. Initially the campaign went even better than expected. For the first six months of the campaign, average sinkings were 630,000 tons per month. Moreover, it took the United States until April to declare war, so Germany had a further two months' start in its race for British collapse. At the end of April, the most destructive month in the whole war with 867,000 tons of merchant shipping lost, British wheat stocks had fallen as low as six weeks, and oil stocks were little more than half the threshold of safety. There were moments of nervousness bordering on panic in Whitehall. Yet the collapse did not occur.

The most important change came with the introduction of convoys in May. Thanks to the success of the initial experiments, by the end of July almost all shipping in the Atlantic was organized on this basis, and by September the rate of loss to U-boats had fallen back to the levels of 1916. Moreover, the German economists had underestimated the number of ships that Britain could marshal and had failed to forecast the rate at which Britain, and more important, the United States, could rebuild their fleets. There was a difficult moment in early 1917 when a whole year's worth of shipbuilding was lost in three months. But that was before the American shipbuilding drive really got under way. In 1918, Britain and America launched 4 million tons compared to losses of 2.5 million tons. But the failure of the submarine war was apparent before that. British wheat stocks were higher at the end of 1917 than they had been a year earlier, and although the losses of merchant ships and their crews continued until the very end of the war, there was never a serious interruption of the vast movement of American resources, both human and material, across the Atlantic.

The entry of the United States into the war turned out to be as decisive as the Allies hoped and as Germany feared. Even before any American soldiers were readied for combat, the change in the position of the two sides was striking. The most immediate result was a further tightening of the Allied blockade. Once the United States joined the war, its concern for the rights of neutrals was transformed into an emphasis on the rights of combatants. Residual shipments of American goods to Germany through neutral countries came to an abrupt end. American exports to Sweden, for instance, fell by more than 80 percent between 1917 and 1918. At the same time, the United States increased its shipment of supplies to the Allies, with ample finance to cover their cost.

Yet for all the change in Allied fortunes, the American entry into the war did not turn it into a rout. If there was any rout in the following year, it was on the Eastern Front, where Russia's collapse into revolution allowed Germany to win a complete victory.

A lopsided treaty was signed at Brest-Litovsk, which left Germany in control of the whole of Eastern Europe up to the frontier of Russia proper.

Before the war, the idea of a German-dominated Central Europe had been little more than a dream. It had taken more concrete shape once the war started, and it became part of German war aims. In 1915, the publication of Friedrich Naumann's *Mitteleuropa* gave the idea a wide popular circulation. The first step would be a customs union with Austria-Hungary and a nominally independent Poland. Other countries of Eastern Europe would inevitably be subsumed into the German-led federation, for there was no future for small countries in a world of global powers: "Sooner or later they must anyway decide with which union they will or can range themselves . . . This is a harsh necessity, a heavy fate, but it is the overpowering tendency of the age, the categorical imperative of human evolution . . . People must submit earlier or later, freely or from compulsion."[20] After Brest-Litovsk, the dream of Mitteleuropa became, briefly, a reality. The Russian empire in Europe was dismantled, and its constituent parts were ruled by German-backed governments. Austria-Hungary and Bulgaria were allies. Serbia and Romania had been conquered. Germany now had almost all the resources it needed for self-sufficiency. Naumann urged General Erich Ludendorff to sue for peace with the Allies in order to hold on to these extraordinary gains:

> So far, our war gain has been the creation and welding together of Central Europe; it means our economic, military, and political inclusion on equal terms among the political associations in the world . . . The Americans and British are deliberately aiming at the destruction of this war gain . . . and they are prolonging the war on this account . . . [The Central European] federation would be broken up for the future by a secession on the part of Austria-Hungary [which] would almost certainly occur if the war were prolonged until 1919.[21]

But Ludendorff thought differently. Victory in the east allowed German armies to be diverted to the west for a final massive offensive that would overwhelm the French and British before the Americans could arrive in force. Equally important, it opened up the prospect of overcoming the Allied blockade. Food could be obtained from the fertile farmlands of the Ukraine. Oil could be obtained from Romania, now in German hands, and from the Russian fields in the Caucasus, on which Turkish troops were rapidly advancing.

If the war had been prolonged into 1919 or 1920, some of these German hopes for new supplies might have become reality. But in 1918, German forces moving into the Ukraine found that the chaos of the wartime Russian economy had drastically reduced agricultural production, and there was no food to be had. Romanian oil was being shipped in reasonable quantities by the middle of the year, but it was no longer sufficient for modern mechanized warfare. Baku (the center of the Russian oil industry, now in Azerbaijan) fell to Germany's Turkish allies in mid-September, too late to make any difference to the outcome of the war. One of the reasons that the German offensive in the spring of 1918 failed was that large numbers of famished German soldiers stopped to loot Allied supply dumps rather than press home their attack. Another was that Germany was never able to field a tank force on the scale of Britain or France. With its chronic shortage of oil, it is not certain that it would have been able to fuel such a force even if it had one. By October, German oil supplies were sufficient for only two further months of mechanized fighting.

The debate over the causes of the German defeat started raging even before the armistice was signed on November 11. Was Germany defeated on the battlefront, or was it "stabbed in the back" by defeatism and revolution on the home front? On October 26, the new foreign minister, Wilhelm Solf, already felt that he had to counter the finger-pointing of the generals. In his view, "Public opinion was so depressed . . . because our military power had been broken. They were now trying to say that our military power would collapse if our national *morale* did not hold out. This attempt to shift responsibility could not be permitted."[22]

This argument, so poisonous and damaging to the stability of the postwar Weimar Republic, was paralleled by an equally important though less contentious debate on the Allied side. Was the war won at sea by the effects of the naval blockade, or on land by the efforts of the Allied armies on the battlefield? In the years after the war, British writing generally argued that it was the blockade that had decided the outcome of the war. This narrative was reassuring to British ears because it gave the major responsibility for victory to the Royal Navy rather than to the French army. More important, it held out the hope that any future war could be won by this relatively painless method of fighting, thereby avoiding a repeat of the awful carnage of the trenches. Subsequent scholarship has modified these views. The blockade is now generally seen as a vital factor in the weakening of Germany, but not decisive on its own. At the end of the war, food supplies in Germany were low, but no lower than in 1917. Oil was in short supply, but not so short as to prevent Germany fighting on, as Ludendorff wanted, especially since the navy still held ample supplies.

The claim that the war was entirely won on the battlefield is also difficult to substantiate. The Allied offensive that started in July had pushed the German line back into Belgium by late October. But the Allied advance had slowed as it moved farther out of the range of logistical support by rail, and after a spate of mass surrenders German resolve appeared to have stiffened as the armies came closer to the German border. At the end of October, Field Marshal Douglas Haig wrote in his diaries that "the enemy has not yet been sufficiently beaten to cause him to accept an ignominious peace."[23] Ludendorff was convinced that the army could hold out, at least long enough to get better terms, and had to be forced from his post before the war could be brought to an end.

The reasons for the German collapse became such a vital issue not just for Germany but for the world because of the role it played in the rise of Nazism. Hitler, like all German nationalists, was convinced that the nation had been betrayed by the "November Criminals." The theory of the "stab in the back" by a pernicious alliance of Socialists, pacifists, and Jews allowed him to discredit the entire Weimar Republic. Yet, if the field of vision is broadened, it is apparent that Germany's collapse was little different from that of other defeated countries.

It is one of the most striking features of the First World War that, in spite of—or perhaps because of—its totality, none of the major combatants was defeated through conquest. In every case they gave up before their armies had been forced to cede any significant national territory. German nationalists made much of the fact that German armies were still outside its borders when the end came. But so too were Austro-Hungarian armies when the Dual Monarchy sued for peace at the end of October. By the time its representatives signed an armistice on November 3, the Habsburg empire had effectively ceased to exist. Its constituent parts had already declared independence amid food riots on the streets and mass desertions in the army. A similar pattern had occurred in Russia the year before. Although Russia had been forced to cede eastern Poland and much of Lithuania to Germany in 1915, the front line thereafter remained largely unchanged, well outside the borders of Russia proper. The fall of the monarchy in February 1917 was prompted by food riots and strikes in St. Petersburg. The tsar's abdication became inevitable when his soldiers refused to fire on the demonstrators and started to join them. The new republican government vowed to fight on but found that the army had had enough. By June, soldiers were refusing to go to the front and were joining the strikers, demanding "peace and bread." When the Bolsheviks grabbed power in October, the front line was still in Lithuania. Lenin immediately sued for peace, but when the full harshness of German demands was revealed, Trotsky at least argued for fighting on for better terms. To no avail: The army had disintegrated. "We have no army; we could not keep the army at the front," Lenin explained to the Congress of Soviets called to ratify the Treaty of Brest-Litovsk in March 1918.[24]

In Germany, as in Russia and Austria-Hungary, it was internal collapse that preempted any thoughts of fighting on. On October 28, sailors at Kiel mutinied rather than take part in a final suicidal battle with the British fleet. By November 4, the sailors had taken over the town. Now it was the turn of the Germans to demand "peace and bread." Within three days, the revolution had spread to Hamburg, Frankfurt, and Munich. It was to prevent a complete disintegration into communist revolution that Friedrich Ebert, the head of the Social Democratic Party, and General Wilhelm Groener, Ludendorff's replacement as head of the Supreme Command, agreed unconditionally to the severe terms of the Allied armistice on November 11.

Before the war, Ivan Bloch had predicted that war would become impossible—not because the leaders of the Great Powers recognized its impossibility but because their soldiers, sailors, and civilian populations would refuse to endure its dreadfulness. Obstinate persistence from above would only lead to revolution from below. Like many of his other observations, this one was remarkable for its acuity. Where Bloch was mistaken was in forecasting—perhaps taking his cue from Marx—that revolution was more likely in highly industrialized countries such as Britain and Germany than in Russia. In Bloch's view, self-sufficiency and sheer backwardness would protect Russia. What he failed to recognize was that backward countries were less able to adapt to wartime pressures. In spite of its prewar agricultural surpluses, Russia was the first country to experience wartime food riots when farm production collapsed as peasants withdrew from the market economy. Moreover, like Marx, Bloch did not understand that advanced industrial societies had more, not less, social cohesion than semi-feudal ones. Russian willingness to fight collapsed before the country was threatened with military defeat. By contrast, German morale held out through hardships just as great as those experienced in Russia because of a greater commitment to the regime and a sense of shared burdens fostered by an efficient rationing system. Only when its eventual defeat had become inevitable did Germany descend into a Russian-style collapse.

In October 1918, the Social Democrat politician Philipp Scheidemann told the German cabinet that the time had come to bring an end to the continuing slaughter on the front and starvation at home. He quoted the old German proverb, "Better an end with horror than a horror without end."[25] The question, not just for Germany but also for the victorious Allies, was how to ensure that such horrors never occurred again.

3

THE FAILURE OF ECONOMIC ISOLATIONISM

Peace? Why, my fellow citizens, is there any man here or any
woman, let me say is there any child here, who does not know
that the seed of the war in the modern world is industrial and
commercial rivalry? . . . The war was a commercial and industrial war. It was not a political war.
                    —WOODROW WILSON, SEPTEMBER 5, 1919

The war to end war failed to solve the economic problems that
had been its root cause.
                    —FOREIGN POLICY ASSOCIATION,
                    War Tomorrow—Will We Keep Out?, 1935

In August 1914, almost immediately after the guns started firing,
H. G. Wells published a small pamphlet titled *The War That Will
End Wars.* He may be credited with having coined the phrase that
gained such wide circulation in the following years. It was crucial, in the minds of almost everyone who lived through the or-
deal, that the war should be the last such terrible conflict to
disfigure the face of the world. Wells's phrase "war to end war"
was used by Woodrow Wilson in his speech to Congress in January 1918 in which he introduced his Fourteen Points on which
lasting peace could be established. But the attempt to craft a
peace settlement that would make war impossible proved unsuccessful, and when hopes for lasting peace were subsequently

dashed, the phrase "war to end all wars" came to be used not with hope but with irony.

At the peace conference at Versailles in 1919, dealing with the immediate cause of the war, the dispute between Austria-Hungary and Serbia, seemed relatively easy. The concept of the multiethnic empire went down to oblivion with the fall of Austria-Hungary. It was replaced by the Wilsonian principle of national self-determination, which was supposed to rule out any future disputes such as those that led to the assassination at Sarajevo.

But everyone knew that there was far more to securing a lasting peace than settling the Balkans. Behind the descent into world war in July 1914 lay two major issues. The first was the problem of Germany. How would it be possible to prevent Germany from threatening the peace and stability of Europe while at the same time allowing it to prosper? The second issue was global: how to resolve the economic insecurities that underlay the antagonisms of the Great Powers. The war had shown that dependence on trade did indeed make countries vulnerable. It therefore seemed to justify their desire to render themselves economically self-sufficient through a network of colonies and spheres of interest. If a way could not be found to reconcile the desire for security with economic interdependence, it was hard to see how a stable and lasting peace could be established. The failure to resolve the problem of Germany may have led to the undoing of the peace settlement in Europe. But it was the failure of Versailles to resolve the question of economic insecurity that led to the outbreak of a global conflict even more devastating than the "war to end all wars."

The basis of the postwar peace negotiations, at least in theory, was Woodrow Wilson's Fourteen Points. In these proposals, economic issues held a prominent place. Wilson's second point stated that there should be complete freedom of the seas so that no country need be afraid of a disruption in its vital foreign trade. The Turkish Straits, the cause of so much friction before and during the war, should be placed under international control and opened to all commercial traffic. To make sure that countries could get unfettered access to raw materials and markets, Wilson's third point required "the removal, so far as possible, of all economic barriers [to trade] and the establishment of an equality of trade conditions." Moreover, Colonel Edward House, Wilson's close adviser, made it clear on his arrival in Europe in October 1918 that the Fourteen Points implied, if they did not explicitly mention, "a fair and equitable understanding as to the distribution of raw materials."[1]

The last part of Wilson's plan, the creation of the League of Nations, was its cornerstone. As House told the Allies, "The principle of a league of nations as the primary essential of a permanent peace has been so clearly presented by President Wilson . . . that no further elucidation is required. It is the foundation of the whole diplomatic structure of a permanent peace."[2]

The reason the league would be "the primary essential of a permanent peace" was not hard to understand. Under the Wilsonian program, nations were to surrender most of the devices by which they had protected themselves in the past. The most visible of these were large armies and navies. His fourth point specified that "national armaments will be reduced to the lowest points consistent with domestic safety." For centuries Britain had relied on its mastery of the seas to blockade its enemies in times of war. Now this weapon too would disappear, for the Fourteen Points prescribed complete freedom of navigation "in peace and in war." Instead of relying on their own forces and alliances to protect themselves, countries would now depend on the new League of Nations, a body that could call for armies to punish aggressors and legally enforce blockades.

The League of Nations was therefore a solution to the question of how to police a multipolar world. But it was also essential to creating economic security. This point was made clearly by the manifesto of the League of Free Nations Association (the precursor of the Foreign Policy Association), established in the United States to support Wilson's peace plans. Without a supranational government, the drive for economic security would inevitably lead to conflict because one country's security could be ensured only at the expense of others.

> The underlying assumption heretofore has been that a nation's security and prosperity rest chiefly upon its own strength and resources. Such an assumption has been used to justify statesmen in attempting, on the ground of the supreme need for national security, to increase their own nation's power and resources by insistence upon strategic frontiers, territory with raw material, outlets to the sea, even though that course does violence to the security and prosperity of others. Under the system in which adequate defence rests upon individual preponderance of power, the security of one must involve the insecurity of another, and must inevitably give rise to covert or overt competitions for power and territory . . . It is obvious that any plan ensuring national security and equality of opportunity will involve a limitation of national sovereignty.[3]

Wilson's Fourteen Points were an impressive shopping list of measures, and in a perfect world they might have put an end to the economic ambitions and fears that had driven the imperial powers toward war. In the circumstances that prevailed after 1918, however, a number of shortcomings doomed his plan to failure.

Although much ink has been spilled on the argument that Wilson's idealism was wrecked on the shoals of unreconstructed European power politics, this is not where the fundamental problems of the economic peace lay. Perhaps the biggest issue endangering Wilson's plans was that America's geopolitical position was quite different from that of any of the countries in Europe. In the first place it was bounded either by vast oceans or by countries that offered no military threat. In the second, it was almost entirely self-sufficient. American agriculture fed not only America but also part of Europe. The country's coal industry dwarfed Britain's, producing over 40 percent of total world output in 1914. The only reason America was not a significant exporter of coal was that its own appetite was so vast. Iron ore production was more than sufficient to feed the giant steel mills of Pennsylvania and Ohio, and to cap it all, America produced nearly two-thirds of the world's petroleum. Thus it was scarcely surprising that in 1913 foreign trade constituted only around 10 percent of GDP in the United States, compared to 50 percent in Britain and 40 percent in Germany and France. In other words, America did not really need the league or any of the other Wilsonian measures to keep the peace and ensure the free flow of essential materials.

This fact was not lost on Wilson's domestic or international audiences. Would his program be acceptable at home, given that it represented the overturning of several long-standing principles of American policy? The least contentious of these changes, perhaps, was the renunciation of any further territorial expansion. Wilson had made this commitment at the beginning of his presidency in order to demonstrate the difference between his principles and those of his Republican predecessors under whom the United States had expanded across the Pacific and into the Caribbean and Central America. The United States would "never again seek one additional foot of territory by conquest," he declared.[4] Still, such a renunciation, although fitting comfortably with America's self-image as a nonimperial power, was a considerable break with what was, in practice, a 130-year history of relentless expansion. More important were the implications of membership of the League of Nations for a country that had, since its formation, a policy of avoiding foreign entanglements and preserving its freedom of action. This proved the ultimate stumbling block. The Republican-dominated Senate refused to ratify the treaty because it might allow the league to commit America to war without the approval of Congress.

Without American participation, the league was never likely to be effective. In 1921, a conference headed by the Italian statistician Corrado Gini was convened to look at the issue of security of access to raw materials. Its report advocated free-trade solutions on Wilsonian lines. Worryingly, however, it concluded that free trade was of little use unless it was backed by a powerful international police force:

> The war and the post-war period have not merely proved the existence of an economic interdependence between the States . . . but have also shown the danger and harmfulness of such a state of affairs, so long as the present political organisation endures . . . Hence, we come to the conclusion that the application of the "free-trade" policy . . . would be politically advisable only if a super-State organisation could guarantee the continuity of this policy even through a period of economic crisis, and if it could also exclude the possibility of wars which would bring it necessarily to an end . . . Even the most optimistic recognise, I think, that such a task would be beyond the present strength of the League of Nations.[5]

The same concern was expressed by Norman Angell in *The Fruits of Victory*, published in 1921 as a sequel to *The Great Illusion*. "So long as there is no real international society organised on the basis of collective strength and co-operation, the motive of security will override considerations of welfare."[6]

There were, however, issues beyond America's rejection of the league that doomed the economic peace settlement. Other cornerstones of Wilson's plan were either missing or severely chipped away. The idea of complete freedom of the seas was rejected outright by Britain before the peace conference began. The country was convinced that it had survived the war only because of its ability to blockade Germany. This was not a right it was willing to surrender to an international body.

Then there was the question of free trade. If freedom of the seas foundered in London, freedom of trade ran aground in Washington even before Wilson set sail for Europe. Protection of American industry had been a hallmark of national policy since the 1820s and had become entrenched under successive Republican governments since the Civil War. Wilson, the first Democrat in the White House since the 1890s, favored free (or at least freer) trade and had reduced import duties in 1913. However, the third of his fourteen points, calling for the removal of barriers to trade, set off a firestorm when he made his speech to Congress. The American Protective League noted "with disapproval and alarm that portion of the President's peace proposals which abandons the time-honored and always successful policy of Protection and the introduction in this country of the false and discredited policy of Free Trade, a policy which has been discarded by every civilized nation."[7] The congressional elections of November 1918 returned Republican majorities in both houses, and by the time Colonel House reached Europe he was already explaining that the American proposal amounted only to the elimination of tariffs that discriminated between one country and another, not the lowering, let alone removal, of tariffs that applied to all countries equally. The elections of 1920 gave landslide victories to the Republicans in both houses of Congress as well as the presidency to Warren Harding, thereby confirming America's rejection of almost all Wilson's ideas, including free trade. The lower tariff rates introduced in 1913 were reversed in the Fordney-McCumber Tariff of 1922, which raised duties to an average of 38.5 percent.

In Europe, matters looked hardly more promising. France had turned away from free trade before the war, and the conflict only confirmed its belief in protection. In 1918, tariff rates were doubled from their prewar levels, reaching a maximum of 40 percent. The new countries of Eastern Europe were all firmly protectionist. Any hope for a revival of commercial freedom rested with Britain. Free trade had been at the heart of Pax Britannica from the moment of the abolition of almost all tariffs and restrictions in the 1840s. British postwar policy was based more than anything on a desire to return to the halcyon days of the prewar period. It might be that Britain had enjoyed a privileged position in that world, but it was a position that had encouraged the growth of general world prosperity. For Britons, it was in the best interest, therefore, not just of themselves but of everyone to return to those key elements that had made the decades before the world war so uniquely successful in human history: the gold standard with London as its epicenter and free trade with the Royal Navy policing the seas.

There was, however, a tension within the British position on trade. As the country's industrial supremacy was threatened in the late nineteenth century by rivals who protected their domestic industries, there was a growing movement to restructure the empire as a self-sufficient economic bloc. Onetime believers in free trade, like the charismatic politician Joseph Chamberlain (father of the future prime minister Neville Chamberlain) and the geopolitical thinker Halford Mackinder, were converted to the cause of a grand imperial federation and customs union or, failing that, a system of preferential tariffs that favored intra-imperial trade. Both men split from the Liberal Party and allied with the Conservatives, who appeared a better proposition for their beliefs. Chamberlain nearly converted the Conservatives to protectionism in 1903, but like Robert Peel, who had sought to convert the party to free trade in the 1840s, he succeeded in splitting the party and thereby handing power to its opponents. In the election of 1906, the Liberals were returned with a commanding majority, and free trade remained a cornerstone of British policy until the war.

The war, however, was a watershed. Tariffs on luxury goods including cars were introduced in 1915, supposedly as a wartime fiscal measure. While this in itself represented a departure from traditional policy, a more important effect of the war may have been a shift in thinking about economic interdependence. The views of Chamberlain, who had died soon after hearing the news of the assassination at Sarajevo, were revived. The rival blockades of the combatants realized people's worst fears about the risks of depending on imports of essential materials, often from unreliable sources. At a meeting of the Imperial War Cabinet in April 1917, as the German submarine blockade reached its height, William Massey of New Zealand argued that "the war had undoubtedly made people realise the dangerous extent to which the United Kingdom had been dependent on foreign countries. This dependence was unnecessary, as the Empire could produce all it required, so long as it retained control of the seas."[8] Even David Lloyd George, a committed free-trade Liberal, was forced to concede that his "general outlook had been altered by things which have happened since the War," and that he was in favor of preferential treatment for the empire—although avoiding discriminatory tariffs that would upset the American allies.[9]

After the war, although the desire to return to the prewar status quo was widely shared, the commitment to free trade was less assured. The Key Industries Act introduced further tariffs in 1919 to support industries deemed essential for national defense. Many Conservatives had been converted to the cause of protection out of a sense of the new fragility of the British economy. Leo Amery argued in 1919 that Britain was "no longer the sort of country that can compete industrially in the open market except in certain industries. We are more in the position of American industries a generation ago, capable of doing tremendous things in our own area."[10] The dominions continued to press for preferential rates for intra-imperial trade, although they did not, for the time being, convince Westminster to follow them. It was the Liberals and the Labour Party that still held the flag for the old verities. Protectionism was part of the neomercantilism that had infected Europe after the 1870s and had been responsible for the ultimately lethal scramble for empire. Leonard Woolf summed up the beliefs of right-minded Socialists:

The theory and practice of protectionism which established themselves between 1870 and 1880, implied that the organisation of the State should be used as a weapon against the industrial and commercial interests of the citizens of other States. A ring fence of tariffs and administrative regulations was to be drawn round the territory under the control of the State in order to reserve within it for its own citizens the markets and the stores of raw materials. These new conceptions, or rather this return to the old conceptions of mercantilism, roused in the capitalist, industrial, and commercial circles of every European nation mingled emotions of cupidity and fear . . . of being shut out from the profitable markets of Europe with its growing population, and of being shut out from the stores of raw materials and food supplies essential for large scale industrial production in towns; the cupidity lay in the desire for profit resulting from success in shutting out your foreign rivals.[11]

With such ideas in mind, it was scarcely surprising that the Labour government of 1923–1924 took a dim view of the idea of imperial preference, viewing it as "a clear violation of the doctrine of economic equality, and this policy, if it is pursued further, will undoubtedly in the course of years lead to great international friction and not improbably to war."[12] The government set about abolishing the wartime tariffs, but its success was fleeting. In 1924, a new election returned the Conservatives to power, and they soon reinstated the tariffs their predecessors had abolished.

If freedom of the seas and free trade had been established under the control of a powerful supranational body, it might not have mattered that the Versailles peace settlement did little to address the question of competition for empire. The empires of the losers were broken up, but there was no suggestion that this should affect the winners. Wilson's idea was that at least the surviving empires should not expand or compete for further territory. At Versailles, lip service was paid to this idea by placing the non-European possessions of the defunct German and Ottoman empires in temporary protectorates run by one of the victorious powers until such time as they were ready for self-government. Their affairs would be run under the auspices of the League of Nations in the best interests of the population and without special economic privileges for the governing country. However, in the eyes of most people, the mandates, far from heralding the demise of imperialism, only increased the global reach of those imperial powers, principally Britain and France, which ran them.

The peace settlement, therefore, did little if anything to assuage anxieties about the lack of self-sufficiency that came with industrialization. The most vocal condemnation of the economic aspects of Versailles came, not surprisingly, from Germany, which lost its colonies, its navy and merchant marine, its iron ore deposits, and part of its coal. In May 1919, the German delegates at Versailles pointed out that "the possession of . . . colonies will be even more necessary to Germany in the future than it has been in the past . . . it is indispensable that Germany should have the possibility of obtaining the raw materials necessary to her economic development, and as far as possible in colonies belonging to her."[13] But there was also dissension among some of the victors—a fact that seemed less significant at the time than it did in the light of subsequent history.

The two dissenters were Italy and Japan, both of which received less than they felt they deserved at Versailles. To wean Italy away from its nominal alliance with Germany and Austria-Hungary, Britain and France had promised it the Dalmatian coast. The deal had been cemented in one of those secret agreements Wilson had sought to ban in his Fourteen Points. At Versailles, Dalmatia was given to the new nation of Yugoslavia in accordance with another fundamental Wilsonian principle: national self-determination. In response, the Italian premier stormed out of the conference. In a separate secret treaty, Japan had been assured of taking over Germany's colonial interests in East Asia, and in 1915 it had annexed Germany's Shandong concession in

China and the string of Pacific island colonies that Germany had itself annexed from Spain in 1898. Following this land grab, it had dictated a treaty with China under the threat of invasion that turned the country into a virtual Japanese protectorate. Yet many of these gains proved short-lived. Under American pressure, the treaty with China was heavily modified in 1917. After the war, Japan was obliged to treat the islands as mandates rather than colonies, and in 1922, it was forced to return sovereignty over Shandong to China.

Underlying the Italian and Japanese anger at the scant regard paid to their claims was a profound divergence of opinion. In theory, Versailles was supposed to put an end to empire building. But to the Italians and Japanese this was, to put it politely, unconvincing.

The lesson of the war was supposed to have been that competition for empire was destructive and futile. But such a view made sense only for Great Powers such as Britain and France, which already had what they needed. Looked at another way, the war had been far from pointless. It had merely had a very high risk-reward ratio. Germany had gambled for high stakes and had lost—but it had nearly won. In early 1918, Germany had temporarily succeeded in realizing its dream of Mitteleuropa. When Germany eventually lost, the cost was enormous—displacing it instantly from the ranks of the imperial powers. Perhaps Germans now regretted the decision to go to war. But that did not mean that all war was futile. It was merely that Germany had miscalculated.

Even more galling was the (willful) blindness of the "Big Three" who ran the peace conference to the realities of the distribution of power. Before the war, the world had been divided unequally among eight imperial powers. At the top of the food chain were Britain, France, America, and Russia, all of them vast in scale, whether continentally or through their overseas empires. Somewhat further down the pecking order was the latecomer Germany—very powerful within Europe but imperially challenged. The position of Austria-Hungary was so complex and precarious that it was hard to tell where it stood in the rankings. At the bottom of the pile were Italy and Japan: both small, both recent arrivals on the scene, and both very short of resources. The war had removed three contestants from the competition, and had dismembered the Ottoman Empire. This had left the troika of Britain, France, and America even more powerful than before—both by the exclusion of rivals, and, in the case of Britain and France, by dividing the German and Ottoman imperial spoils. Italy and Japan, their wartime allies, far from being rewarded with sufficient gains to bring them into the hallowed circle of truly great powers, were denied even the territorial gains they had been promised. If the world war had been about competition for resources, the imperial hierarchy was now more unequal than before—consisting of three giants and two pygmies. It was a world of "haves" and "have-nots."

As the Versailles conference convened, the Japanese delegate and future prime minister Prince Fumimaro Konoe gave a clear indication of how the lesser powers thought in his article "Reject the Anglo-American-Centered Peace":

No doubt the condition before the war was satisfactory from the viewpoint of Great Britain and America, but it cannot be said so, when considered from the viewpoint of justice and humanity. As may be seen in their history of colonization England and France occupied most of the less civilized countries long ago and made them their colonies. In consequence Germany and other late comers could hardly find any land to secure for their expansion. This state of things was contrary to the fundamental principle of equal opportunity and a right to the equal existence of different countries. The writer considers it right and just for Germany to have tried to destroy this state of things. He does not endorse the measures taken by her, but expresses sympathy for her in the position which compelled her to act as she did. In short, the British and American principle of peace was the same as that advocated by those desirous of maintaining the *status quo* and had no connection whatever with the principles of humanity and justice. Nevertheless, the Japanese, enchanted by the beautiful and high-sounding words uttered by the British and American statesmen in their declarations, have been misled to thinking that peace is equal to justice, in spite of Japan being in a position like Germany to wish for the destruction of the *status quo*, and are drunk with an Anglo-American peace welcoming the idea of a League of Nations like a heaven-sent gospel. This attitude of the Japanese people is ignoble and greatly to be detested.[14]

Konoe's article, originally written for a Japanese audience, was picked up by an American journalist and translated into English, causing a considerable stir. However, Konoe's views were widely shared, and the more emollient Anglophone journalist Kiyoshi Kawakami made similar points in his 1921 book, published in America, *The Real Japanese Question*:

Here is Japan, struggling to solve, partly at least, her population problem by becoming an industrial and trading nation, and yet harassed by lack of three essential materials of industry—oil, iron, and coal. If she steps an inch out of her narrow precincts and tries to obtain, say in Siberia or China, the privilege of working such mineral resources, down comes the sword of Damocles in the shape of protest, official or otherwise, from the Western nations . . . [The] question is, is the existing world order right, allowing a few nations to monopolize vast territories and enormous resources, and compelling others to eke out an existence out of their limited lands and scanty resources?

Kawakami's answer to his rhetorical question was, unsurprisingly, that the existing world order was not right. He proposed two solutions: "It is obvious that a program to establish permanent peace with justice should contain one of two propositions, namely, a more equitable distribution of territory, or the removal of the exclusive policy adopted by Western colonial Powers against Asiatic peoples."[15]

Since it was unlikely that a more "equitable distribution of territory" would be remotely acceptable to the three Great Powers, Japan argued at the conference for the inclusion of a racial equality clause in the Covenant of the league. Its main purpose would be to put an end to the anti-Japanese immigration policies applied by America and Australia, and it foundered on their opposition. The opposition in Australia, whose population at the time was only five million compared to fifty-five million in Japan, was based on the fear that unrestricted Japanese immigration could eventually turn the country from a British dominion into a Japanese one. One thing was clear: The issues that had driven imperial expansion before the war had not been resolved by Germany's defeat. Unless a lasting solution was found, they could erupt again.

The Japanese view on access to raw materials and migration (although not on racial equality) was also widely held in Italy. It was Italy that had attempted to insert a clause into the Covenant of the League of Nations about equitable access to raw materials. And it was the Italian Corrado Gini who had drafted the 1921 league report on the issue, which had noted that the questions of resources and migration were intimately connected. The war had disturbed the flow of raw materials, leaving resource-poor but manpower-rich countries with excess populations that needed an outlet.

The Italian Fascists took up the issue of migration, but in less measured tones than Professor Gini. In a speech in Milan, Mussolini praised the fecundity of his people: "The Italian people are all too fertile. I am glad of it. I shall never encourage birth-control. The fact that other countries have fallen into a decline should make us proud of our flourishing increase . . . As our population increases there are three outlets: to condemn ourselves to voluntary sterility—and Italians are too intelligent for that; to wage war; or to place our surplus population elsewhere."[16]

Luigi Villari was even blunter about the political implications of Fascist emigration policy: "In the present temper of the Italian nation it would no longer be enough to admit a certain number of Italian workers to foreign countries where they would be gradually denationalized and lost to their mother country. A different solution is needed, and will certainly be found."[17] Villari was implying the need for colonies under Italian control. Libya was not enough. He had his eyes on neighboring Tunisia, nominally under French rule but with a larger Italian than French population. He envisaged a "Texan" solution—a reference to the American immigrants into Mexican territory in the 1830s, who, once a majority, had declared independence from Mexico and subsequently joined the United States.

Until the 1930s, however, these dissatisfactions of the have-nots rumbled on largely below the surface. The German and Japanese governments were in the hands of moderates, who thought it better to adapt to the postwar order, even if at heart they disagreed with it. It was Italy that first fell into the hands of radicals when the Fascists forced their way into power in 1922. But during the 1920s, Mussolini was mostly concerned with appearing a statesman worthy of a place among the Great Powers, and his foreign policy stances more often than not coincided with Britain's. However, the resentments were still dormant, and when the peace settlement crumbled in the early 1930s, they reemerged in more virulent form, eventually provoking a second world war more terrible than the first.

The collapse of the peace settlement was due, more than anything else, to the failure to resolve the question of how to deal with Germany. For France, at least, questions of trade and economic security were secondary to this issue. The French view was straightforward and concrete: Germany was the threat to world peace, and the only real question that needed to be addressed was how to tame German aggression. The issue was all the more urgent because the French were well aware that the war had weakened France more than Germany, not just because the battleground had been on French soil, or because France had lost a greater percentage of its male population than Germany, but because Russia, France's vital ally, had disintegrated into revolution and civil war and was no longer a threat to German security in the east.

To deal with a likely future German threat, French policy had three strands. The first was a question of territory and industrial resources. France understood only too well the military implications of Germany's prewar dominance of steelmaking, not to mention its wartime seizure of France's iron ore and coal-producing areas. The return of Lorraine would deprive Germany of the most important source of its prewar metallurgical dominance, but it was not sufficient. The coalfields and steelworks of the neighboring Saar should be handed to France to complement the iron ore of Lorraine. In addition, France should get free deliveries of coal from the Ruhr. This way French steel production would come close to, or even exceed, Germany's. Ideally, the whole of German territory west of the Rhine should revert to France so that the country could reclaim its "natural" frontiers as in Roman and Napoleonic days. But, if not, the Rhineland on both sides of the river should become an independent country so as to create a buffer zone between France and its overmighty neighbor. As a last resort, the area, although remaining part of a unified Germany, should be demilitarized and placed under international administration. A minority view, held by some on the left of French politics, was that France should use its temporary control of the region to persuade Germany to enter into a cooperative sharing of industrial resources, which might in itself lead to long-term peace between the two countries. But the core of French policy always remained the taming of its enemy, especially since the attitude of the German delegates at Versailles suggested to the French that they were dealing with an unrepentant country that did not believe it had been truly defeated on the battlefield.

The second French objective was to replace the defunct Russian alliance with an Anglo-American security pact. The French prime minister Georges Clemenceau would accept a newfangled league of nations but, he told the National Assembly, "There is an old system which appears to be discredited today, but to which . . . I am still faithful . . . Here in this system of alliance . . . is the thought that will guide me at the conference."[18] One of the tragedies of the interwar years is that a Franco-American security agreement could quite likely have passed the US Senate, given that Henry Cabot Lodge, the leader of the Senate Republicans, supported it. But Lodge was not willing to accept the League of Nations without reservations that Wilson refused to accept. In the end both the treaty and the security pact fell together, and France was left with no American support in any form.[19] For the durability of the postwar peace, this was a disaster.

The final French aim was to make Germany pay reparations for the immense damage it had done to France. This would serve several purposes: rebuild France, weaken Germany, and provide funds to repay France's war debts to America and Britain. The three strands of French policy were flexible up to a point. Insofar as its allies agreed to sign a formal alliance and forgo payment of war debts, France would be willing to scale back its territorial and financial demands on Germany. As it turned out, America and Britain were willing to accept the allocation of the Saar coal mines to France and the demilitarization of the Rhineland area for a period of fifteen years, but no more. Neither country joined a security pact with France, Britain subtly making its participation dependent on America's. Furthermore, America refused to countenance any reduction of its war loans. France was therefore left depending on punitive reparations payments as its main vehicle to secure the peace. This too was to sow the seeds of disaster.

Against the French view that Germany had to be contained,

others believed that it should be rehabilitated. It was true that German militarism, which had provoked the cataclysm, had to be excised. But it was equally important to restore Germany economically so that the European and world economy could recover its prewar pattern of growth and prosperity. It was the largely unknown John Maynard Keynes who made this point in his bestselling *Economic Consequences of the Peace*, in which he lacerated the Versailles Treaty. Before the war, it was "on the prosperity and enterprise of Germany the prosperity of the rest of the Continent mainly depended."[20] If the victors pursued a "Carthaginian peace," they would not only feed German resentment without which there could be no long-term peace but also condemn Germany to poverty, and with it the rest of Europe. What the continent desperately needed was the recovery of foreign trade, for, as Herbert Hoover, in charge of American relief efforts, noted, "A rough estimate would indicate that the population of Europe is about 100,000,000 greater than can be supported without imports, and must live by the production and distribution of exports."[21]

After the Second World War, the containment and integration of a reformed and prosperous Germany within the Western world was one of the principal hallmarks of a successful peace settlement. After the First World War, the failure to resolve the German problem was the rock on which the peace settlement foundered. And the main cause of the failure was the toxic interconnection between reparations and trade policy.

The reparations section of the Versailles Treaty was contentious right from the beginning because of Article 231, the so-called war guilt clause, which forced Germany to accept responsibility for the "damage to which the [Allies] have been subjected as a consequence of the war imposed upon them by the aggression of Germany and her allies." The issue was propelled to prominence not just by German outrage at its one-sided allocation of blame for the war but also by Keynes's focus on the economic consequences of its enforcement. Much ink has been spilled over whether reparations were morally or economically defensible. However, the true issue was not reparations per se but the combination of reparations with inter-Allied war debts.

America ended the war with more than $10 billion owed to it by its allies. At the same time, Britain, France, and Italy were owed reparations by Germany that amounted in theory to $32 billion, or more realistically to $12 billion.* The overall result of reparations and and war debts would, therefore, be a westward flow of funds starting in Berlin, passing through Rome, Paris, and London, and ending in Washington.

A portion of the reparations could be settled in kind, by coal deliveries to France or by confiscating the German merchant fleet in compensation for wartime submarine sinkings. But most would have to be paid in cash. The obvious way to make payment possible was for the debtor countries to run trade surpluses and the creditor countries to run corresponding deficits. It soon became apparent, however, that the countries that were supposed to be on the receiving end of the westward money flow did not like the idea of resolving imbalances by adjustments to international trade. The United States did not wish to reduce its trade surplus with Europe, and neither Britain nor France wished to boost the exports of a trade rival that had already proved more than a match for them before the war. In 1922, the United States passed the Fordney-McCumber Tariff Act, which further disadvantaged European industrial exports. If the restoration of free trade was to be the fundamental principle of the peace settlement, it fell at this first hurdle.

In the absence of adjustment to trade flows, the only other solutions were debt forgiveness, further loans, or default. By 1922, all-around war debt cancellation was openly advocated by Britain, but rejected by America, which clung to the sanctity of its

---

* The nominal amount of reparations was 132 billion gold marks, or $32 billion. However, most of this sum was in the form of deferred obligations without interest, which everyone knew were unlikely ever to be paid. The Belgian premier George Theunis joked that they could be safely left on his desk since no thief would be tempted to steal them.

claims on its wartime allies with the same tenacity with which France clung to its claims on its wartime enemy. By 1923, an impasse was reached. Germany failed to make scheduled payments, France occupied the Ruhr Valley to collect them by force, and Germany moved from high inflation to hyperinflation as it printed money to pay its bills.

Thereafter a semblance of normalcy was restored. In 1924, the French admitted defeat and retreated from the Ruhr in exchange for a reduced reparations schedule, which was effectively financed by American loans. Germany got a new currency and a new moderate government with foreign policy run by Gustav Stresemann. Over the following two years, the German, British, and French currencies returned to the gold standard, and international trade started to recover, growing by almost 6 percent per year between 1924 and 1929, helped by some modest bilateral deals that reduced tariff barriers within Europe. Even the Franco-German steel dispute found a temporary compromise through a cartel agreement that greatly reduced Germany's prewar dominance.* In 1926, Germany was admitted to the League of Nations. Two years later, the Kellogg-Briand Pact was signed by the countries that had fought in the war to "condemn recourse to war . . . and renounce it, as an instrument of national policy in their relations with one another."

Yet beneath the surface, the unresolved financial imbalances lay like a land mine. After 1924, Germany paid its reparations and the Allies paid their war debts only because of new American loans to Germany. In fact, American money flowed eastward in double the amount required to finance reparations, leading to an unhealthy boom. Instead of the current account surplus that

---

* The cartel, which included Belgium and Luxembourg, allocated 40.5 percent of annual production to Germany and 38.5 percent to France. However, France's position of near equality with Germany hinged on the Saar Valley, which had 6.5 percent of production. When the Saar reverted to Germany in 1935, France's production fell while Germany's increased so that it was 50 percent higher than France's.

Germany needed to pay reparations on a sustainable basis, it ran a deficit. After 1928, there was what economists call a "sudden stop." Americans stopped sending their money abroad—initially because the rates offered on loans to finance speculation on the booming Wall Street market were too attractive to ignore, subsequently because the ensuing crash made lenders averse to risk of any kind.

It was at this point that the shallow foundations of the return to normalcy in the late 1920s were exposed. The German economy went into a tailspin as soon as the inflows of foreign money came to an end. An international commission headed by the American businessman Owen Young renegotiated the reparations schedule over a longer period, making it coincide exactly with the amounts required to repay the Allies' debt to the United States. But this was a meaningless gesture given the near impossibility of Germany making any payments in the absence of credit or a major change in trade patterns.

The German government compounded the problem by pursuing a policy of self-imposed austerity. Memories of the inflation of the early 1920s prevented any resort to devaluation, deficit spending, or monetary easing as a way to counteract the financial shock. The result was a downward economic spiral that led to a banking collapse in late 1931, sharply rising unemployment, and the inevitable rise of political extremes. In September 1930, the entry of the Nazi party into the Reichstag with almost 20 percent of the popular vote showed clearly that the postwar order was at risk.

The crisis gave a sharp boost to the forces of protectionism. In 1927, the World Economic Conference in Geneva, attended by every major country, had issued a declaration calling for a general reduction in tariff barriers as the way to restore world prosperity. The declaration passed largely unheeded. In 1928, France increased some tariffs even though it was running a trade surplus as a result of the undervalued exchange rate at which it had returned to the gold standard two years earlier. In 1930, America responded to the economic downturn that followed the 1929 stock market crash by passing the notorious Smoot-Hawley Tariff, which raised duties to 60 percent in spite of an unprecedented campaign by 1,028 leading American economists urging the government "to consider the bitterness which a policy of high tariffs would inevitably inject into our international relations . . . A tariff war does not furnish good soil for the growth of world peace."[22] President Hoover also opposed the bill but was persuaded to sign it by his party, which remained almost universally protectionist. Smoot-Hawley probably had less direct economic effect than sometimes imagined because most of the items covered were already subject to such high tariffs that there was little trade in them. Moreover, many American imports were outside the compass of the act. But its enactment by a country that was less dependent on foreign trade than any other industrialized country and whose current account was in regular surplus set off a backlash. Canada instantly raised duties on its main imports from America. France and Italy did likewise. World trade started to spiral downward, falling 30 percent in volume by 1932. In other words, Smoot-Hawley was less significant in itself than as the trigger for a chain reaction.

Perhaps the most important domino to fall was Great Britain. Driven by its desire to restore the bases of its Victorian preeminence, Britain had followed a postwar regimen of rigorous deflation and fiscal austerity so that sterling could regain its prewar value and return to the gold standard at the old exchange rate. It had been rewarded by a decade-long economic depression and an overvalued currency that left the country with an uncompetitive economy and a precarious international financial position. In 1925, Keynes had unleashed another of his broadsides, *The Economic Consequences of Mr. Churchill*, aimed at the decision of the chancellor of the exchequer to return to gold. The focus on Winston Churchill was unfair since the fixation with reclaiming the nation's place at the high table of international finance was widely shared—among others by the Labour Party. Yet Keynes was right to point out that a further revaluation of sterling in order to return to the gold standard would make the country less competitive at a time when it was still struggling with high unemployment and a chronic trade deficit. The British return to gold in 1925, won at heavy cost, turned out to be a Pyrrhic victory. The international boom of 1927–1928 helped cushion the British economy, but the economic crisis that followed soon made the country's position untenable, and in September 1931 the decision was taken to let sterling float. Its value promptly fell.

In the light of history, most economists agree that this was the best decision that could have been made. The devaluation of sterling restored international competitiveness to the British economy. More important, the country was no longer forced to maintain high interest rates to protect its gold reserves—over the following months the Bank of England's lending rate was reduced from 6 percent to 2 percent. As a result, Britain was the first of the major economies to start recovering from the Depression.

Yet at the time, the devaluation of sterling was a profound shock to the global system. For centuries sterling had been the world's strongest and most reliable currency, and it had always been assumed that any deviations from its gold parity (such as had occurred, for instance, during the Napoleonic Wars) would be temporary. But now, the currency, whose strength and solidity had made it the anchor of the international trading system, was being set adrift. Worse, it was being allowed to fall to a level even lower than was required to restore the competitiveness of its exports—settling around 30 percent below its old parity. Before the war, Britain had maintained a staunch commitment to free trade when its rivals were moving toward economic nationalism. Even after the war it seemed that the country would continue to be one of the props of a relatively open trading system, in spite of the qualms of many on the right. Now, with the Labour government giving way to a national government dominated by the Conservatives, in August 1931 Britain leapfrogged over its more protectionist rivals and was indulging what looked like a beggar-thy-neighbor currency war. This impression was compounded in

March 1932 when a general tariff was introduced on goods from sources outside the empire. Later in the year, the Imperial Economic Conference in Ottawa formalized a system of imperial preferences. The new British policy led to a reorientation of trade toward the empire, which by the end of the decade provided 40 percent of British imports compared to 30 percent at the beginning.[23]

It looked as if Joseph Chamberlain had finally had his way. And just as Chamberlain had been a Liberal free trader before his conversion to protectionism, so other notable Liberals now abandoned their old beliefs and joined the ranks of the economic isolationists. Perhaps the most shocking of the defections was that of Keynes. In June 1933, he wrote an article in which he turned the old arguments of the free-trade Liberals on their head. Ever since the days of Richard Cobden, and before him of Jeremy Bentham as far back as the 1790s, it had been argued that international trade must foster peace. To Keynes's mind such arguments were wrong.

> It does not now seem obvious that a great concentration of national effort on the capture of foreign trade [and] a close dependence of our own economic life on the fluctuating economic policies of foreign countries are safeguards and assurances of international peace. It is easier, in the light of experience and foresight, to argue quite the contrary. The protection of a country's existing foreign interests, the capture of new markets, the progress of economic imperialism— these are scarcely avoidable in a scheme of things which aims at the maximum of international specialization.

His conclusion was that if countries wanted peace, they should aim for self-sufficiency. "I sympathize, therefore, with those who would minimize, rather than those who would maximize economic entanglement between nations."[24]

By the time Keynes wrote his article, the postwar settlement had unraveled. The Young Plan of 1929 was denounced by the

German right as a continuation of the "enslavement of the German people." A referendum in December, introduced by the right-wing businessman Alfred Hugenberg, repudiated the entire Versailles Treaty, albeit on too low a turnout to give the referendum legal force. By 1931, the futility of attempting to make reparations or interallied debt payments was recognized by a moratorium arranged by President Herbert Hoover. A conference held by Britain, Germany, and France in Lausanne in 1932 agreed to cancel reparations permanently as long as America could be persuaded to cancel its debt claims. Yet it seemed that American intransigence about war debts was even harder to overturn than French intransigence about reparations. The US Congress rejected the Lausanne proposals in December, although the decision was largely totemic given that no further payments of either reparations or interallied debts were made anyway.

In any case, the ending of postwar financial obligations could not stop the economic decline that followed from the fiscal and monetary responses pursued by the German and American governments. By 1932, German unemployment topped 35 percent of the workforce. In the election in July, the Nazis became substantially the largest party, winning over 37 percent of the votes—compared to 21 percent for the Social Democrats (SDP), who had always formed the backbone of the Weimar Republic. In January 1933, Hitler became chancellor of a right-wing coalition government. By June he had repudiated the financial clauses of the Versailles Treaty, and in October Germany withdrew from the League of Nations.

Not much more help to the international economic order was forthcoming from across the Atlantic. By some process of quid pro quo, the world's greatest creditor and its greatest debtor were the two countries worst affected by the Depression. By 1932, America's unemployment rate exceeded 40 percent, and in November the country elected a politician as determined as Hitler to tear up the economic rule book. Franklin Roosevelt's first hundred days in office witnessed a whirlwind of measures, not all of them coherent, designed to stop the economic rot. His greatest success was in stabilizing the banking system, putting an end to the waves of bank collapses that had progressively contracted the supply of credit. Far more controversial, then and now, was his attempt to reflate the economy by raising prices across the board. Following the advice of George Warren, an obscure agricultural economist, he decided that the way to do this was by devaluing the dollar against gold—as if all commodity prices must automatically rise in tandem with gold. His policy failed in its implausible objective (although it may have contributed to the economic recovery by scaring the Federal Reserve into lowering interest rates and increasing the money supply). To the outside world, Roosevelt's monetary policy appeared as yet another nail in the coffin of international economic cooperation. In July 1933, an international conference was convened in London to revive the world economy—only to be scuppered by a "bombshell message" from Roosevelt in which he announced that he would place America's needs first: "The sound internal economic system of a Nation is a greater factor in its well-being than the price of its currency in changing terms of the currencies of other Nations."[25] To drive the point home, Roosevelt inaugurated a policy of driving down the value of the dollar—nominally against gold but in practice against all foreign currencies—not stopping until the dollar had fallen by 40 percent. At this point, the dollar had outdone the devaluation of sterling two years earlier. It was now valued at a level far below that required for international competitiveness since the country was running a surplus in both its trade and current accounts, even if reduced from the levels of the 1920s.

Before the financial crisis of the early 1930s, it was already apparent that, whatever their statements to the contrary, neither Britain nor the United States, the only two countries that could truly be described as world powers, was fully committed to free and open world trade. American politicians might talk about the "open door" and freedom of the seas, but they were unwilling to open the country's own doors by lowering tariffs, or to accept a current account deficit as the necessary concomitant to the payment of reparations and war debts. Britain's policy was less overtly protectionist, but support for free trade was shallow. Now, in the aftermath of the financial crisis, both countries showed that they could not be relied upon to prop up the system of global trade on which so much of prewar prosperity had depended. Other nations were bound to take note.

The collapse of the world economy after 1929 and the move of Britain, America, and France toward economic nationalism revived the dissatisfactions of the have-nots. How were they to cope in a world of protectionism? One solution was to attempt to become more self-sufficient themselves. The first moves in this direction were made even before the economic crisis struck. Mussolini started his "Battle for Wheat" in 1925, designed to increase domestic grain production. Japan invested heavily in rice production in Taiwan. In Germany, Hitler's rise to power was followed by a turn toward economic autarky guided by Hjalmar Schacht, head of the Reichsbank since 1924 and now minister of economics. Confronted with the difficulty of finding foreign exchange through conventional means, Schacht responded in an unorthodox manner by defaulting on foreign debts, establishing rigorous capital controls, and setting up a series of bilateral trade agreements with countries in Eastern Europe and Latin America, which obviated the need for foreign currency. Instead of devaluing the reichsmark, as might have been a logical response in a world of free trade, Schacht maintained its value so as to maximize the amount of imports that Germany could obtain for the minimum amount of exports. Hitler's plans to revitalize the German economy by spending on infrastructure and rearmament were financed by issuing off-balance-sheet paper claims to suppliers—which in theory were redeemed by reichsmarks but in practice were allowed to mount up. The practice was potentially highly inflationary, but in the short term it worked wonders. Unemployment fell from six million to less than one million by 1937. Germany's economy outperformed all others in recovery from the Depression. It was a recovery, however, without any stimulus from foreign trade, which before 1914 and after 1945 played such a large part in Germany's economic advance.

Parallel to these financial measures to isolate Germany from the world economy, steps were taken to prepare for shortages of essential raw materials by stockpiling and developing substitutes. During the First World War, Friedrich Naumann had celebrated the necessary turning of Germany away from dependence on international trade toward autarky. Shut off by the Allied blockade, "we Central Europeans shall have learnt and endured something definite and peculiar, for we have actually been a 'self-contained commercial State' . . . Our enemies wished to do us an injury, but God . . . has turned it into a blessing."[26] Under Hitler, Naumann's dreams of a socialist war economy started to come true. Production facilities for synthetic fuel and synthetic rubber were set up, using Germany's abundant supply of coal as a base. Exploitation of Germany's limited sources of iron ore was intensified, so that by 1938 the country could satisfy 30 percent of its demand without having to conquer France. At the Nazi party conference in September, Hitler boasted that "all thoughts of a blockade against Germany may as well be buried now, for it is an entirely useless weapon."[27]

Yet, although economic self-sufficiency was a possibility for continental giants such as America and Russia, for a country of Germany's size autarky was never going to be an adequate remedy for its shortage of critical materials. This was even more true for Italy and Japan, both smaller and less well endowed with resources. It was inevitable that attention would turn toward another solution: the acquisition of territory, either peacefully or by force.

The first to take the plunge was Japan. After 1929, those who believed in a peaceful rise through trade lost influence, while the militarists who believed that Japan could prosper only through territorial expansion grew more vocal. "Our national state of affairs has reached an impasse," an army officer declared in 1931. "The critical problems of population and foodstuffs seem all without solution. The only answer . . . is boldly to open up Manchuria and Mongolia."[28] In September 1931, a group of conspirators in the army engineered an incident in Manchuria that was used to justify the military occupation of the province. In 1932, Japanese control was cemented by setting up a puppet state of Manchukuo, which declared independence from China. The reaction of the League of Nations amounted to feeble protest. Emboldened by the Japanese example, Italy followed suit in 1935, invading Ethiopia, to which it felt that it had a long-standing right, on the justification that it needed the area for its economic survival. Once again the League of Nations proved itself toothless. The issue of the distribution of resources now became the focus of an intense international debate.

The Italian position was clear. Britain (which not coincidentally had taken a lead in protesting the invasion of Ethiopia) was to blame. Its empire spanned the world and hogged the lion's share of resources without regard to the rights of others. A propaganda leaflet showing John Bull bestriding the globe declared that "England has in its hands or controls almost all the raw materials produced in the world: from cotton to wool, from petroleum to diamonds, from coal to gold." Because it was aware that without its empire it would be a third-rate power, "England has used the great riches in its possession to impede in every way those who, less favored by nature, have attempted, as is their right, to find new sources of riches and work." This was not fair, and it could not be tolerated. "At the base of every war and especially those which are being fought nowadays, there is an economic claim. Peoples less rich in raw materials, or densely populated nations, need to procure all that is indispensable for their existence, or to seek in less inhabited territories an outlet for their always growing population . . . No one can deny to any people the right to life . . . We Italians in particular do not wish to be exposed forever to every possible form of economic suffocation because we lack oil or coal or iron or rubber or wool."[29]

A somewhat less strident Italian analysis of the distribution of world resources purported to show that the "richest empire in raw materials is the British Empire, which in eight of the twenty-four products listed, accounts for more than half the world production, in another twelve more than a quarter and only in the remaining four less than one-fifth."[30] Even Corrado Gini was starting to sound a note unlike his measured tones in the 1921 League of Nations report. In 1937, he published an article claiming that Italy had the right to expand for the good of civilization—and would do so by force if necessary:

> Italy, a country with high demographic density and deprived of essential raw materials, superior, moreover, to the Slavs and Iberians in many technical and cultural aspects, justly claims the means of exploiting its endowments not only for its own interests but also for those of mankind . . . Willingly or not, one must recognize that, today as in the past, there does not seem to be any possibility of an equitable distribution of population and raw materials without the use or at least the threat of force.[31]

In Germany, the Nazi writer Anton Zischka wrote bestselling books about the Anglo-Saxon monopolists who threatened Germany's welfare, and the heroic efforts of German scientists to overcome them by creating substitute materials. His *Wissenschaft bricht Monopole* (Science Defeats Monopoly), published in 1936, sold 616,000 copies.[32] A more reasoned line of argument for international consumption was put forward by Hjalmar Schacht, who retained an audience in the United States even after he gave his allegiance to Hitler. In 1937, he published an article in *Foreign Affairs* in which he revisited one of his pet subjects: the return of

Germany's colonies. In spite of his association with a policy of autarky, Schacht was aware of the limitations of domestic self-sufficiency, especially in a country of Germany's size.

> Much is said nowadays to the effect that Germany is striving for autarchy. People entirely forget that this autarchy has long since been achieved by such countries as France and Great Britain, not to mention Russia and the United States . . . As against these great economic domains stand countries with large populations and limited territories . . . These two kinds of countries have lately been classified as the 'Haves' and the 'Have-nots'.

What was needed to maintain the peace was for Germany to become as self-sufficient as the other great powers: "So long . . . as the problem of colonial raw materials is not solved for Germany, so long she will remain a source of unrest despite all her love of peace. It is that love of peace which still permits her to entertain the hope that she can solve the colonial problem peacefully and that she can take her place in the ranks of the Haves."[33]

Britain was caught somewhat unprepared for these assaults on its global position, not least because it found many in the United States to be among its critics. In 1937, Norman Angell published *This Have and Have-Not Business: Political Fantasy and Economic Fact*, addressed largely to an American audience, in which he reported that on a tour of the country he "had found a very widespread feeling that Great Britain was almost as much to blame as Italy for the war in Africa, as much to blame as Japan for the war in China and as much to blame as Germany for the unrest in Europe." The common image was of "a bloated and blood-sucking John Bull owning a vast estate, while starvelings clamour at his gate."[34]

To counter these charges, Britain had several lines of defense. One was to refer the matter to another League of Nations conference, which found that any problems of obtaining supplies had more to do with difficulties of getting foreign exchange than with trade restrictions, and recommended the return to full currency convertibility—while admitting that its report "could not, unfortunately, form the subject of any international action in the present circumstances."[35] Indeed, since neither America nor any of the have-nots were members of the league, it was even more toothless than before.

British writers focused on the fact that the raw materials were very far from being in short supply. To the contrary, it was a time of oversupply. All producers, including the British colonies, were happy to find buyers for their commodities at almost any price. If there were problems of foreign exchange, they were largely a result of the self-destructive economic policies of Dr. Schacht:

> Germany's difficulties are of her own making; . . . if she had had the sense, like the British Empire and most of the raw material producing countries, to devalue her currency she would have been able to import just as easily as anyone else; [but] if she persists in pursuing an eccentric monetary policy, based on peculiar political and psychological motives, and condemned by almost every economist in the world, she should not blame other people for the consequences.[36]

The motives behind Germany's policy of autarky were clear: to prepare for war. Any problems with supply were simply the result of attempts to stockpile vast quantities of materials in preparation for conflict. As Angell observed, the argument of the have-nots was circular:

> Why do you need to go to war?
> To have raw materials within our borders.
> Why do you need to have them within your borders?
> In order that we may go to war.[37]

Further arguments were trotted out: Germany's trade with its colonies had always been negligible anyway; no one could contemplate returning the colonies to the care of an avowedly racist government; why, furthermore, was Germany not asking Japan for the return of its East Asian colonies? And for its American critics, British writers countered that it was no good taking a holier-than-thou stance when it was itself a bastion of economic nationalism.

All this was true. There was, however, a note of unease, and occasionally of self-reproach, in the British and American positions. It could not be denied that together the United States and the British Empire already had their hands on a very large percentage of the world's resources. And not content with those within their official borders, the two powers had spent the postwar years acquiring a near total worldwide dominance of the material whose importance had been propelled into the limelight by the war: petroleum.

The United States had always held a dominant position in world oil production—a position that not only blessed the country with energy independence but also conferred a high degree of leverage against less well-endowed rivals. It was Britain whose situation was massively reinforced by events after 1914. In the Middle East, Britain's wartime occupation of Iraq was converted into a league mandate, further extending its control of the Gulf region. The government owned 51 percent of the Anglo-Persian Oil Company, which not only controlled the whole of Iran's oil industry but also held 50 percent of the Turkish Petroleum Company formed to prospect in Iraq, and 50 percent of the Kuwait Oil Company. Another oil giant, Royal Dutch Shell, although headquartered in the Netherlands, had acted almost as a branch of the British government during the war. It dominated oil production in the Dutch East Indies, owned 25 percent of the Iraqi concession, and at the end of the war it succeeded in establishing major positions in Mexico and Venezuela—the two largest oil-producing countries outside the United States and Russia. By the early 1920s, the extent of British control of worldwide oil assets was causing some alarm even in America, which was beginning to worry that its thirst for petroleum might begin to outrun even its vast reserves. In 1919, the *Philadelphia Public Ledger* published a speech by a senior British oil executive who predicted that in ten years' time America would be forced to pay $1 billion per year for oil imports, almost all of which would find its way into British pockets.[38]

The Americans were particularly worried about Britain's near total domination of the Middle East. Their response was to challenge the validity of the Turkish Petroleum concession, agreed to by the Ottoman government but not formally signed before the outbreak of the war. As a compromise, Anglo-Persian ceded half its 50 percent interest to a consortium of American oil companies. American concerns about excessive British control of international oil were also reduced when Standard Oil of New Jersey managed to get a large stake in Venezuela's oil fields. By the late 1920s, both Venezuela and the Middle East (the latter more a prospector's dream than a reality) had been stitched up under Anglo-American control. Subsequent American inroads into the Middle East via concessions in Bahrain and Saudi Arabia did nothing to change that fundamental picture. In 1940, three-quarters of world oil exports came from either the United States or Venezuela, and most of the remainder came from areas under British or American control.

Confronted with criticism of such global dominance, British and American writers were forced to admit that not all was right. Norman Angell conceded that if the claims of the have-nots were to be countered, no country, including Britain, could make economic policy solely on the basis of its own self-interest. The Labour Party argued for the return of multilateral trade and the ending of imperial preferences. The American writer Frank Simonds argued that the United States had to take a lead in securing world peace, and that this would entail major changes to existing policy:

The price of peace . . . is . . . the assurance of economic security to the peoples of all of the great powers . . . In the absence
of such security . . . the world will presently be condemned to
witness new struggles between the great powers, some seeking to acquire, others to retain, those resources in raw materials
and minerals essential to modern industrial life . . .

Patently this price of peace must be paid by those nations,
of which the United States is the most striking example,
whose material resources bestow the largest measure of economic self-sufficiency. What is, moreover, the most astounding
detail in the performances of the American peacemakers is
their failure to perceive the implications for world peace of
the tariff and monetary practices and policies of their own
country . . .

Italian Fascism, German National Socialism, and Japanese Imperialism, despite their common doctrine of violence,
have done no more to make future wars inevitable than has
the American Democracy by means of the Hawley-Smoot
Tariff, the war-debt policy, and its performance at the London Economic Conference.[39]

Fortunately, in the United States at least, these were not lone
voices crying in the wilderness. The Roosevelt administration
may have started its term in office with a display of heavy-handed
economic nationalism, but Cordell Hull, Roosevelt's secretary of
state, was an opponent of the interventionist aspects of New Deal
economics and a strong advocate of free-trade internationalism.
Under his influence, an act was passed in 1934 that for the first
time gave the president a free hand in negotiating tariff agreements with other countries without congressional authorization.
The stranglehold of the protectionist lobby on American trade
policy was loosened. After the events of 1935, Hull became convinced that a reversal of protectionism and economic nationalism
was the only way to stop the descent toward war. He started to
pressure Britain for an agreement between the two major powers to

take a lead in the reestablishment of freer trade and lower tariff rates. In view of the darkening international situation, Anglo-American trade cooperation "would probably mark the difference between war and peace in Europe in the not distant future."[40]

It was a hard task. Now that it had been converted to the cause of economic self-sufficiency, Britain felt more comfortable within the bosom of the empire. The British global position, however impregnable it may have appeared from outside, felt very much less so from within. The First World War had left deep psychological scars. The German submarine blockade and the bombing raids on British cities had shown that being an island nation and having the Royal Navy were no longer a guarantee of safety. Although the future support of the dominions in a war could not be taken entirely for granted, it was infinitely more to be relied upon than the support of the United States. While the State Department pushed for a return of economic internationalism as the only way to ensure global security, other acts of the American government pulled in entirely the opposite direction. The Neutrality Acts of 1934 and 1937 were based on the belief that it had been the allure of profits from supplying and financing the Allies that had dragged America into the last war. Henceforth no trade was to be undertaken with any combatant except if paid for in cash and transported in non-American ships. That way it would not matter if they were sunk by U-boats. The Neutrality Acts may have played well in Peoria, but they were scarcely likely to reassure a nervous Europe that America was committed to preserving the peace.

The same calculations applied on the economic front. From a British perspective, imperial preferences were not a perfect answer to its problems. The dominions were independent and since the beginning of the century had been busily fostering their own industrial development through protective tariffs. At the Ottawa Conference in 1932, they had used their leverage with the mother country to drive a hard bargain. The result of imperial preferences was increased intra-imperial trade, but mostly in the form of

Canadian and Australian exports to Britain. On the other hand, Britain at least enjoyed the "exorbitant privilege" of issuing the currency used by the entire sterling bloc, which included countries outside as well as inside the empire. It could therefore finance itself with ease.

By contrast, the American offer of economic détente did not seem very attractive. Hull was willing to consider making a trade-off in which reductions in imperial preferences were compensated by a reversal of the post-1934 undervaluation of the dollar. However, the offer was blocked by Henry Morgenthau, the secretary of the treasury, who called Hull's proposal "one of the most anti–New Deal broadsides" he had "seen in a long time."[41] Moreover, Hull was a hard bargainer on tariff rates and was largely immune to arguments that, as the party with the chronic trade surplus, the United States should do most to lower its still high duties.

An Anglo-American agreement was eventually signed in late 1938, the British accepting a relatively poor trade bargain ($300 million of trade concessions against $140 million in return) in the hope, as expressed by Hull, that the agreement might send a signal of "economic appeasement, which in turn would facilitate political appeasement."[42] Coming shortly after the ill-fated Munich Agreement allowing Germany to take over the Sudetenland, it was equally futile as a method of forestalling war.

The truth was that, despite Hull's belief that a return to free trade by America and Britain would mollify the have-nots, Hitler was never interested in free trade. He was not really even interested in the return of the Germany's colonies—using them only as a pawn in negotiations and as a useful propaganda tool. His view, already clearly expressed in *Mein Kampf*, was that Germany's future lay in the East. In his analysis, there were four possible solutions to the problem of a growing German population: limitations on fertility, the more efficient use of existing territory, dependence on foreign trade, and territorial expansion. He dismissed all except the last. Limitations on family size, as practiced for example by the French, were a recipe for long-term decline. More efficient exploitation of internal resources was possible only up to a point. Dependence on foreign trade left Germany vulnerable to blockade, and any attempt to protect itself by building a world-class navy was bound to provoke the enmity of the geographically better placed Britain. Hitler dismissed the prewar German belief that it could achieve "the peaceful conquest of the world by commercial means" while simultaneously pursuing a naval arms race as "the most completely nonsensical stuff ever raised to the dignity of a guiding principle in the policy of a State." The only solution was territorial expansion, not in overseas colonies but to the east, thereby avoiding British opposition:

> Such a territorial policy [could not] find its fulfilment in the Cameroons but almost exclusively here in Europe . . . If new territory were to be acquired in Europe it must have been mainly at Russia's cost, and once again the new German Empire should have set out on its march along the same road as was formerly trodden by the Teutonic Knights, this time to acquire soil for the German plough by means of the German sword and thus provide the nation with its daily bread. For such a policy, however, there was only one possible ally in Europe. That was England.[43]

Hitler's emphasis on territorial expansion in the interest of self-sufficiency was the reason Hjalmar Schacht's influence was destined to come to an end. Schacht always understood that his policy of domestic autarky was an imperfect improvisation for difficult times. In 1936, he advocated a reintegration of Germany into the world economy so that the country could grow on a more sustainable basis. Hitler thought otherwise and handed oversight of the German economy to Hermann Goering, who set about preparing for war. Rather than buy cheap raw materials through foreign trade, the production of costly synthetic substitutes was rapidly increased. In November 1937, Hitler held a secret conference at Hossbach at which he reiterated his belief that there was "a pronounced military weakness in those states who base their existence on export . . . This explains the great weakness on our food situation in wartime. The only way out . . . is the securing of greater living space . . . The space required for this can only be sought in Europe."[44] For Hitler, even the unification of Germans under one roof was secondary to this goal. In March 1939, having achieved his declared goal of liberating the Sudeten Germans, Hitler took over the dismembered rump of Czechoslovakia, clearly showing that conquest rather than ethnic reunification was the aim. In May, as he was demanding that Poland hand over Danzig (Gdansk) with its largely German population, he told his inner circle that "Danzig is not the subject of the dispute at all. It is a question of expanding our living space and of securing our food supplies."[45] To achieve Hitler's goals, war was inevitable. The only question was when.

Given the revisionist views about the world order expressed by Prince Konoe at the end of the First World War, a second war in the Far East also appeared likely at some point. When Japan took over Manchuria in 1931, it stepped over a threshold that Germany crossed in March 1939. From then on, it was only a matter of time until some further act of expansion drew it into war with Britain and America. The issues that drove conflict in the Far East were even more clearly about resources than those in Europe.

Japan's strategic position was one of precarious balance. The country was deficient in almost all industrial raw materials except coal. It had to import two-thirds of its iron ore, mostly from China and British Malaya. It had almost no oil and depended on the United States for over half its supply. Moreover, by the early twentieth century, the country was no longer self-sufficient in food. The more Japan industrialized, the more it depended on security of supply. This gave it incentives that drove it in opposite directions. The acquisition of an empire would reduce its dependence on trade with potentially hostile suppliers. On the other hand, colonies could be acquired only through force, and in a war the country's dependence on sea imports made it vulnerable. In 1935, a Japanese official summed up the problem in terms designed to reassure a foreign audience:

> We are told sometimes by our foreign friends that we are in the forefront of the outbreak of nationalism that has occurred in the world in recent years. It would be well to point out, however, that our political nationalism, such as it is, has been largely brought into being by economic nationalism elsewhere. We are not, as we cannot be, economic nationalists. Our economic future depends on supplies of raw materials which we can obtain economically only from foreign countries. Thus our progress is inevitably bound up with that of the countries from which we must buy. Only the richly endowed nations can be economic nationalists, and we are not of their number.[46]

The Japanese strategy was gradually to expand the empire's sphere of control on the nearby mainland, by force if necessary, but only insofar as this did not arouse a military response from the Great Powers. The takeover of Manchuria was followed by a series of small steps pushing farther into Chinese territory, while always stopping short of war. The government of China under Chiang Kai-shek was too preoccupied with fighting the Communists under Mao Zedong to respond with force to any of these provocations. The three outside powers that might have opposed Japan were in no mood to take on foreign military entanglements. Russia was attempting to create socialism in one country through the turmoil of collectivization and forced industrialization. The two greatest wishes of the British and American public were to reduce domestic unemployment and avoid any repeat of the last war. Little did they imagine that the war they were seeking to avoid would eventually provide employment for all. Even when yet another "incident" led to full-scale Japanese invasion of China in 1937, there was no meaningful international opposition.

By 1939, Japan had had some success in turning its growing

empire to good account. Agricultural production in Korea and Taiwan was increased, making Japan self-sufficient in rice. Manchuria, in particular, was designed to form a crucial part of the Japanese economy. A five-year plan was established in 1937 that envisioned a fourfold increase in iron ore production and a threefold increase in coal. But none of this solved the oil problem. There were only two solutions: an expansion north up the eastern coast of Siberia, or an expansion south into Southeast Asia. The northern solution was favored by the army, but there were two objections. First, although Japanese companies held oil concessions in Sakhalin Island, the industry was in its infancy and finding sufficient quantities of oil there would take a long time. Second, the Russians were proving themselves no pushovers, roundly defeating a Japanese army when it attempted to annex a portion of Mongolia in the summer of 1939. The southern strategy was favored by the navy. Its crucial objective was the Dutch East Indies, which produced around 3 percent of world oil output, sufficient to cover Japan's needs.

Some Japanese justified the creation of a self-sufficient Asian empire under Japanese "leadership" as a contribution to world peace. In a world that no longer recognized free trade, economic isolation through the creation of autarkic blocs was the only answer. Hashiro Arita, a relative moderate in the ranks of the militaristic hard-liners, put forward arguments that echoed Hjalmar Schacht:

> When the doctrines of freedom of communications and trade prevailed the world over, enabling men and goods to move from one country to another with comparative ease, regardless of the status of their countries, it was possible even for small nations . . . to maintain a respectable existence side by side with the great Powers . . . Now, however, that such doctrines have all but disappeared with the great Powers' closing or threatening to close their doors to others, small countries have no other choice left but to strive as best they can to form

their own economic *blocs* or to found powerful states, lest their very existence be jeopardized. . . .

The establishment of *blocs* is the stage or method through which war is to be done away with and peace maintained, thereby assuring the advancement of world civilization and culture in general . . . The *bloc* system as proposed by Japan for East Asia . . . is a step forward for world peace, since it is a . . . method of guaranteeing peace by abolishing those grave economic disparities which have so often been the source of conflict.[47]

The problem with Arita's Greater East Asia Co-Prosperity Sphere, as it was disarmingly called, was that its creation led not to peace but to warfare and violence. This was not just because it had to be imposed on Asian peoples who, like the Chinese, had no desire for Japanese domination. It was also because Japanese expansion into Southeast Asia would inevitably run up against the military opposition of Britain and America. The area's raw-materials riches were vital to many countries. A Japanese attempt to corner them would run afoul of the problem described by the League of Free Nations Association in 1918: The economic security of one country could be secured only at the expense of others.

From the British and American perspective, the most important material produced in the area was not oil but rubber. This apparently inconsequential vegetable product of the Amazon rain forest had been propelled to the forefront of world attention by the rise of the automobile. Britain had understood its importance early on, and by planting extensively in Malaya produced three-quarters of world output by the early 1920s. Over the following decade, Malaya's near monopoly was somewhat reduced by rival plantations in the Dutch East Indies, but between them these two areas controlled 98 percent of the world market. For Britain, rubber had an additional importance since it was its single largest source of dollar earnings. For America, the region was also vital for its production of tin—one of the few metals in which it was deficient. The economist Eliot Janeway put the strategic implications of Asian raw materials bluntly:

> The American economy, and with it American defense, cannot be operated without rubber and tin, which at present cannot be obtained in adequate quantity except from the British and Dutch colonies in southeastern Asia. And Japan today commands the trade route connecting the west coast of the United States with the Malaysian Straits . . . Here, ready to hand for Japan, is a safer and more powerful weapon against the United States than the folly of naval attack.[48]

For the Japanese, the strategic calculations were delicate. The Nazi-Soviet Non-Aggression Pact of June 1939 had allowed Russia to concentrate additional forces against Japan in the East. By contrast, Britain was fully occupied with the European crisis, which in September finally erupted into war. America was still isolationist at heart, economically as well as politically. *Fortune* magazine conducted a survey in which two-thirds of Americans agreed with the idea that the country should "try to develop its own industries to the point where it does not have to buy any products from foreign countries."[49] Against this head-in-the-sand attitude, government strategists were warning that America found itself "so violently and overwhelmingly dependent on southeastern Asia that our entire foreign policy must be adjusted to that fact . . . It is not an exaggeration to say that the United States would be compelled, for its existence as a major industrial state, to wage war against any power or powers that might threaten to sever our trade lines with this part of the world."[50] But in 1939 it was not clear that such a pragmatic view of America's global interests would win out over a deeply entrenched isolationism.

From a Japanese perspective, the balance of risk versus reward pointed toward a "southern strategy." The outbreak of war in Europe in September 1939 offered a once-in-a-thousand-years opportunity to replace European domination of Southeast Asia. Nakahara Yoshimasa of the Navy General Staff was almost exultant: "Finally the time has come. This maritime nation, Japan, should today commence its advance to the Bay of Bengal! Moss-covered tundras, vast barren deserts—of what use are they? Today people should begin to follow the grand strategy of the navy . . . (We should not hesitate even to fight the United States and Britain to attain that end.)"[51]

But others were more cautious. The calculus of risk and reward in the southern strategy was made more difficult by the fact that America, unlike Russia, held a crucial weapon: It could shut off most of Japan's oil supplies at will. The stage was set for one of the most desperate military gambles in history.

4

ECONOMIC WARFARE, 1939–1945

We shall become the most self-supporting State, in every respect, . . . in the world . . . Timber we shall have in abundance,
iron in limitless quantity, the greatest manganese-ore mines in
the world, oil—we shall swim in it! And to handle it all, the
whole strength of the entire German manpower!

—ADOLF HITLER, AUGUST 1942

Hitler's ambition to make Germany a self-sufficient empire was
destined to remain unfulfilled. But for a tantalizing period between 1941 and 1942, as German tanks rolled across the plains of
Russia, it seemed that his dream might come true. Russia and its
hinterland were to become the new frontier—a vast land of unexploited riches that would remove the threat posed by the two
looming self-sufficient giants—the United States and the Soviet
Union.

The river of the future is the Danube. We'll connect it to the
Dnieper and the Don by the Black Sea. The petroleum and
grain will come flowing towards us . . . Add to this the canal
from the Danube to the Oder, and we'll have an economic
circuit of unheard-of dimensions . . . Europe, and no longer
America, will be the country of boundless possibilities . . .
There is no country that can be to a larger extent autarkic
than Europe will be.[1]

As he visualized this wondrous scene, Hitler was reflecting, and only slightly distorting, the theories of the geopolitical thinkers of the late nineteenth and early twentieth centuries. The ideas of Halford Mackinder had received a more welcoming reaction in Germany than they ever did in his home country. His concern that sea empires like Britain's could be challenged by the rise of land-based empires controlling the Eurasian "heartland" elicited an understandably warm response in German thinkers such as Karl Haushofer, professor of geography at the University of Munich. Haushofer took over Mackinder's vision and added to it a particularly Germanic concern with race and ethnicity. It was via Haushofer that Hitler encountered the idea of Lebensraum: the living space necessary for a people to thrive. The fertile, resource-rich expanses of Ukraine and Russia were needed for the German race to fulfill its destiny. It was an inconvenience of history that the Slavs had already colonized the area. The dream of a German-dominated Mitteleuropa, which had inspired the strategists of the First World War, was too penny-pinching. Eurasia was the ultimate prize, and in the end one of two nations must end up controlling it: Russia or Germany. Hitler, with his disdain for Slavs and hatred of communism, was determined that it should be Germany. The reward for his daring vision would be the transformation of his adopted country from a vulnerable European state surrounded by enemies and still dependent on trade across seas it could not control, into an invulnerable, self-sufficient empire.

Hitler's view on how to run this great empire was firmly rooted in the nineteenth-century imperial mind-set. Germany would be the manufacturing center; its newly conquered colonies would be restricted to supplying raw materials and markets. In his worldview, the slow diffusion of industrialization beyond its original European homeland was a looming disaster, threatening the bases of the continent's prosperity and power.

It would be a wise policy for Europe to give up the desire to export to the whole world. The white race has itself destroyed its world commerce. The European community has lost its outlets in other continents. Our manufacturing costs prevent us from meeting foreign competition . . . To their misfortune, the English have industrialized India. Unemployment in England is increasing, and the English worker gets poorer.

No such mistake would be made in a German-run Eurasian empire. As his armies wrapped up their conquest of Ukraine in September 1941 and prepared to advance on Moscow, Hitler gave his dinner audience a glimpse of how he saw the future of the Third Reich:

> The country we are engaged in conquering will be a source of raw materials for us, and a market for our products, but we shall take good care not to industrialize it . . . I insist on the fact that it's on our own soil that we must organize the production of whatever is vitally essential . . . All deliveries of machines, even if they're made abroad, will have to pass through a German middleman, in such a way that Russia will be supplied with no means of production whatsoever, except of absolute necessities.[2]

In the autumn of 1941, before the onset of a bitter winter in Russia and before Pearl Harbor, Hitler's vision of the future brimmed over with optimism. The postwar world would provide boundless opportunities for the development of a vast, resource-rich empire under German control. "Once this region is organized for us," he told Walther Funk, his minister for economic affairs, "all threat of unemployment in Europe will be eliminated." There would be enough work to keep industrious German colonists busy for fifty years.

But in the meantime, there remained the job of winning the war. And for all his hopes for the future, Hitler was aware that the war was about resources, and its outcome would depend on their control. "Despite all its efforts, the side that hasn't got the natural riches must end by going under."[3]

The outbreak of the First World War had been greeted by a combination of shock and an outburst of patriotic enthusiasm. The Second World War was ushered in merely with a dull sense of inevitability. Unlike in 1914, there was no financial panic. War was anticipated (Lloyd's of London had stopped covering marine war risk after Italy's invasion of Ethiopia in 1935), economic and financial interdependence had been reduced by the economic balkanization of the 1930s, and people already knew how to run the economy on a war footing.

The horrors of a war of attrition among industrialized nations were too well known for anyone to be fooled again into thinking that the troops would be home by Christmas. As Paul Einzig, the expatriate Hungarian economist, noted in *Economic Problems of the Next War*, published as the skies darkened in 1939, "There may have been some excuse during the last war for assuming that hostilities would come to an end within a few months. There can be no excuse for any statesman or government official falling into the same error when the next war breaks out."[4]

In the corridors of Westminster, there was one glimmer of optimism. The First World War had been won, in large part, because of the British naval blockade. There was some reason to think that this relatively painless military strategy might succeed again. After all, the situation was in some ways more favorable than last time. Germany had lost all its colonies (not that they had been of any use in the last war) and, more important, a portion of its European territory as well. It was now even shorter of foodstuffs and essential raw materials than before, primarily through its loss of iron ore reserves to France, and to a lesser extent through the loss of coalfields to Poland. Moreover, the country no longer had any gold or overseas assets with which to purchase foreign goods even from neutral countries. Einzig noted that, unlike in 1914, the German population was already underfed after years of Nazi economic policies that favored "guns instead of butter."

"Accordingly a shortage of food will produce a quicker and more devastating effect than it did in the last war," he predicted.[5] It was therefore no surprise when, on the first day of the war, Winston Churchill, the newly appointed First Lord of the Admiralty, announced a blockade of Germany. Nor was it a surprise that Germany responded with the announcement of a counterblockade of Britain and France.

Yet, viewed in the round, there was not much reason to expect a straightforward reenactment of the economic war of 1914–1918. For one thing, Germany was determined not to allow a repeat of the errors that had led to defeat in 1918. Even though Hitler's prewar claim that his policies of autarky had made Germany immune to blockade was an exaggeration, this did not disguise the fact that several important steps had been taken to reduce the near-term risk of economic strangulation. Production of synthetic oil and rubber was rising and already amounted to around one-third of oil consumption and half of rubber consumption. The creation of stockpiles further reduced the country's dependence on imports in the short term. Oil reserves in 1939 were six to eight million tons, sufficient to cover import requirements for between eighteen months and two years.

Hopes for a rapid success of the Allied blockade were further undermined by Hitler's surprise rapprochement with Stalin in August 1939. The Nazi-Soviet Non-Aggression Pact ensured Hitler an easy victory over Poland without the risk of a major two-front war.* A similar calculation was made by Stalin, who was now able to concentrate his forces against Japan in Mongolia without fear for his western frontier. Equally important in Hitler's

---

* Hitler did, however, face a minor two-front war. France declared war as soon as Germany invaded Poland and immediately sent troops into the Saarland, where they encountered only marginal opposition because the large majority of the German army was in the east. Unfortunately, the French then decided to retreat behind the Maginot Line and fight a defensive war. At the Nuremburg trials, General Alfred Jodl stated that France could probably have won the war in September 1939 had it mounted a full-scale offensive.

calculations were the two German-Soviet commercial agreements of August 1939 and February 1940, which allowed Germany to import significant quantities of Russian grain, oil, iron ore, and other strategic materials. By the middle of 1940, Russia was responsible for half of Germany's imports. "The conclusion of this treaty has saved us," declared Colonel Eduard Wagner, the quartermaster general of the army.[6]

Militarily, the equation was also different. There was a general determination, particularly in Berlin, to avoid the drawn-out carnage of trench warfare. The development of mechanized warfare made possible tactics of mobility and deep penetration. Such ideas were taken particularly seriously in the German army, where they evolved into a strategy of blitzkrieg (lightning war). It was well understood in Berlin that the shorter the war, the smaller the probability that its outcome would be decided by shortages of raw materials. A new imponderable was introduced by the extraordinary advances in air power in the interwar period. These not only altered the balance on the battlefield but also made possible the deep penetration of enemy territory. The full consequences of air power were hard to foresee—although the devastation of civilian life by bombers had been regularly foretold. Air power might neutralize the effectiveness of sea power by making warships vulnerable. On the other hand, it might amplify the effectiveness of a naval blockade by making possible the destruction of warehouses and transport links onshore. Two things were for sure: Air power would be vital, and it would require very large quantities of aviation fuel.

The conquest of Poland in September 1939 gave rise to an immediate improvement in Germany's strategic position. It regained the coalfields of Silesia, which it had lost in 1919, became self-sufficient in zinc, and reduced its food deficit. One of the remaining weak spots on which Allied strategy could focus was Germany's increased dependence on Swedish iron ore for its steel now that French imports were cut off. Without steel, Germany's war machine would grind to a halt. Germany and the Allies both turned their attention to Norway, whose North Sea port of Narvik was the only year-round transshipment point for Swedish ore. Britain and France made plans for an expeditionary force through Norway and Sweden that would help Finland in its war with Russia (and incidentally secure control of Narvik and the Swedish mines). But these were stalled by Norwegian and Swedish hesitancy. Churchill became so frustrated by Prime Minister Neville Chamberlain's kid-glove approach to Scandinavian neutrality that he argued for mining the sea channel along the Norwegian coast in spite of Norwegian opposition. But before Chamberlain could be persuaded to take action, Hitler launched a surprise invasion in April to forestall this looming threat to his supply lines.

Two years later, the invasion of Norway was described by Hitler as one of the most decisive campaigns of the war. It not only secured Swedish iron ore for Germany while denying it to Britain but also provided forward bases for the U-boats, enabling them to patrol deep into the Atlantic. In reality, the invasion's importance was overwhelmed by Germany's subsequent conquest of France and the Low Countries in May and June. Hitler now had access to all the iron ore and coal deposits that Germany had controlled in the last war, bringing the Reich closer to self-sufficiency. However, Swedish iron remained critical for German steel manufacture throughout the war, not just to make up quantities but also because of its very high quality. As the war progressed, Hitler was willing to supply Sweden with coal even at the cost of reducing domestic fuel consumption in order to ensure access to this critical resource. The Allies remained powerless to stop the trade, no matter how much moral pressure they applied to the Swedish government, until the last months of the war.

For a while, the fall of France appeared to be a prelude to the fall of Britain. A massive invasion force was prepared on the French coast while the Luftwaffe was given the task of clearing the Royal Air Force from the skies so that German planes could fend off the British navy during the invasion. In practice, however, the invasion stood little chance of success. The German navy was a shadow of its former glory before 1918. Although it had been partly rebuilt after the Anglo-German Naval Agreement of 1935, its forces were limited to 35 percent of the tonnage of the Royal Navy, and even this limit was never reached. After Munich, Hitler discarded the agreement and authorized the building of a surface fleet that would rival Britain's, but it was too late to make an impact on the war. At the outbreak of war, the German navy was only 200,000 tons compared to the 1,300,000 tons of the Royal Navy. The invasion of Norway had gambled the entire strength of the German fleet, and losses sustained in the Battles of Narvik and elsewhere had reduced it to a handful of serviceable ships. Meanwhile, the Luftwaffe proved incapable of achieving control of the skies—and even if it had, it was unlikely it could have defended the invasion fleet from the Royal Navy, in particular from its large fleet of torpedo boats that were virtually immune to air attack because of their size and speed.[7] On September 17, Operation Sea Lion, as the German invasion was code-named, was postponed indefinitely.

The failure to wrap up the war in Western Europe, however, did not appear to be any reason for Hitler to lose much sleep. His main frustration continued to be the obtuse stubbornness of the British in failing to see where their self-interest lay. Instead of hazarding their whole empire in an outdated concern to keep Europe disunited, they should have agreed to divide the world between their sea-based global empire and his land-based Eurasian empire. In the meantime, the Reich looked indestructible. Germany's prewar dependence on oil imports should have rendered it highly vulnerable to blockade, but the British efforts were having almost no effect. On the contrary, oil stocks had increased slightly during 1940. Of the six million tons consumed, more than half was now produced by the synthetic oil plants set up by I.G. Farben. Romania provided another eight hundred thousand tons and Russia six hundred thousand.[8] The remainder had come from captured oil reserves in Holland and France. Iron ore supplies seemed secure, and détente with Russia made available almost all the other materials required by Germany. Hungary, Romania, and Bulgaria had been drawn into the German economic sphere of interest before the war and had now become members of the Axis. Before the war, Romania had shipped 40 percent of its oil to Britain; now its supplies would go exclusively to Germany. Even the shortage of gold, necessary to buy supplies through neutral countries—in particular, Switzerland—was resolved, partly by looting gold stocks in conquered countries, partly by stealing the assets and even the gold fillings of Jews.

Yet even so, Hitler could not feel entirely safe. In the words of the historian Adam Tooze, "Despite the extraordinary extent of the Wehrmacht's victories, the space under Germany's control in the autumn of 1940 was not, therefore, the self-sufficient *Lebensraum* of which Hitler had dreamed."[9] The conquest of Western Europe was a remarkable achievement, but it meant that Germany now ruled a vast area that was historically dependent on imports and was now subject to blockade. In some ways it might have been easier, for instance, to have Holland remain neutral, as it had been in the last war, so that it might act as a surreptitious funnel for imports into Germany. The consumption of conquered populations could be, and was, held down, but even so, grain reserves were shrinking over the winter of 1940–1941.

Hitler's focus, therefore, had to turn to Russia. It was hard to see how the Nazi-Soviet Pact could endure. Hitler had played a remarkably duplicitous game with Stalin, not only deceiving him about Germany's long-term military intentions but also profiting as far as possible from the trade agreements. Like all Germany's trade deals since 1933, these had been arranged on the basis of barter. In exchange for Russian raw materials, Germany was committed to supplying not just coal but also machine tools and blueprints for advanced military technology such as the battleship *Bismarck* and the planned Messerschmitt Me 209. During 1940, Germany found excuses for falling behind on its commitments and therefore did considerably better in the overall exchange. However, by 1941, the Russians were demanding that the accounts be balanced, and this increasingly posed the risk of handing over the wherewithal to strengthen the Russian military in a conflict that, in the end, was inevitable. It was not just that in Hitler's worldview communist Russia was the archenemy. It was also that Hitler's ultimate ambition was a self-sufficient German empire, and this objective could never be fulfilled while the country and its European possessions were dependent on imports from Russia. There was also the oil situation. Germany had balanced its accounts so far only by looting captured stocks and by holding down civilian consumption in the occupied territories to bare subsistence. Moreover, Romanian oil was essential to long-term security of supply, and although the country was firmly in the German camp since the takeover of power by the Fascist-leaning Ion Antonescu in September 1940, its oil fields were perilously close to the Russian border, especially since Stalin had taken advantage of the Nazi-Soviet Pact to annex those parts of northeastern Romania that Russia had lost in 1918.

So the die was cast, and in June 1941, Hitler launched Operation Barbarossa. The initial German strategy was to destroy the Russian army and capture Moscow. Oil and other resources would then flow naturally to the new imperial masters. That this meant starving Russia of necessary resources did not matter. The invasion plan of May 1941 was shockingly direct about the results of diverting Ukrainian grain to Europe:

> Many tens of millions of people in this territory will become superfluous and will die or must emigrate to Siberia. Attempts to rescue the population there from death through starvation by obtaining surpluses from the black earth zone can only be at the expense of the provisioning of Europe. They prevent the possibility of Germany holding out till the end of the war, they prevent Germany and Europe from resisting the blockade. With regard to this, absolute clarity must reign.[10]

Barbarossa appeared to come tantalizingly close to success, but it failed to land the anticipated knock-out blow, and over the winter a regrouped Russian army under Marshal Georgy Zhukov pushed the Germans back from Moscow. In the meantime, the sheer scale of the forces and the vast distances covered had eaten up large quantities of German oil stocks. When Hitler launched his second offensive in 1942, the priorities were clear: The oil fields of the Caucasus were to be the main focus—to acquire them for Germany and to deny them to Russia. "Unless we get the Baku oil," he told Field Marshal Manstein, "the war is lost." Once again it looked for a time as if he might succeed. By August, the German forces had reached the Caucasus, and the Maikop oil fields near the Black Sea were captured. But by this stage the army was desperately short of oil and found that the Maikop fields, instead of offering fresh supplies, had been methodically sabotaged by the departing Russians. The route to Baku over the Caucasus mountains was too well defended for the reduced German forces to take and, failing in their attempt, they had to move north to help counter a growing Soviet counterattack around Stalingrad. After the bitter winter battle for control of the city had ended with the loss of an entire German army, it was clear that hopes of getting control of Russian oil were effectively over. Maikop was retaken by the Russians in January.

The winter of 1942–1943 was also the turning point in Hitler's other major war front: in the Atlantic. Germany declared a blockade of Britain as soon as the war broke out. However, its initial efforts were relatively modest. The interwar period had seen an attempt to put the genie of total war back in the bottle, particularly attacks on civilians. Unrestricted submarine war had been banned by the London Naval Treaty of 1930, which required the safe passage of crews before a merchant ship could be sunk. Like the inhibitions against bombing civilians, such reticence about taking civilian life was soon overcome in the heat of war. Nonetheless, as in the First World War, Germany had to worry about alienating American opinion. The first U-boat victim of the war was a passenger ship, the SS *Athenia*. Worried about the impact of the death of its American passengers, Hitler reiterated orders against attacking civilian ships without warning. Moreover, Germany had few submarines available for ocean patrol. Between the wars, most naval planners felt the U-boats had failed to achieve their objectives and that the new British technology of sonar rendered them vulnerable to detection and attack. Few merchant ships were sunk in 1939, and in early 1940 the German submarine force was largely focused on assisting the invasion of Norway.

The successful invasion of France changed the equation. While Germany allowed the defeated French a sliver of consolation by agreeing to a reduced but nominally independent state, it was careful that the boundaries of Vichy France should not include any part of the Atlantic coastline. The strategic importance of Atlantic ports was immediately clear to Admiral Karl Dönitz, the commander of the submarine fleet. From his experience at the end of the First World War, he had seen that the convoy system could be beaten only by a countervailing concentration of submarines employing "pack tactics." But to be effective, it would require very large numbers of submarines patrolling in the Atlantic in groups for long periods. This would be far easier from bases on the French coast. As for sonar, he noted that it worked only against underwater targets, and his proposed method of attack was on the surface at night.

As soon as Dönitz's "wolf packs" were introduced in late 1940, the British found themselves in difficulty. They had not prepared for such tactics, and it took a long time to develop successful countermeasures. Sonar proved largely ineffective, and there had been insufficient preparation for convoy protection between the wars. Paradoxically, it may have been the instinctive preference of all navies for the traditional glamor and well-understood military ethics of surface warships against the cramped squalor and questionable morality of submarines that helped save the day. The Kriegsmarine devoted much of its energy to building powerful commerce raiders such as the *Gneisenau*, *Scharnhorst*, and *Bismarck*. These would make short work of any convoy they encountered, while dispersing the convoys rendered them even more vulnerable to U-boats. It turned out to have been a mistaken strategy. Convoys could be protected by diverting equally powerful British warships to escort them. Moreover, the anxiety provoked by the power of the ultramodern German warships meant that every effort was made to hunt them down and put them out of action. *Bismarck* cost as much as fifty U-boats, and it was destroyed without sinking a single merchant ship. German surface warships were responsible for only 2 percent of all the Allied tonnage sunk during the war.

The climax of the Battle of the Atlantic came after America entered the war. Hitler had declared war on the United States on December 11, 1941. The reason, other than solidarity with his Japanese allies after Pearl Harbor, was to allow Germany a freer hand in enforcing the sea blockade. The passing of the Lend-Lease Act in February 1941 meant that in material terms the United States had aligned itself unequivocally with Britain, and subsequently with Russia. Its destroyers were already acting as escorts for the Atlantic convoys, making German submarines hesitant to strike. The impressive rate of sinkings in the first part of the year fell off as the year progressed. It was useless for Germany to fight the Battle of the Atlantic with one hand behind its back in the vain hope that the Americans might not enter the war formally.

The declaration of war on America changed the focus of the battle. The remaining commerce raiders were withdrawn from France to Norway to help threaten the Arctic convoys to Russia. In the meantime, the U-boats enjoyed the "happy times" afforded by the easy prey of unprotected American shipping on its Atlantic seaboard. The highest rate of sinking in the whole war was in the first half of 1942, before the American naval command recognized the necessity of arranging convoys and of enforcing blackouts of coastal towns.* Even after these unnecessary failures had

---

* The U-boats were able to sit offshore and pick off the merchantmen as their silhouettes passed across the lights of the towns. This was the only time when the Allied losses during the Second World War equaled those incurred in the early months of 1917 before the convoy system was introduced.

been remedied, the threat was not over. The submarine-building program, which had cranked up to a level of twenty boats a month in 1941, was starting to give Dönitz a sufficiently large operational fleet to use his wolf packs on the scale he always wanted. Until the spring of 1943, it seemed as if the Atlantic convoy system could still be overwhelmed. Unlike in the First World War, when the U-boat threat was largely surmounted by the simple expedient of the convoy system, the solution in the Second World War was far more complex, involving advances in tactics, weaponry, detection systems, and code breaking. Above all it was air power that turned the tide. The crucial change in 1943 was the establishment of complete air cover across the Atlantic by protecting convoys with aircraft carriers and equipping their aircraft with precision radar that could identify U-boats on the surface at a distance. In the first three weeks of May, Germany lost thirty-two submarines. In August, more U-boats than merchant ships were sunk. As Dönitz later recorded in his memoirs: "Radar, and particularly radar location by aircraft, had to all practical purposes robbed the U-boats of their power to fight on the surface. Wolfpack operations against convoys in the North Atlantic . . . were no longer possible . . . We had lost the Battle of the Atlantic."[11]

In practice, the German blockade never came as close to success as was sometimes feared. While not as dominant as before the First World War, the British merchant fleet was still by far the largest in 1939, with more than 30 percent of world tonnage. It was joined in 1940 by much of the Norwegian and Dutch fleets, which refused to hand themselves over to the Germans, adding a further 10 percent of world capacity. There was, therefore, a considerable initial cushion to sustain losses. Sinkings almost always outpaced new building in the first years of the war, but they were never enough to seriously dent the capacity of the fleet. The tonnage of the British fleet fell from 17.2 million in late 1940 to 14.3 million at the beginning of 1943, but the addition of foreign ships by chartering or requisition meant that the total available tonnage was still over 18 million.[12] And this was without counting the American contribution to the transatlantic fleet after 1941. Once the American shipbuilding program got going in earnest in the second half of 1942, any successes of the U-boats were comparatively insignificant. By the end of the year, the total Allied fleet was growing far faster than the U-boats could sink it. Moreover, the Allies were able to adjust by speeding up the time spent in port so that the same volume of shipping tonnage could go farther. Average round-trip times across the Atlantic fell from seventy-eight days in 1942 to forty-eight days by 1944.[13]

There were two main preoccupations of the British authorities: oil and food. With the exception of 1942, when they fell 10 percent below 1938 levels, oil imports were always higher than before the war. In conjunction with a modest rise in British synthetic oil production, total supply rose during the course of the war. But so did consumption, in spite of strict domestic rationing. There were nervous moments at the height of the U-boat campaign after the American entry into the war. From the beginning of 1942 until the spring of 1943, consumption exceeded supply almost every month.[14] But oil stocks never fell so low as to affect military capacity, and Britain always had far larger reserves than Germany even at the zenith of the Reich in 1941. The situation with food was similar to the First World War. After the surge in domestic food production in 1917–1918 in response to the blockade, British agriculture had reverted to its prewar patterns, so that by 1939 Britain once again imported two-thirds of its calories. But the decline of agriculture between the wars also meant that Britain had untapped possibilities of food production. Pasture was once again converted to arable land, allowing a rapid increase in grain production, and the population was encouraged to "Dig for Victory" in their gardens and allotments. The net domestic output of food calories doubled during the course of the war, allowing a nearly 50 percent reduction in food imports without any fall in nutrition. The cost was a monotonous carbohydrate-rich diet, but it has been argued that, as a whole, the population was better fed than before the war.

On the other hand, Dönitz had some justification for blaming the failure of the blockade on the shortsightedness of the German high command. He had argued for years that a fleet of three hundred long-distance submarines was necessary to find all convoys and attack them in force. Before 1943, he was compelled to work with a far smaller number of ships, partly because of the mistaken focus on building commerce raiders. When he finally reached something approaching his target in 1943, advances in defensive technique rendered his U-boats too vulnerable to be effective. If Germany had started building submarines at the rate of fifteen per month as soon as the war started, instead of achieving that rate only in late 1941, the outcome of the blockade might well have been different. As Dönitz mused in his memoirs, "After three and a half years of war we had brought the British maritime power to the brink of defeat in the Battle of the Atlantic—and that with only half of the number of U-boats that we had always demanded . . . In reality our leaders had learnt nothing from the First World War."[15]

If the first front of the economic war was on the open seas, its second front was in the even vaster expanses of the skies. It was not long after the development of air power that its possibilities outside the battlefield were understood. Airplanes could penetrate behind enemy lines and across frontiers, thus attacking targets of strategic importance unreachable by other means. This meant that bombers, in particular, shared a moral conundrum with submarines. As weapons beyond the battlefront, they would inevitably kill civilians. This had already been made apparent by the German bombing raids on England during the First World War. As with submarines, there had been an attempt between the wars to put the genie back in the bottle. The rival powers declared that bombing raids on civilians had no place in their plans, even as they prepared air forces that could deliver them and took defensive measures against them. Germans had conflicting feelings about the issue. With memories of the Allied blockade still raw, they could, and did, claim that bombing civilians was no worse than starving them. General Horst von Metzsch epitomized this thinking in 1933 in a chilling indication of what might occur in a future war: "There is no reason to think that a future war will be more barbarous than the World War. Although future air raids will be directed against the civilian population more than was the case in the World War, it must not be forgotten that a starvation blockade, which affects women and children, the aged and the sick, is incomparably more barbarous."[16]

On the other hand, Hitler was wary about starting a tit-for-tat bombing war. Fixated on the collapse of morale that had led to the "stab in the back" of November 1918, he was worried that the German population might buckle under a concerted bombing campaign. In practice, however, the pressures of war meant that in Germany, as elsewhere, any moral or other inhibitions about the use of bombers, like those about the use of submarines, were set aside.

A problem with bombing was that it was stuck in a technological halfway house. Between the wars, air war theorists identified two separate, and in many ways incompatible, objectives. In 1921, the Italian Giulio Douhet advocated the use of bombing as a pure terror weapon. He did not consider this inhumane. On the contrary, noting that Germany's defeat in 1918 had been precipitated by a collapse of morale on the home front, he argued that the speed at which a civilian population could be terrorized by bombing would bring wars to a rapid end, thereby avoiding the carnage of the last war: "The end would come with merciful speed. Future wars might prove more 'humane' than those of the past because they might, in the long run, shed less blood."[17] A second strand of thought rejected such notions as immoral but thought that the focus of bombing should be to amplify the effectiveness of economic warfare by striking at production and transport nodes behind the enemy lines. In the wake of the Depression, American strategists, in particular, were well aware of the fragility of modern economies and thought that well-directed bombing of such targets could cripple a country's war-making capacity.

With the advantage of hindsight, it is easy to see where the problem lay. Douhet's vision of "peace through terror" was impossible until the advent of nuclear weapons made bombs so destructive that nations became afraid to make war on each other. The alternative vision of victory through economic decapitation was not viable until the advent of "smart" weapons made precision bombing possible. In the Second World War, governments decried terror bombing and advocated the targeting of factories and railheads, but the available technology was primitive and could be used only at the cost of massive civilian casualties. As a result, the line between the two strategies was blurred, and governments were tempted, without admitting it directly, to see if Douhet was right. They found, horrifically, that he was not yet right. The bombs available in World War II were powerful enough to kill hundreds of thousands of civilians but, until August 1945, not powerful enough to terrorize them into submission.

The awful logic that drove strategic bombing in the Second World War first became apparent in the Blitz. When the Battle of Britain failed to achieve air superiority over the south coast of England, Goering changed tactics and started bombing the London docks in daylight. The Luftwaffe soon found that the losses incurred in daytime raids were unsustainably high and therefore turned to nighttime attacks, which were inherently less precise. A few experiments showed that targeting an entire area was more likely to achieve results than attempting pinpoint accuracy. Such bombing had the additional advantage of destroying the houses of the workers who inevitably lived close to their workplaces. Then it was found that incendiaries were more effective than high explosives in destroying large areas. The inexorable progress toward what became in effect the bombing of civilians, even if never officially part of Luftwaffe strategy, is demonstrated by the rise in the use of incendiary bombs from 13 percent in September 1940 to 92 percent by December, culminating in an air raid that set off the "Second Great Fire of London" at the end of the month (a raid so devastating that it immortalized the photograph that seemed to demonstrate that only St. Paul's Cathedral remained, miraculously, unscathed).

The Blitz did not achieve Hitler's objective of knocking Britain out of the war. It is uncertain whether it could have done so given the technology available at the time. Military production was dispersed to safer quarters, and, contrary to expectation, the morale of the population did not buckle. German air power might have been more effective if it had concentrated on supporting the sea blockade. German planes were enjoying considerable success against merchant shipping in late 1940 and early 1941, and Dönitz argued for the creation of combined air-sea tactics to concentrate on bombing ports and patrolling the seas. Rather too late in the day, in March 1941, Goering was persuaded to change the focus of bombing raids to Britain's Atlantic ports. But he strongly resisted any dilution of his control over the Luftwaffe, and after May almost all Germany's air power was diverted to the Russian campaign.

As Russia grappled with the bloody job of beating back the German military machine, Stalin argued repeatedly for an Allied invasion of France to take pressure off the Eastern Front. But until 1944, the only possible British and American contributions to the European war (other than tying up some German forces in North Africa and Italy) were to keep Russia supplied with food and war matériel, and to bring the war to Germany from the air. The military logic that led to strategic bombing was already set out by Churchill as early as July 1940:

> When I look around to see how we can win the war I see that there is only one sure path. We have no Continental Army which can defeat the German military power. The blockade is broken and Hitler has Asia and probably Africa to draw from. Should he be repulsed here or not try invasion, he will recoil eastward, and we have nothing to stop him. But there is one thing that will bring him back and bring him down, and that is an absolutely devastating, exterminating attack by very heavy bombers from this country upon the Nazi homeland.[18]

Like the Luftwaffe, the RAF soon found that daytime bombing attacks were suicidal—the more so because British planes had
to operate beyond the range of fighter protection. For some time
even attacks at night were ineffective because the British lacked
the techniques of nighttime navigation and targeting developed
by the Germans. By 1942, however, RAF navigational methods
had caught up, and Bomber Command was ready to put into effect the conclusion it had drawn from the Blitz: The only effective
strategy was "area bombing" conducted by massed formations of
planes that would overwhelm any possible defenses on the ground
by their sheer numbers. "The bomber," as Prime Minister Stanley
Baldwin had foretold gloomily in 1932, "will always get through."
Civilians would not be targeted per se (that remained taboo), but
they would be the inevitable casualties of raids designed to wipe
out urban areas surrounding vital war industries. Their morale
would surely crumble, and they would force their government to
surrender—or so ran the theory.

Nighttime area bombing proved every bit as destructive but
not nearly as effective as imagined. Cities were laid waste, but
there was modest impact on war production. If there was any erosion of civilian morale, it had no effect on government policy.
When the US Army Air Force joined the fray in early 1943, it
attempted to avoid the moral black hole that had sucked in the
Luftwaffe and RAF. However, the USAAF too had to abandon
precision daytime raids after unsustainable losses to German
fighters over the summer. It was only when the long-distance P-51
Mustang fighter became available to the Allies and was put to use
as part of a concerted bombing campaign against German aircraft production in February 1944 that the balance of forces
changed. From that point, the Luftwaffe ceased to offer adequate
protection against daytime raids, and the Allies could finally concentrate on what, ideally, should have been the focus of the economic air war all along.

The most important targets were readily selected. After the
failure of Hitler's 1942 Russian campaign, it was clear that oil

remained the fundamental weakness of Nazi Germany. Its vulnerability lay not so much in immediate shortfalls, which were offset by increases in synthetic production and further reductions in civilian consumption, but in the fact that oil production was centered in a handful of highly visible locations: the Ploësti refinery in Romania and the nine large synthetic oil plants in Germany. As soon as Germany found itself on the defensive, this potentially lethal weakness became a cause of concern. As Field Marshal Erhard Milch reported at a meeting in April 1943: "The hydrogenation plants are our most vulnerable spots; with them stands and falls our entire ability to wage war. Not only will planes no longer fly, but tanks and submarines also will stop running if the hydrogenation plants should actually be attacked."[19]

Once the threat of Luftwaffe fighters had been largely eliminated by the spring of 1944, the Allies started a series of bombing attacks on the oil plants, which reduced their output by more than 90 percent by September. Albert Speer, Hitler's minister of armaments and war production, responded by a frantic rebuilding program and by moving production to smaller, hidden facilities. But the major damage was done, and in the last months of 1944, total oil supplies were only one-third of the level a year earlier. For the rest of the war, German military operations were hamstrung by shortages of fuel. The Ardennes Offensive (December 1944–January 1945), the last great attempt to stop the Allied advance in the West, depended for its success on capturing Allied oil stocks since German supplies were inadequate to maintain the initial thrust. The slow strangulation caused by the attacks on the synthetic oil plants was compounded by attacks on Germany's rail network. By the end of 1944, the Ruhr had been more or less cut off from the rest of Germany.

After the war, the official British history of the economic blockade concluded, "Thus it was in the last phase of the war the full range of economic weapons was at last being used with the deadly effect that the early economic-warfare planners had postulated; and the German fuel disaster proved that there was after all an Achilles heel. But it had been struck by the bomber and not by the blockade."[20] It was precision attacks, not area bombing, that had struck the vital blow. During his postwar interrogation, Speer was asked to rate the effectiveness of different bombing strategies on German war potential. He placed attacks on oil production first, attacks on transport second, and area attacks on cities only fifth out of eight.

The success of the Allied attacks on Germany's oil and transport infrastructure did not, however, put an end to area bombing. By this time so much had been invested in strategic bombing forces that there were far more bombers and bombs available than were needed for precision attacks. The destruction of cities continued right up to the end of the war. By the time Germany was finally compelled to surrender in early May 1945, its urban landscape had been reduced to piles of charred rubble.

A similar fate was to overcome Japan. When the war broke out in Europe in 1939, the idea of a move into Southeast Asia looked tempting to the Japanese military, but still dangerous. The sweeping German victories of 1940 changed the balance of risk and reward. France and the Netherlands had fallen, leaving their Asian empires virtually undefended. Britain was facing a fight for its very survival and could not afford to leave large forces in the Far East. In September 1940, Japan took advantage of France's weakness to force the Vichy government to allow Japanese troops into Indochina. Their only likely purpose was to act as a springboard for an attack to the south. By July the following year, further Japanese advances down the coast of Indochina so alarmed the United States, as well as Britain and the Dutch government in exile, that they froze Japanese assets and, crucially, restricted Japanese access to oil. But the oil weapon backfired. From the point that it was triggered, Japan was forced to decide whether to press on or admit defeat. Dependence on imports counseled the latter, but the combination of economic insecurity with military strength was a powerful incentive to fight. The fateful decision to go to war with the United States and the British Empire simultaneously was based on the gamble that the Japanese navy could land a speedy knockout blow to the American Pacific fleet based in Hawaii.* This would allow Japan the time to conquer the rich but lightly defended colonies of Southeast Asia and convert them into a powerful, self-sustaining empire before the Anglo-Saxon powers could get together the forces to oppose them. Adventurers such as Teiichi Suzuki, the head of the Planning Board, swept aside the concerns of doubters who were "uneasy because we are short of raw materials . . . But there is no reason to worry. In 1943 the materials situation will be much better if we go to war."[21]

The gamble on war worked better than anyone dared imagine. The devastating surprise attack at Pearl Harbor delayed the American naval forces' arrival in the Far East for five months. During that window of opportunity, the Japanese conquered the Philippines, British Malaya, Singapore, the Dutch East Indies, Borneo, New Guinea, and a string of Pacific islands. For a time it looked as if Japan's dreams of a self-contained East Asian empire might be fulfilled. Taken together with Germany's equally remarkable conquests in Europe and Russia, the world seemed to be witnessing a transfer of global power even faster and more wide-reaching

---

* The moment was advantageous for naval reasons. In 1922, in an attempt to put an end to the arms race of the prewar era, the Washington Naval Conference had agreed to strict limits on naval forces. Britain, for so long used to having by far the world's largest navy, had to swallow its pride and agree to parity with the United States, which had gone on a major building spree during the war and now threatened to surpass the Royal Navy. Japan was allowed a force equal to 60 percent of the two naval superpowers. This gave it the world's third-largest navy—a remarkable achievement for a relative newcomer. However, Japan's naval strength created an unstable balance of power in the Far East. Its forces were large enough to dominate the area most of the time—especially since the United States had agreed not to turn its refueling base at Subic Bay in the Philippines into a permanent naval presence. On the other hand, they were not large enough to assure control of the region if America and Britain concentrated their fleets. In 1941, both Britain and America had moved most of their forces to the Atlantic, leaving Japan with a temporary naval predominance in the Pacific that would, however, disappear once America completed its naval building program.

than the conquests of Alexander the Great, Khalid ibn al-Walid, or Genghis Khan.

The most urgent goal of the conquest of Southeast Asia was to achieve self-sufficiency in oil. Between them, the Dutch East Indies and British Borneo produced around nine million tons of oil per year. In theory this was more than enough to cover Japanese consumption of five to six million tons. In the short term, the objective of self-sufficiency was set back by the destruction of the oil fields and refineries by the departing Dutch and British engineers. However, the Japanese were prepared for such sabotage and set about repairing the damage with a massive application of manpower. In 1942, production was down by 60 percent, but by 1943 it had returned to nearly 80 percent of its prewar level. Imports into Japan were still limited, but the navy, by far the largest consumer of oil, could refuel at will. Prime Minister Tojo announced that the oil problem had been solved.

Japan's hope was that the astonishing speed and completeness of their military success would force the Western powers to come to terms with the reality of Japanese regional hegemony. They failed to realize that such an outcome was unlikely not only because it ran up against a determination to redress what was seen as an affront to national pride but also because it challenged powerful Western economic and geopolitical interests. Japan's conquest of Southeast Asia not only secured resources for Japan, it also denied them to Britain and America. The United States secured 90 percent of its tin and 98 percent of its rubber from the area. For Britain, its Malay colonies were not only sources of raw materials but also vital generators of foreign exchange. Moreover, Japan's ambitions did not appear to stop in Southeast Asia. It was already threatening India and Australia.

It turned out that Japan's attack on Pearl Harbor had not been overwhelming enough. America's aircraft carriers escaped destruction because they were out at sea, and the Japanese failed to destroy the easy target of the base's fuel supplies. As a result, America was able to mount a serious naval threat within months, whereas Admiral Chester Nimitz reckoned that the destruction of the oil tanks alone would have set the United States back by the better part of two years. But in the end it is hard to see how much difference it would have made. With an overwhelming advantage in industrial potential, the United States could afford to take its time. Nor did the loss of Asian rubber bring America to the negotiating table as some Japanese hoped. Tires were the first item rationed once war was declared, recycling was increased, and a crash program of synthetic rubber production was set up. An emergency government stockpiling program put in place in late 1940 ensured that America had accumulated sufficient reserves to get through the first eighteen months of the war before synthetic rubber production really took off.

It can never be certain whether economic warfare on its own would have succeeded in defeating Germany. In the end, the Nazi regime was brought down by invasion. In the Pacific War, however, the position was different. Japan surrendered while it was still territorially intact and with most of its wartime conquests still in its hands. If it had not been for Douglas MacArthur's insistence on the reconquest of the Philippines, for reasons as much of emotion as hard-headed strategy, the only important actions undertaken by the US Army would have been the capture of a string of small Pacific islands necessary to bring the war close enough to Japan to strangle it through a combination of naval and air power.

The relative success of Germany in holding out against Allied economic pressure demonstrated, among other things, that contiguous land-based empires are harder to blockade than islands. This had always been Hitler's point when he argued for expansion to the east rather than a return to the futile nineteenth-century policy of overseas colonies. Japan, however, was an island nation and every bit as dependent on seaborne trade as Britain. It was therefore a perfect target for a naval blockade. In many ways, Japan was even more vulnerable than Britain. Its merchant fleet was only six million tons, compared to the twenty-one million tons available to Britain at the end of 1940. Nor did Japan have a ship-building industry as large as Britain's. It was therefore less able to make up losses. Moreover, Japan lacked a powerful ally like the United States that was able to provide not only cargoes for British convoys but also, as the war progressed, merchant ships and military protection.

Surprisingly, given the example of the Battle of the Atlantic, neither Japan nor America had prepared for a sea blockade. The US Navy authorized unrestricted submarine warfare on the first day of war, but it had relatively few boats available, and those mostly operated in tandem with surface fleets. Moreover, American torpedoes proved defective, and it took a long time for complaints from submarine commanders to bring about a redesign. It was only in 1943, and especially in 1944, that the blockade became really effective. Even more puzzling, for a country so dependent on sea trade for its food and other vital materials, was the lack of preparation by the Japanese. They had made no provision for convoys, and when convoys were instituted in 1943, there was little consideration of the kind of escorts best suited to protect them. In particular, the Japanese made no provision for air cover, which was proving critical to Allied success in the Atlantic.

The Pacific submarine war was on a smaller scale than the Battle of the Atlantic. America deployed fewer submarines than Germany, and sank fewer ships. But it scarcely mattered when Japan had so much smaller a margin for survival than Britain. After 1943, Japan's shipping losses mounted. By the end of 1944, in spite of a frantic building program, its merchant fleet was reduced by over one-half. By the end of the war, Japan had less than one-quarter of its fleet left. The last convoy of oil tankers left for Japan in March 1945, never to arrive. By late 1944, oil supplies were so low that they had to be conserved in the most extreme ways. Kamikaze tactics were adopted in part because one or two planes on a suicide mission could accomplish the same as ten or more in a conventional attack. Moreover, they did not need fuel for the return journey.

Japan's food supplies were also progressively squeezed by the blockade. By the end of 1944, rice shipments from Taiwan and Southeast Asia had been reduced to a trickle, and even those from Korea had fallen by more than one-half. The loss of food imports compounded an underlying problem with Japanese agriculture. Unlike Britain's underutilized countryside, Japan's farmland had no margin for increased production. Almost all available agricultural land was already in use, and its output was stretched to the maximum by high inputs of fertilizer. Moreover, the country was already on a largely carbohydrate diet, so there was no room to increase calorie output by switching land away from meat production. The result was that the Japanese civilians, already on meager rations at the beginning of the war, were surviving on a mere 290 grams of food per day by its end.[22]

Could Japan have been blockaded into submission? Might the Pacific War have ended with soldiers and civilians taking to the streets demanding "peace and bread" (or in this case, "peace and rice"), as occurred in Russia and Germany in the First World War? It seems uncertain given the extraordinary resilience of the Japanese war spirit in the face of hardships far greater than those endured by Russia or Germany thirty years earlier. But in the end the question is unanswerable because it was never put to the test. Japan was bombed into submission instead.

Bombing raids started far later than the naval blockade because of the great distances involved. It was only with the introduction of the B-29 Superfortress long-range bomber in 1944 that reaching Japan became feasible, and regular large-scale raids did not start until the end of the year when the Mariana Islands had been recaptured and equipped with suitable airfields. The early bombing attacks focused on precision targeting of military targets. However, as in Germany, it was soon found that they were not as effective as hoped. The B-29s were able to bomb in daytime even without fighter cover, thanks to their very high altitude and speed, which made them virtually unreachable by Japanese fighters. However, this meant that they had to fly high above Japan's regular cloud cover, negating any advantage in accuracy achieved by flying in daytime. In late February, it was decided to switch tactics to area bombing with incendiaries conducted at low altitudes at night. The firebombing raids proved devastatingly effective in destroying Japan's cities with their wooden houses, but their impact on the Japanese war economy to some extent only duplicated the effects of the blockade. The US postwar survey of the air campaign noted that "most of the oil refineries were out of oil, the alumina plants out of bauxite, the steel mills lacking in ore and coke . . . Japan's economy was in large measure being destroyed twice over, once by cutting off imports, and secondly by air attack."[23] In many ways, the most militarily effective use of B-29s may have been in assisting the blockade by dropping more than twelve thousand mines around Japan's coastline in the bluntly named Operation Starvation. In the last year of the war, air attacks and mines were as important as submarines in tightening the blockade—especially in severing Japan's sea links with Korea. However, the air attacks had an objective that went beyond the immediate damage they caused. By the end of 1944, Japan had, in effect, already been beaten, but according to a postwar American survey, only 10 percent of Japanese accepted that the war was lost.[24] The air war was necessary to bring home the truth of defeat to a population kept almost entirely in the dark about the true state of affairs, and to a government in which the pragmatists were opposed by militarists determined to fight to the end. Only if the Japanese accepted the reality of defeat would it be possible to compel the country to surrender without an invasion.

After May, there was a lull in the bombing of Japan's cities, and the early results of the survey of the bombing campaign in Germany suggested that the focus should be placed firmly on transport. However, the desire to bring the war to a speedy end gave the air war a renewed urgency that brooked no limits. A new campaign was launched in late June focusing on smaller cities not already hit. This campaign had an explicitly psychological aspect: The raids were prefaced by drops of leaflets naming the possible targets and suggesting that they be evacuated before they were destroyed, so that the lives of innocent civilians would not be sacrificed in the vain cause of propping up a militarist government. Among the cities on the list of possible targets were Hiroshima and Nagasaki—left aside in readiness for the atomic bombs that were being prepared in New Mexico. Finally, on August 6 and 9, area bombing reached its logical conclusion with the dropping of two bombs so powerful that they changed forever the way strategic bombing was viewed. Here, finally, was a weapon so devastating that Douhet's theory of terror bombing as a deterrent to war might become reality.

Whether Little Boy and Fat Man actually brought the war to an end is bound to remain uncertain. Emperor Hirohito specifically referred to the bombs in his address to the public on August 15 announcing his decision to surrender. However, there will always be alternative explanations: from the cumulative effects of the naval blockade and air bombardment, to the Russian invasion of Manchuria on August 9, and the looming US invasion of the home islands. What is certain is that no one on the Allied side assumed that the invention of the atomic bomb eliminated the need to craft a lasting peace settlement. If anything, the new weapon made it even more urgent to ensure that this latest conflict was truly the "war to end all wars."

5

PAX AMERICANA AND THE SECOND ERA OF GLOBALIZATION

Either men may set up a common league to keep the peace of the earth, or one state must ultimately become so great and powerful as to repeat for all the world what Rome did for Europe two thousand years ago.

—H. G. WELLS, *In the Fourth Year: Anticipations of World Peace*, 1918

When H. G. Wells brought up the example of ancient Rome while speculating about the post–World War I peace settlement, he was not advocating a modern-day Pax Romana. If countries failed to resolve their differences under the auspices of a league of nations, as was then being proposed by the Allies, the grim alternative, as he saw it, was to fall under the jackboot of Teutonic imperialism. In the brave new world Wells envisaged, imperialism was out and cooperation was in. He did not consider the possibility that the new world order might need a hegemon to run it. Yet it turned out that it was precisely a new Rome that the world required.

Two decades later, it was clear that the Versailles Treaty had failed in its objective of ensuring that the conflict was the "war to end all wars." But now there was a second chance to bring about lasting peace. This time the need to do so was even more urgent than in 1918, since advances in technology had made the Second

World War more devastating than the first, and a third world war would be even worse.

The Wilsonian formula for lasting peace in 1918 had been based on three elements: (1) the disarmament of aggressor nations, to be followed by their rehabilitation as peace-loving members of the international community; (2) an end to the inexorable expansion of empires and the removal of barriers to trade so that all nations could feel confident of access to raw materials and markets; and (3) the establishment of a worldwide league of nations to arbitrate disputes and keep the peace. In practice, Wilson's ideals had been put into effect at best partially. The aggressors were disarmed, but far from being rehabilitated, they refused to see the justice of the new world order, not least because other empires appeared to be expanding. Economic nationalism and protectionism were not abolished; in fact, trade was less free than before the war. Most important of all, the League of Nations, the linchpin of the new world order, was doomed from the start by the failure of Wilson's own country to join it. How were the Allies proposing to do better this time?

In some ways, their plans did not look so very different from Wilson's. Their manifesto was the Atlantic Charter, drawn up by Roosevelt and Churchill in August 1941. Even though its publication preceded America's entry into the war, the charter became the foundation of Allied policy for the postwar settlement, and all members of the anti-Axis alliance, now known as the United Nations, were required to sign up to its principles. Like Wilson's Fourteen Points, the charter renounced territorial aggrandizement and endorsed the principles of national self-determination, the disarmament of aggressors, and freedom of the seas. While the Fourteen Points had attempted to lance the boil of economic nationalism through the removal of "all economic barriers and the establishment of equality of trade conditions," the charter addressed the same issue by committing to "further the enjoyment of all States, great or small, victor or vanquished, of access, on equal terms, to the trade and to the raw materials of the world which are needed for their economic prosperity." This time the reference to raw materials was specific—scarcely surprising after the war of words between haves and have-nots in the run-up to war.

The most telling absence in the Atlantic Charter, when compared to the Fourteen Points, was reference to the League of Nations or any international body. This might seem surprising given that the charter became the founding document of the United Nations as a military alliance, and thereby of the United Nations as a world intergovernmental body. The omission is explained by the fact that the United States was not a member of the League of Nations, and in 1941 it was almost impossible for an American politician to imply that the country should join such a body. Churchill's first draft of the charter included a commitment to maintaining the peace in the postwar world "by effective international organization," but Roosevelt cut it out. The internationalism of his administration was still controversial within the country. The most he would accept was a reference to the possible "establishment of a wider and permanent system of general security" sometime in the future.[1]

However, the tide was turning. The Second World War brought about a gradual but profound change of opinion in America. The fall of France in 1940 and the threatened invasion of Britain brought home the alarming possibility of a hostile German empire controlling not just Europe but the Atlantic as well. In the presidential elections of that year, the Republican Party turned away from its isolationist wing and chose the internationalist Wendell Willkie as its candidate.

In February 1941, Henry Luce, the founder of *Time*, wrote an article titled "The American Century," calling for the country to take up the challenge of global leadership:

> We can make a truly *American* internationalism something as natural to us in our time as the airplane or the radio. In 1919 we had a golden opportunity, an opportunity unprecedented

in all history, to assume the leadership of the world . . . We did not understand that opportunity. Wilson mishandled it. We rejected it . . . To lead the world would never have been an easy task . . . Nevertheless, with the help of all of us, Roosevelt must succeed where Wilson failed.[2]

His message was reinforced by a book by the American diplomat James Cromwell with the audacious title *Pax Americana.* Both authors were strong supporters of the internationalist policies of Franklin Roosevelt. Yet Roosevelt himself was forced to proceed with caution. His policy was to push the country ever closer to war without taking the final step—even when German U-boats attacked American ships in the Atlantic. As the German ambassador reported to Berlin, "The American Government, in contrast with Wilson in 1917, does not make the question of war or peace dependent upon incidents on the high seas, but uses these incidents, which by its policies have become unavoidable, to dramatize its propaganda in order to break down public opposition to its present course of action."[3]

In early December, the threat of a Japanese invasion of Southeast Asia was so great that Roosevelt was on the verge of asking Congress to declare war on Japan to protect vital American interests. But in the end, the Japanese were the first to pull the trigger, and Roosevelt reacted to Pearl Harbor with shock, but also with some relief that his speech was no longer necessary.

Once America was at war, public opinion swung rapidly toward internationalism, now aided by powerful voices from the Republican Party. In June 1942, ex-president Herbert Hoover published *The Problems of Lasting Peace,* which became an instant bestseller. The book discussed the ways peace might be maintained after the war, none of which were feasible without American involvement. In early 1943, Wendell Willkie published *One World,* which sold even more copies. In it he argued strongly against isolationism, stating that America had "sacrificed a magnificent opportunity for leadership" in 1919, and it was now time to "determine whether America will assume its proper place in world affairs."[4]

After 1942, therefore, America's long-term participation in the peace settlement seemed certain. Moreover, the country's economic dominance, and its role as wartime banker and supplier to its allies, put it in a very strong position to ensure that the terms of the settlement were to its liking. Whereas most other countries involved in the war had seen their economies devastated, the United States emerged from the war with its economic output almost 70 percent higher than in 1939, and now accounted for around half of total world production. The way seemed clear for the establishment of a true Wilsonian world order under American leadership. Yet the path to a durable peace was far more complex than this simple paradigm suggests.

It was not the original intention of the American framers of the peace that the country should be more than first among equals. The idea was to maintain the three-power alliance (or in some iterations, the four-power alliance including China) as the world's police force. James Cromwell's *Pax Americana*, written before Russia's entry into the war, envisaged what was in reality a Pax Anglo-Americana—a permanent alliance between the United States and the British Empire. Herbert Hoover's book recognized that a United States–dominated Pax Americana was a possible solution to the problem of lasting peace, but he rejected the idea in favor of ongoing enforcement by the major wartime allies. As the war progressed, such ideas took concrete shape. The alliance was named the United Nations, open to all who subscribed to the Atlantic Charter, and plans were put in place to transform it into a permanent body to replace the failed League of Nations. The role of the major allies in policing the peace was to be formalized as the Security Council of the new body. The members of the United Nations and the Security Council would work in harmony to maintain world peace. Looking back from the perspective of the 1950s, a study of American foreign policy by the Woodrow Wilson Foundation commented on

the almost utopian quality of much official American thinking in the wartime years when the United Nations Charter
was under discussion . . . It [was] assumed that our special
responsibility for maintaining world order was discharged
with the establishment of the United Nations, in which the
United States would be only *primus inter pares*, acting as impartial arbiter of possible disagreements among the other
members and keeping a benevolent but detached interest in
the operation of the world organization.[5]

The word "utopian" may be too charitable a description of the
sometimes very hard-nosed negotiations about how the postwar
world was to be ordered, but it certainly reflects the fact that the
peace that emerged was not entirely the one that was conceived
during the war.

Nowhere were the negotiations about the postwar order harder
fought than over the issue of economic nationalism. This was arguably the area in which the Versailles settlement had most con-
spicuously failed to eradicate the underlying causes of war.

By this time, the views of Cordell Hull, the longtime advocate
of free trade, had become accepted policy within the administration. His attempts to forestall the war by measures to restore
international trade had proved futile, but it was agreed in Washington that such measures would be fundamental to creating a lasting
peace after the end of hostilities. In Hull's view, it was impossible
to "separate the idea of commerce from the idea of war and peace."
As early as January 1940, long before the United States had joined
the conflict, he declared publicly that after the war the country
must apply all its "moral and material influence in the direction
of creating a stable and enduring world order" so that international
politics did not again "assume such a character as to make of them
a breeding ground of economic conflict, social insecurity, and,
again war."[6]

What was needed was an end to policies that aimed at creating
autarkic empires, or self-sufficient blocs, and a return to multilat-

eral trade open to all. The idea, shared not just by Germans and Japanese but by many in Britain and the United States, that self-sufficiency would reduce the causes of international conflict, was fundamentally wrong. In words that echoed back to Richard Cobden and Frédéric Bastiat, Hull argued that "without expansion of international trade . . . there can be no stability and security either within or among nations . . . The withdrawal by a nation from orderly trade relations with the rest of the world inevitably leads to . . . preparations for war and a provocative attitude toward other nations."[7]

In an influential book, *The Reconstruction of World Trade*, published in 1940, the economist John Condliffe pointed out that autarky was an illusion in the modern world. It was hard enough for industrial nations to be self-sufficient in food, but "the distribution, particularly of mineral resources, in the world is such that it is less possible to develop national self-sufficiency in this respect than in respect of foodstuffs."[8] The same point was made in 1942 by Herbert Hoover:

> Nations do like to have sovereignty over areas of raw materials so that they may have an outlet for population and . . . a place in the sun. It also gives still more assurance of supplies in war . . . But even a redistribution of colonies would not provide everybody with raw materials. Anyone familiar with their distribution in the world would realize that to give parts of all the different raw-material areas to everybody is wholly impossible.

The only solution, therefore, was a return to free and open multilateral trade: "The whole experience of the past hundred years shows that the assurance of supplies of raw materials requires only a dissolution of monopoly controls, an assurance of equal prices, open markets—and peace."[9]

This sounded simple, but it was not. If international trade was to be restored, it was not sufficient to defeat the Axis powers.

There was strong opposition to the idea of free trade within the ranks of the Allies themselves. It was not just a question of Soviet Russia, which since the 1917 revolution had more or less ceased to be part of the international economy at all and whose interest in rejoining it was extremely uncertain. The biggest disagreement was between America and Britain.

The main target of Hull's economic diplomacy was the British imperial trade preferences that had been in place since 1932. At times, the rhetoric from the State Department made it seem as if they were as great an obstacle to world peace as the Nazis themselves. The Lend-Lease negotiations in 1941 were particularly rancorous on this point. The State Department was determined to use American leverage over Britain to bring about the end of the empire as an economic bloc. Article 7 of the draft agreement specified that "the terms and conditions upon which the United Kingdom receives defense aid . . . shall provide against discrimination in either the United States or the United Kingdom against the importation of any product originating in the other country."[10] This implied, even if it did not explicitly require, the end of imperial preferences.

British opinion was almost universally hostile to the American position. The biggest reason was the deep sense of economic insecurity that pervaded the country. Even before the war, Britain had lost its old confidence in its ability to compete internationally. The war not only made the long-term prospects for the economy worse; it also showed that the best way to survive in hard times was through a centrally managed economy. The Labour Party, which had traditionally been supportive of free trade, swung against it. Keynes, now working for the government for the first time since 1919, thought that Britain needed to copy the economic system set up in Germany by Hjalmar Schacht: "The underlying idea is sound and good. In the last six months the Treasury and the Bank of England have been building up a system which has borrowed from the German experience all that was good in it. If we are to meet our obligations and avoid chaos in international trade after the war, we shall have to retain this system."[11] Sent to negotiate with the Americans about Lend-Lease, Keynes argued that Britain would need exchange and trade controls for years after the war while its industry turned from manufacturing munitions to producing goods for export. He described any agreement that involved the immediate abolition of controls as a "lunatic proposition."[12] Exposing the country to the bracing winds of free international trade immediately after the war would be disastrous.

There was a second reason for British hostility to the American position. Although Hull recognized the need for tariff reductions, he viewed this as secondary to the ending of imperial preferences. To British eyes this was mere hypocrisy. American tariffs remained extremely high and fell precisely on the manufactured products that Britain needed to export if it was to feed itself. In the end, Britain was forced to accept the Lend-Lease clause, managing only to add a phrase tying the elimination of preferences to the "reduction of tariff and other trade barriers." But this still left British exports to the United States at the mercy of the US Congress, which had the final say on tariffs. As the American ambassador to London reported in 1944,

> [the British] consider that the extension of preferences in the early thirties was primarily a response to the Smoot-Hawley tariff, and they wonder whether Congress will be prepared to make the very substantial cut in tariffs which the U.K. public, in view of the anticipated postwar balance of payment difficulties, would consider as a necessary offset to giving up all or a substantial part of preferences. Therefore, they do not respond favorably to a frontal attack from Americans on preferences per se, particularly if there seems to them to be an implication that the adoption of preferences was a more heinous offense than the erection of a very high wall around a market of continental dimensions.[13]

The reference to Congress was significant. Hull might believe in general tariff reductions, but there was considerable opposition throughout the country, and especially in Congress, where, as Hull noted, attempts to reduce tariffs invariably "resulted in higher tariffs because the special interests enriched by high tariffs went to their respective Congressmen and insisted on higher rates."[14]

The issue of trade barriers and tariffs was intimately connected to a second source of dispute among the Allies: the problem of currency. The fixed exchange rates and absence of capital controls that had made the first era of globalization so successful before 1914 had been replaced in the 1930s by a patchwork of restricted currencies. Sterling was used with the British Empire and the sterling bloc. Germany traded by means of barter without resort to any international currency at all. Dollars were used only for trade with America and were perennially scarce because of America's persistent trade surplus. Gold, which had formed the ultimate means of settlement in the old monetary system, had fled to America during the crisis years and had been locked up in vaults. Countries such as Germany had justified their resort to bilateral trade by the difficulty of obtaining foreign exchange. The League of Nations conference on raw materials in 1937 had reported that there were more concerns about access to foreign exchange to pay for commodities than about their availability. If multilateral trade was to be reestablished after the war, some monetary arrangement would have to be set up that would satisfy a global need for a stable and liquid means of payment.

In the eyes of Americans, this could be based only on the dollar. Since only America had sufficient gold, the dollar, convertible into the yellow metal for international settlement purposes, would have to do. The British had other ideas. They objected to anything that risked a return to the deflationary bias of the interwar gold standard, which had forced deficit countries to contract their economies while surplus countries had no corresponding obligation to expand theirs. If multilateral trade was to be restored, it must be with provisos that avoided self-defeating deflation. Keynes came up with a strikingly original proposal for a new supranational currency for international settlements administered by an International Clearing Union. The "bancor" was, as its name suggested, to be based on gold. However, the risk of deflationary adjustments was limited by three devices: First, exchange rates, although fixed, would have a margin of flexibility; second, countries would have the automatic right to borrow from the ICU to cover balance of payments deficits; and third, financial penalties would be imposed on countries that ran persistent trade surpluses as well as those that accumulated deficits.

Such ideas had little appeal across the Atlantic. The ICU would have $26 billion in overdraft facilities, of which the United States, as the dominant creditor nation, could find itself responsible for up to $23 billion. It was a debtors' charter. At the Bretton Woods conference in 1944, a solution acceptable to Washington was hammered out. The dollar, not the bancor, was to be the fulcrum of the postwar international financial order. Instead of the ICU, there was to be the International Monetary Fund, which would lend money to countries to cover short-term balance of payments problems, but only on conditions that would place the burden of adjustment on their shoulders. Moreover, America's commitment to the fund would be limited to $3.2 billion. To handle the anxieties of Britain and other European countries about the availability of dollars, given that America was likely to continue to run a trade surplus for years after the war, there was a "scarce currency" clause, which allowed countries to limit trade with countries whose currency was difficult to obtain.

A further round of difficult Anglo-American negotiations occurred when the Lend-Lease program, which had kept Britain afloat during the war, came to an abrupt end in September 1945. Keynes's last job, before his premature death in 1946, was to negotiate a loan from the United States to cover the inevitable period of postwar adjustment. The bargaining, once again, was hard. Washington finally agreed to $3.75 billion, but only on the condition that Britain made its currency fully convertible for trade by

1947. As with the Lend-Lease negotiations, the loan caused an uproar in Parliament, where it was debated in tandem with signing up to Bretton Woods. Members described it as a "financial Dunkirk" and "the Boston Tea Party in reverse." By this time Keynes had been reconverted to the idea of multilateral trade. Whatever his misgivings about the terms to which Britain had been forced to agree, it was better for the future of the world than to continue with a system of economic blocs. He helped sway the parliamentary debate by pointing out that the "determination to make trade truly 'international' and to avoid the establishment of economic blocs which limit and restrict commercial intercourse outside them is plainly a condition of the world's best hope . . . I beg those of you who look askance at these plans to ponder deeply and responsibly where it is they think they want to go."[15]

The question is: Did these hard-headed negotiations amount to an American attempt to emasculate, if not destroy, the British Empire? After all, there was a sound Wilsonian logic for doing so. If imperial rivalries were the root cause of the wars that had riven the world since 1914, the best answer was surely to abolish *all* empires, whether or not they had been aggressors. The fact that neither the British nor the French had started the war could not disguise the fact that they were the cause of belligerency in others. The argument of Germany, Italy, and Japan before the war had been clear. The "satisfied powers" were unlikely to start a war, precisely because they already had what they wanted. It was the dissatisfied powers, the have-nots, that felt compelled to use force to obtain their fair share of the world's resources. Even if the British Empire did not start the war, jealousy of its position ranked high on the list of underlying causes.

There were other emotions that drove American attitudes toward Britain. The United States had been born in a struggle for liberation from the empire. It saw itself, rightly or wrongly, as a nonimperial, even an anti-imperial, nation. There was an understandable revulsion at the idea of American lives being expended across the Pacific just to restore the colonial possessions of the

Europeans. Lurking behind such idealistic thoughts was a jealousy of the extraordinary reach of the British Empire (colored in the 1930s and early '40s by a considerable overestimate of its strength) and the natural desire of a rising power to displace a declining one.

American anti-imperial feelings were apparent in Wendell Willkie's *One World*. The tour of allied countries on which it was based managed to bypass Britain while visiting Egypt, India, and China. Willkie's vision of the postwar world had no place for empires. "After centuries of ignorant and dull compliance, hundreds of millions of people in eastern Europe and Asia . . . are no longer willing to be Eastern slaves for Western profits . . . They are resolved, as we must be, that there is no more place for imperialism within their own society than in the society of nations. The big house on the hill surrounded by mud huts has lost its awesome charm."[16]

It is relatively easy to interpret US wartime policy as a deliberate attempt to destroy the British Empire, and given the fact that the empire did dissolve after the war, it is easy to make a causal connection between wartime policy and postwar outcome. However, the situation was more complex than this simple historical narrative suggests. American views of Britain were undoubtedly colored by suspicion, rivalry, and even antipathy, but there was also a strand of Anglophilia within the administration and the country in general, nurtured by a common language and alliance against common enemies. Empires might be bad from an American perspective, but the British was almost certainly the best of the bunch. Moreover, feelings about independence for Asia scarcely extended to Africa, whose peoples were generally considered a long way from being able to govern themselves. In the State Department, it was not the political position of the colonies that upset officials but rather the system of imperial trade preferences. Self-governing dominions like Canada and Australia caused far more Anglo-American friction, even though there was no objection to their political status, than did the whole of colonial Africa.

In any case, Britain was a vital ally in the war and would undoubtedly remain one afterward. It could be pressed only so far. Churchill was adamant that the empire would not be dissolved on his watch and that Britain would regain all it had lost in the Far East. Roosevelt was a pragmatist, and in the end he acceded to Churchill's position. The claims of the Dutch to their old colonies were also accepted but those of France were rejected. In Roosevelt's view, France "had been [in Indochina] for nearly one hundred years and done absolutely nothing with the place to improve the lot of the people."[17] At the Cairo Conference in December 1943, which planned the postwar settlement in Asia, all were agreed that Indochina should become an international mandate. Yet by the end of the war, the determination of the restored French government to reclaim its old colony was so strong that it was allowed to do so. Were the Allies really prepared to oppose one of their members by force?

In practice, the attempts of the American administration to create a postwar order based on free multilateral trade without empires or economic blocs did not advance very far in the immediate aftermath of war. The Bretton Woods system existed on paper, but it could not operate until the European economies had recovered to a point where free international trade and convertible currencies were possible. In 1941, Britain had committed in principle to end imperial preferences, but as Winston Churchill noted in 1945, "I did not agree to Article 7 of the Mutual Aid Agreement without having previously received from the President the definite assurance that we were no more committed to the abolition of Imperial Preference, than the American Government were committed to the abolition of their high protective tariffs."[18] In practice, little was done on either front. As for the European empires, while they had clearly been shaken by the events of the war, they were still intact.

What about another major pillar of a lasting peace: the disarmament and subsequent rehabilitation of the aggressors? There was certainly no doubt about the former. Germany and Japan had to accept unconditional surrender and occupation by Allied armies. There was no immediate chance of their disturbing the peace again. Nor was there any possibility this time of Germans arguing that they had not truly been defeated on the battlefield and had lost the war only because of a stab in the back. But did the completeness of their defeat in 1945 mean that they would be reconciled to the postwar order? The first steps taken by the Allies were not altogether promising. Germans had resented losing Silesia and Danzig in 1919; how were they likely to respond to the loss of entire eastern provinces to Poland in 1945? They had resented reparations in the 1920s; they were scarcely likely to be happy about reparations in the 1940s. At Yalta, a figure of $20 billion was proposed—lower, it is true, than the $32 billion demanded after the First World War but far larger than the $5 billion actually paid. The country most adamant about receiving reparations this time was Russia rather than France. As soon as the war ended, it set about the wholesale dismantling of German industrial equipment and sending it back home. The other Allies did the same on a smaller scale in their zones of occupation. This method of extracting reparations fitted in with the Allied plan to reduce German industrial might so that the country could never again become a military threat to its neighbors. The Quebec Conference in late 1944 openly discussed a plan suggested by Henry Morgenthau for converting Germany from an industrial powerhouse "into a country primarily agricultural and pastoral in its character."

Moreover, France was once again committed to laying its hands on Germany's coal mines and industrial resources. French policy in the aftermath of liberation was dominated by the desire to reassert its position as a great power and by an equally strong determination never again to be subjugated by its neighbor. In 1946, Jean Monnet, later revered as a founding father of the European Union, put forward a plan for the economic revival of the country. The Saarland with its coalfields was to be separated from Germany and handed to France as a protectorate. The Rhineland

and Ruhr were to become an independent country under French or international control. With secure access to Germany's coal, France would increase its steel output to fifteen million tons a year, while Germany's was reduced to six million tons.[19] Once again the war to control Europe's coal and steelmaking capacity was in the balance, and this time France intended to be the victor. In sum, it looked as if the peace was set to be just as Carthaginian as the one that Keynes had attacked so memorably twenty-seven years earlier.

A similar set of prescriptions was being followed in Japan. The country was not only to be demilitarized and democratized, it was also to be defanged economically. As in Germany, overly powerful industrial groups were deemed to have been behind its militarism. The American Initial Post-Surrender Policy for Japan in September 1945 ordered that the great conglomerates (zaibatsu) such as Sumitomo and Mitsubishi be broken up. It also declared that the Japanese would have to rebuild their economy unaided, and that the country could not expect to enjoy a standard of living higher than its (relatively poor) neighbors.[20] In 1946, a plan for reparations was prepared, proposing that Japanese industrial equipment be sent to the countries it had occupied during the war. Japanese industry should not be allowed to recover to the point that would "allow her to gain control, or to secure an advantage, over her neighbours."[21] In the meantime, the Japanese economy, far from recovering, was plagued by shortages and hyperinflation.

None of this looked very promising for the prospects of a lasting peace. Germany and Japan might have been thoroughly defeated and disarmed, but they were far from rehabilitated. Looking at the postwar world, they would have seen all their worst fears justified. The peace settlement was entirely lopsided, involving the loss not only of their wartime conquests but a good portion of their prewar territory as well. Their industry was destroyed, and their conquerors seemed determined that they would never again become great industrial powers. Their access to raw materials was still at the mercy of haves, who were now even more powerful than before. The British Empire was weakened, but America was correspondingly strengthened. Between them the Anglo-Saxons still controlled vast portions of the world's resources, and much of what was left was controlled by the Russians. Moves toward free and unrestricted trade remained largely theoretical, whatever the fine sentiments of the Atlantic Charter. Trade was less free in 1946–1947 than in the 1920s, let alone before 1914.

What changed this pattern, above all, was the Cold War. The precise date at which this conflict started will always remain a point of debate. The Potsdam Conference in July 1945 was already tetchier than either Tehran or Yalta as the postwar settlement of Europe replaced the defeat of Hitler as the main topic of discussion. Churchill's "Iron Curtain" speech in March 1946, given in Truman's presence and with his informal assent, marked for many the end of their illusions about the possibility of continuing Soviet-American cooperation. The US State Department had already changed its mind in February with the arrival of George Kennan's "long telegram," which described Soviet foreign policy as a dangerous amalgam of long-standing Russian territorial ambitions and the Marxist belief in the eventual worldwide victory of socialism. But in terms of policy, the true beginning of the Cold War was in March 1947, when Truman addressed Congress about the urgent need to take over from an exhausted Britain the protection of Greece from the risk of a Communist takeover. Pointing to those European countries that "recently had totalitarian regimes forced upon them against their will," he declared, in what became known as the Truman Doctrine, that the United States should "support free peoples who are resisting attempted subjugation by armed minorities or by outside pressures." The reference to the Soviet Union was oblique but clear. Some pretense of cooperation between the onetime allies continued for a while, but this came to a definitive end with the Soviet blockade of West Berlin in June 1948.

The changes brought about by the Cold War were enormous. First of all, the idea that the postwar era could be policed by the continuing cooperation of the wartime allies fell by the wayside. The Security Council of the newly established United Nations turned out to be constitutionally incapable of effective decision making. The granting of veto power to its permanent members now meant that it was permanently gridlocked. The one time the UN took action against aggression in accordance with its avowed purpose was in response to the North Korean invasion of the South in 1950. Russia boycotted the meeting of the Security Council in the hopes of challenging its legitimacy. It never made the same mistake again. As for the United States, any idea that it could take a backseat in the postwar era evaporated. It was now going to have to maintain, and even reinforce, its leadership role in the non-communist world. For this reason, liberal internationalists such as Averell Harriman looked back on the start of the Cold War as a moment not of fear but of celebration:

> It has now been seven years since the United States embarked upon a positive and active course of world leadership in time of peace with the object of preserving freedom and preventing another world war. The date that took place was March 12, 1947, when President Truman asked Congress . . . for economic and military and advisory aid to Greece and Turkey and proclaimed what became known as the Truman Doctrine . . . Those who had long and anxiously awaited such an historical turning will never forget the elation of those days in the spring of 1947.[22]

Equally important were the changes to the way Germany was treated. It became essential to rehabilitate it both politically and economically so that it could help the fight against communism. Reparations were now out of the question. Instead Germany received infusions of American money through the Marshall Plan. The postwar balance of accounts for West Germany is estimated to be $1 billion paid in reparations versus $4 billion received in aid. By contrast, the smaller and poorer eastern sector under Soviet occupation is reckoned to have paid around $7 billion in reparations to Russia.[23]

Nor was the punitive competition for coal and iron ore reserves pursued by France acceptable. The Saarland was once again ceded to France for a time, but there was no more question of an independent Rhineland or of handing the resources of the Ruhr to France. If Germany was to be rehabilitated as an industrial power, it would need them. But at the same time, it was essential to find some way to resolve once and for all the perennial conflict over who was to control Europe's coal and steelmaking capacity. If the threat from the East was to be faced, it was no longer acceptable for the only possible outcomes to be an overmighty Germany confronting an intimidated France, or a resurgent France crippling Germany's ability to support itself. The only viable solution was to share these crucial resources. The problem was made more urgent by the rise in support for Communist parties in Western Europe over the harsh winter of 1946–1947. The Marshall Plan introduced in the summer of 1947 specifically required that European countries cooperate to come up with a plan for use of American aid in a manner that would restore the economy of the whole continent. This implied the equitable allocation of coal and iron ore. When the western zones of occupied Germany were granted self-government in 1949 as a federal republic, it was made a condition of autonomy that the resources of the Ruhr were to be shared with the country's neighbors under the supervision of an international authority. By this time France had been won around to the view that only European integration could resolve the chronic conflicts that had beset the continent. Jean Monnet, once the author of a plan that would have hobbled the German economy in the interests of France, now became, with Robert Schuman, the leading light behind the European Coal and Steel Community in 1951. It was the resolution of the eighty-year struggle for possession of coal and iron ore that led the way to the Treaty of Rome and the European Union. The Schuman Declaration of May 1950, which led to the ECSC, made clear the relationship between the struggle for coal and steel and the struggle for peace:

> The pooling of coal and steel production should immediately provide for the setting up of common foundations for economic development as a first step in the federation of Europe, and will change the destinies of those regions which have long been devoted to the manufacture of munitions of war, of which they have been the most constant victims.
>
> The solidarity in production thus established will make it plain that any war between France and Germany becomes not merely unthinkable, but materially impossible.[24]

The Cold War also put paid to any concerns about an American military withdrawal from Europe. NATO was founded in 1949. Its primary, if unstated, objective was to protect against the risk posed by the Russian armies sitting behind the iron curtain. Indirectly, however, it also meant that, unlike after Versailles, America and Britain were now bound as guarantors of French security. Lord Ismay, NATO's first secretary-general, described its purpose as "to keep the Russians out, the Americans in, and the Germans down." This explains why it was initially so popular in France. Ultimately, however, the incorporation of Germany into NATO (in 1955) was essential for its success. The United States and Britain became convinced that without German manpower, the Western alliance could not hope to counter Russia. The Cold War therefore led to Germany's military as well as its political and economic rehabilitation.

Events in the Far East followed a similar pattern. By 1947, it was becoming apparent that the continuing economic chaos in Japan was merely boosting the local Communist Party. The country's economic revival was essential. In 1948, the Johnson Committee recommended ending reparations and taking measures to increase Japanese manufactured exports. Attempts to break up the zaibatsu were quietly ignored. The rehabilitation of the country became even more urgent in 1949 with the loss of China to the Communists. The following year, the Cold War turned hot with the outbreak of war in Korea. Japan suddenly became central to the global struggle. Thanks to the occupation, it provided a ready-made base for American troops to counter the invasion. In the longer term, Japan was also a vital bastion of the democratic-capitalist world in what suddenly looked like a hostile Asian environment. From the Japanese point of view, the Korean War was an economic turning point. American orders for trucks and ships poured in, establishing the bases of Japan's postwar miracle. In 1951, the Treaty of San Francisco formally recognized the newly independent, postimperial Japan, which now became an ally of its wartime enemy.

The Korean War put an end to America's belief that it would need only modest military forces after the war. Until 1949, it had assumed that it could rely on its monopoly of nuclear weapons to deter aggressors. The Russian test of an atomic bomb in August, years earlier than anticipated, shattered that assumption. In any case, the Korean War showed that the possession of nuclear weapons meant little if their use was taboo, and that large conventional forces were also needed. By the late 1940s, demobilization had reduced the size of the American armed forces from 12 million to 1.5 million men. In the aftermath of Korea, the number doubled. At the end of the Second World War, the US Navy had grown to an enormous size, with around 1,200 warships and an equal number of landing craft. Three years later, demobilization had reduced the number of ships to 267. The rationale was that there was no naval threat from any other country and that nuclear weapons were rendering navies obsolete. In 1946, an underwater nuclear test at Bikini Bay sank or severely damaged seventy-three surplus warships anchored there. However, Korea showed once again the importance of navies for sea landings, air strikes, blockade, and supply. The navy was rebuilt until it reached six hundred ships.

Another result of the Cold War was that countries that might otherwise have opposed American leadership were now prepared to accept it. In Japan, Shigeru Yoshida, prime minister for most of the first postwar decade, crafted a policy that turned Japanese dependency on American military protection into an asset. The country's new constitution renounced the use of military force. It could therefore focus on economic development while the US Navy protected its vital sea trade. Yoshida's view was that "Japan should and could live as a maritime nation and that cooperation with [the United States] would be the best way to acquire access to the world market and its resources and to safeguard her sea routes."[25] Unrestricted access to Western markets that had been closed to it before the war was a more than adequate compensation for being prohibited from trading with China. By the late 1950s, the Japanese shipbuilding industry, revitalized by the Korean War, had grown to the point that it was putting American and British shipbuilders out of business. In Germany, the muted acceptance of the Allied occupation was transformed by the events of 1948. The introduction of the Deutsche mark into the Western occupation zones in June was strongly opposed by the Russians, who blockaded West Berlin in response. This attempt to starve Berlin into submission ended any residual appeal of Soviet communism in West Germany, and the Allied airlift to supply the city turned the Americans and British into heroes.

Probably the country most reluctant to accept American supremacy was not one of its defeated opponents, but its ally France. From the moment that France was liberated in 1944, its government had one objective above all others: to restore the country's rightful place as a Great Power. This meant ensuring not only that its colonies in the Far East were reclaimed and that it had its own zone of occupation in Germany, but also that it maintained an independent foreign policy that did not simply follow the lead of America. France attempted to adhere to a position midway between the United States and the Soviet Union, and its diplomats did not entirely despair of reviving the pre-1914 three-way alliance among France, Russia, and Great Britain as an offset to dependence on America. The Cold War scuppered such plans, based on a world order that no longer existed.[26] French intellectuals might continue to proclaim their admiration for the communist dream and their disdain for all things American, but their impact on national policy was marginal.

By uniting the Western world against a common enemy under American leadership, the Cold War was instrumental in achieving what the Atlantic Charter on its own, for all its good intentions, could not: an end to the cycle of world wars for resources. America's allies, old and new, accepted the necessary fact of American supremacy on the understanding that the new hegemon would not abuse its military and economic power to exclude them from the global marketplace. This was an unanticipated result of the postwar settlement, and to no one did it come as more of a surprise than Stalin. To his dying day he stuck to the Leninist orthodoxy that capitalism meant imperialism, and imperialism meant war. After all, this theory had looked more than plausible for the first part of the century. In his speech for the 18th Party Congress in 1939, Stalin argued that the world situation conformed exactly to Lenin's thinking:

> The [1929–1933] crisis had already . . . sharpened the struggle for markets and sources of raw materials. The seizure of Manchuria and North China by Japan, the seizure of Abyssinia by Italy—all this reflected the acuteness of the struggle among the powers. The new [1938] economic crisis was bound to lead, and is actually leading, to a further sharpening of the imperialist struggle. It is no longer a question of competition in the markets, of a commercial war, of dumping. These methods of struggle have long been recognized as inadequate.

It is now a question of a new redivision of the world, of spheres of interest and colonies, by military action.[27]

After the war, Stalin remained confident that attempts to create lasting peace must founder on the basic contradictions of capitalism. His economic adviser, Eugen Varga, however, suggested that the old rules might no longer apply now that the capitalists were confronted by a powerful communist bloc. They might be scared into cooperating. In 1948, Varga was attacked at a meeting of Soviet economists for "deviating from the Lenin-Stalin theory of imperialism," and the following year he publicly recanted his heretical views. But in private he continued to advance them— correctly arguing that: (1) the capitalist countries had learned from the war, (2) the rising power of communism was forcing them to ally (or, as he put it, "the mutual interest of the bourgeoisie in this particular historical moment is greater than its mutual contradictions"), and (3) the United States was so much more powerful than any other capitalist country that there was unlikely to be a war between them.[28]

Stalin was having none of this. In 1952, he published *Economic Problems of Socialism in the U.S.S.R.* to put a definitive end to the debate. Its chapter "Inevitability of Wars Between Capitalist Countries" is worth quoting at length.

Some comrades hold that, owing to the development of new international conditions since the Second World War, wars between capitalist countries have ceased to be inevitable. They consider that the contradictions between the socialist camp and the capitalist camp are more acute than the contradictions among the capitalist countries; that the USA had brought the other capitalist countries sufficiently under its sway to prevent them going to war among themselves and weakening one another; that the foremost capitalist minds have been sufficiently taught by the two capitalist world wars . . . not to involve the capitalist countries in war with one another again . . . Outwardly, everything would seem to be "going well": the USA has put Western Europe, Japan and other capitalist countries on rations; Germany (Western), Britain, France, Italy and Japan have fallen into the clutches of the USA and are meekly obeying its commands.

But this subservience would not last.

Britain and France . . . are imperialist countries. Undoubtedly, cheap raw materials and secure markets are of paramount importance to them. Can it be assumed that they will endlessly tolerate the present situation, in which . . . American capital is seizing raw materials and markets in the British and French colonies and thereby plotting disaster for the high profits of the British and French capitalists? . . .

Germany (Western) and Japan . . . are now languishing in misery under the jackboot of American imperialism . . . Yet only yesterday these countries were great imperialist powers . . . To think that these countries will not try to get on their feet again, will not try to smash the US "regime" and force their way to independent development, is to believe in miracles . . .

After the First World War it was similarly believed that Germany had been definitely put out of action . . . In spite of this, Germany rose to her feet again as a great power within the space of fifteen or twenty years after her defeat, having broken out of bondage . . . The United States and Britain assisted Germany's economic recovery . . . with a view of setting a recovered Germany against the Soviet Union . . . But Germany directed her forces in the first place against the Anglo-French-American bloc . . . Consequently, the struggle of the capitalist countries for markets and their desire to crush their competitors proved in practice to be stronger than the contradictions between the capitalist camp and the socialist camp . . .

It is said that Lenin's thesis that imperialism inevitably generates war must now be regarded as obsolete, since powerful forces have come forward in defense of peace and against another world war. That is not true . . . It will not be enough because, for all the successes of the peace movement, imperialism remains in force—and consequently, the inevitability of wars will also continue in force.[29]

The fact that Varga's analysis, rather than Stalin's, was the correct one did nothing to lessen the danger in which he had placed himself. He was lucky that the great dictator died the following year. Before his death, he was planning another purge in which Varga would almost certainly have been a victim.

The outbreak of peace among Western nations was obviously good in itself, but it would have meant little if the struggle for resources that had driven their antagonisms was simply transferred to the new conflict between East and West. Fortunately that was not the case. The conflict between communism and capitalism could remain "cold" in part because the economic forces that had driven the industrialized countries to war did not apply.

Marx had argued that the socialist revolution would occur in the most advanced capitalist nations. Had that been the case, the first communist state would most likely have been a country like Britain, which was fully integrated into the world economy and heavily dependent on overseas trade. This historical nonevent would have shown whether communism and international trade were really compatible. Instead, the revolution broke out in Russia, a country that was not only economically backward but also largely self-sufficient and had vast mineral resources.

Before the First World War, Russia's trade consisted of grain and oil exports in exchange for manufactured products. As the world's largest exporter of grain, the country was integrated into the global economy, but even so its total foreign trade amounted to under 15 percent of GDP compared to around 40 percent for Germany and France, and 50 percent for Britain. The level of trade in the late tsarist period represented a high-water mark that was not equaled until the late 1970s. Under communism, foreign trade fell to a point where in the late 1930s it represented no more than 0.2 percent of GDP. If any country in the world was an autarky in the 1930s, it was Stalin's Russia. The reasons for this fall in commerce with the outside world lie partly in the general collapse of world trade. But there were other factors, specifically connected to communism, that contributed to the isolation of Russia from the global economy.

The 1917 revolution and ensuing civil war reduced Russian foreign trade almost to zero as internal chaos was exacerbated by foreign embargoes. In 1922, Lenin's New Economic Policy attempted to revitalize the moribund economy by accepting many aspects of the free market, among them international commerce. By the late 1920s, foreign trade had recovered to around two-thirds of the prewar level. However, such dalliance with the ways of capitalism was never supposed to be more than a temporary expedient, and in 1927, Stalin decided to force the pace of change by establishing complete state control of the economy. Agriculture was collectivized, and industrialization was pushed forward by rigorous five-year plans that forced down consumption so as to support a large rise in investment. Imports of machinery were initially required for this great leap forward, but the ultimate ambition was to render Soviet Russia independent from the West.

This aim was accelerated by the evaporation of Russian export earnings. This was partly the result of the worldwide depression that lowered the price of grain, Russia's major source of foreign exchange. But domestic and international politics were equally to blame. The disruption of agriculture caused by collectivization reduced the amount of grain available for export to less than two million tons, compared to up to nine million before 1914. The Nazi takeover of Germany meant that Russia's largest trading partner was now ruled by a party dedicated to achieving economic self-sufficiency, and in any case antagonistic to trading with Bolsheviks. After 1934, Soviet policy decreed that autarky was the immediate goal. The Second Five-Year Plan stated that Russia "must be converted into a country that is independent in a technical and economic sense."[30] The reduction in trade was heralded as a sign of success: "The USSR has fulfilled the grandiose plans of the Second Five-Year Plan, with the aid of an insignificant volume of imports, and in the future we can fulfill our plans, without the need for imports. Nearly everything that is at all needed for a powerful country—everything—is being produced in the USSR."[31] At the same time, Germany's attempts at autarky were ridiculed. Capitalism, it was argued, was incapable of achieving true self-sufficiency because of its reliance on the free market. This was a shortsighted assessment of the situation. Russia, with its vast resources, was naturally self-sufficient in a way that Germany could never be. Hitler's evaluation of Germany's position was far more realistic.

After the war, Stalin was confronted by a new geopolitical landscape. Lend-Lease had reintroduced Western goods into Russia, and the United States was intent on increasing world trade as a means of preserving the peace. Had Stalin wished to turn Russia back toward foreign trade, the way to do so was clear. On the other hand, the expansion of Russian power into Eastern Europe meant that the idea of socialism in one country was no longer necessary. Russia could create its own economic bloc—and thereby avoid the pitfalls of international commerce. If Russia's new satellites were allowed to trade freely with the countries of the West, Stalin feared that they would gravitate toward them politically as well.

The crux came with the Marshall Plan in 1947. By this stage relations between the two superpowers were deteriorating fast, but American aid was nonetheless offered to all European countries, including Russia. The sting in the tail was that aid was to be given on the basis of plans agreed among the recipients to rebuild the European economy as a whole. This implied the restoration of intra-European trade. The offer was, to some extent, a trap. If Stalin allowed the countries of Eastern Europe to take up the offer, their economies would probably be orientated toward the West. If he forbade them to do so, the blame for the division of Europe, by now almost inevitable in American eyes, would fall on Russia. The summoning of the still-multiparty Czechoslovakian government to Moscow to prohibit it from taking part in the plan was the definitive moment when the illusion of Eastern European independence was shattered. It was no surprise when a coup forced the noncommunists out of the government a few months later. The Stalinist ideal of autarky was now extended to include the whole Soviet bloc. As an official textbook of 1954 put it, "The world democratic [i.e., communist] market has at its disposal sufficient resources to provide every country with everything necessary for its economic development."[32] The economic isolation of the communist world during the Cold War was only increased by the Western embargo on exports of arms and strategic materials.

After Stalin's death, communist dogma about trade was to some extent rethought. Commerce with the outside world was no longer entirely discouraged; even so, it recovered only modestly. Until 1970, trade with the noncommunist world was barely over 1 percent of GDP. The problem was that even when the Soviet Union was not pursuing a policy of strict autarky, international trade never fitted comfortably within the communist system. Trade with the West was limited by a desire to avoid dependence on the capitalist world. Whereas in the Western countries, trade was the spontaneous interaction of parties seeking economic benefits, in the Soviet bloc trade was a state monopoly governed largely by political considerations, a point made succinctly by Khrushchev in 1957: "We value trade least for economic reasons and most for political purposes."[33] This was particularly true of Soviet trade with the third world, which was governed almost exclusively by a desire for influence. In any case, a true evaluation of economic costs and benefits was almost impossible when prices in the Soviet Union were entirely different from those set by the market. Even inside the communist world, trade was muted. Attempts to rationalize economic activity within the So-viet bloc ran up against the desire of its members to be self-sufficient. Where trade did exist, it was complicated by artificial prices that varied between countries, so that "following estab-lished prices and exchange rates produced losses, not gains." The process was later characterized as little more than an "exchange of inefficiencies."[34]

The result was that for the first quarter century after the Sec-ond World War, the Soviet Union remained largely isolated from the global economy. Even after Stalin's death, when it no longer shunned all trade, the inherent incompatibility of communism with free trade combined with the natural self-sufficiency pro-vided by the empire's vast resources kept commercial contact with the noncommunist world to a minimum. This meant the Soviet Union had little reason to take part in the kind of struggle for raw materials and markets that had propelled the First and Second World Wars.

The Cold War therefore resolved itself into a standoff between two mutually incompatible blocs: a communist world under Rus-sian domination that remained a virtual autarky, and a capitalist world under American leadership that depended on international trade. Just as the communist bloc's autarky was to some extent the result of Russia's natural self-sufficiency, the dependence of Western countries on trade was the natural result of their reliance on imports of basic materials. In the aftermath of the war, the United States was also joining the ranks of the have-not nations. Its appetite for raw materials was outstripping its ability to pro-duce even those resources in which it was abundant, such as oil. This gave the establishment of Hull's vision of a world united by the bonds of unfettered international trade greater urgency.

The importance of trade in the Western economy increased continuously during the decades of the Cold War. After a halting start, progress in reducing barriers was slow but persistent. The initial American plan, conceived at Bretton Woods, for an Inter-national Trade Organization to oversee the reduction in tariffs was rejected by the US Congress. But the General Agreement on Tariffs and Trade was established in 1947 (bypassing congressional ratification) with an initial round of tariff reductions agreed by the member states. Successive negotiations from 1949 onward reduced rates further. By the end of the 1960s, the American dutiable rate (inherited from the infamous Smoot-Hawley Tariff) had fallen from 60 percent to 10 percent. Ten years later it was 5.7 percent. Rates in other countries were reduced in tandem. One result was that the British imperial preferences, the cause of so much Anglo-American tension in the 1930s and '40s, became increasingly meaningless. Another, not surprisingly, was a rapid growth in international trade. By 1980, overseas trade represented around 40 percent of GDP in Britain, France, and Germany— levels once again approximating those prevailing before 1914. In the United States it was around 18 percent of GDP— approximately double the level of the 1900s and four times that of the late 1930s. The original American postwar ideal of a world free of trade blocs was diluted by the creation of the European Economic Community in 1957. The United States accepted and even encouraged the EEC as a further cement for peace in Europe. In any case, the EEC was not allowed to threaten a return to the 1930s because its tariffs with the outside world were continually lowered as part of the GATT negotiations.

The growth of trade was supported by a return to stable international monetary arrangements. Here, once again, progress was gradual. The Bretton Woods system, agreed to in principle in 1944, did not really come into effect until 1958. In the late 1940s, the United States continued to run a massive trade surplus with the war-ravaged countries of Europe, which had neither gold nor dollars with which to pay. There could be no hope of convertible currencies until this fundamental imbalance was resolved. Free-trade flows were first reestablished outside the dollar area: within the sterling bloc and then within Europe through the creation of a multilateral clearing union for intra-European trade in 1950. Before convertibility with the mighty dollar could be ventured, realistic exchange rates had to be set. The attempt to restore sterling convertibility at the official rate in 1947 proved disastrous. The run on the pound as soon as controls were lifted meant that they had to be reinstated within weeks. Two years later, first sterling and then a further twenty-three currencies were devalued against the dollar by up to 30 percent. The "scarce currency" clause of Bretton Woods turned out to be redundant. The dollar shortage was resolved, first by the Marshall Plan and other forms of American aid and then by the move of the United States from current-account surplus to deficit in the wake of the Korean War. By 1958, the distribution of international reserves had reached a point where the Bretton Woods ideal of convertible currencies for trade could come into effect in Europe. Japan followed suit in 1964.

In a curious way, the Cold War reconciled two apparently incompatible visions of peace. Within the Western world, the belief of liberal free traders held sway, justifying their hopes that economic interdependence was the route to peace. On a global scale, however, it could be said that the advocates of economic independence had also been proved right. The bipolar system was inherently stable because the two blocs had no economic reasons to go to war such as those that had propelled the two world wars. Moreover, even if they had wanted to fight, their possession of nuclear weapons that assured their mutual destruction acted as a powerful restraint. Yet the two rivals were not content merely to scowl at each other across the iron curtain while they waited for the internal contradictions that they perceived in each other's systems to hand them a bloodless victory. There remained an unresolved question about the postwar order that was to provide fertile ground for the rival blocs to spar without actually going to war with each other.

The future of the European empires was uncertain in 1945. Their colonies in the Far East had been reclaimed. But their wartime loss to the Japanese had been a profound blow to the prestige of the old imperial powers. Japan's use of the language of liberation to justify its conquests, however cynical it may have been, struck a chord with nascent liberation movements, which, even if they disliked the Japanese, could not help responding favorably to an Asian country beating the Europeans at their own game. The Americans had also employed a considerable amount of anticolonial rhetoric during the war, and had backed their words with deeds by promising full independence to the Philippines as soon as the war ended. The Atlantic Charter's third clause, which asserted "the right of all peoples to choose the form of government under which they will live," was taken by independence movements to imply the end of empire, even if the British government hastened to deny that the clause applied to its colonies. With so much encouragement for the idea of decolonization, it was hard to foresee a long and stable future for the colonial empires in the Far East. Indonesia and Vietnam declared unilateral independence as soon as the Japanese left, and the Dutch and French were able to retake them only by force. In India, the movement for independence, already difficult to contain peacefully before the war, had become so powerful that Britain had to offer the carrot of postwar autonomy in a barely successful attempt to keep the country under control during the critical years of the war.

If decolonization had consisted of devolving power to local governments that were based on Western precepts and that retained close political and economic ties to the mother country, the process would have caused few headaches in Western capitals. This is what occurred in colonies of white settlement such as Canada and Australia, for instance. But where empire meant the rule by a tiny privileged elite of Europeans over the indigenous populations of previously autonomous societies, such an outcome was not certain. Many of the potential leaders of such ex-colonies might well translate their resentment of imperial rule into a rejection of the economic system that accompanied it and look elsewhere for inspiration.

They could, in theory, have looked east to Japan, whose success in avoiding the humiliations experienced by other Asian countries in the nineteenth century made it an obvious model for neighbors seeking to respond to the challenge of the West. But the Japanese example was tarred by the fact that Japan had absorbed not only Western capitalism but also Western imperialism. By the end of the Second World War, the brutal record of Japanese occupation had inoculated the minds of nationalists throughout East Asia against copying the Japanese path to modernity.

A more attractive alternative lay to the west. After the Russian Revolution of 1917, communism acted as a siren song for colonial subjects seeking independence. Socialism had a natural appeal for those who felt themselves to be poor and exploited, and Lenin had skillfully positioned communism as the ideological antithesis of colonialism when he equated capitalism with imperialism. One of the advantages of this equation was that America could be described as imperialist just as easily as Britain or France. After the war, Communist parties were set up in almost every country in East Asia by radical young nationalists, a number of whom were to become household names after 1945. Ho Chi Minh learned about communism in postwar Paris, where he was present at the founding of the French Communist Party in 1921, before returning to Indochina and setting up the Thanh Nien (Vietnamese Revolutionary Youth Movement) in 1925. Zhou Enlai also discovered communism in Paris after the war, and in 1921 he and Mao Zedong participated at the first meeting of the Chinese Communist Party.

It soon became clear that the decolonization of East Asia might not run smoothly. China had been fought over since the 1920s by the Nationalists and the Communists, both of which espoused some combination of socialism, nationalism, and anti-imperialism. The Nationalists were more acceptable in Western eyes largely because they were not pro-Soviet. The two parties put their differences behind them while dealing with the Japanese occupation, but as soon as Japan was defeated they returned to their struggle. Communism was also a threat in Korea, where Russia had managed to take over half the country in the final days of the war. In Vietnam, the Communists under Ho Chi Minh declared independence immediately after the Japanese surrender, before any Western forces could arrive. It was soon apparent that the French were not going to be able to reassert their position in the country without a long, hard struggle. Communist parties had gained popular support in a number of countries as a result of their opposition to Japanese occupation. In the Philippines, the postindependence government had to deal with the insurgency of the Huks, an anti-Japanese guerrilla force that subsequently transformed itself into the armed wing of the Communist Party. In Malaya, the MPAJA (the Malayan People's Anti-Japanese Army) became the MNLA (Malayan National Liberation Army), which started a fully fledged insurgency in 1948 in opposition to British plans for a guided progress toward independence.

The West's fear of the impact of communism on decolonization was that the process might lead not simply to the political independence of former colonies but to their complete separation from the global economy. Like the countries of Eastern Europe, they might be absorbed into the black hole of Soviet autarky. The consequences for the West would be dire, as Vice President Richard Nixon warned in 1958: "If it succeeds in extending Communist rule throughout Africa and Asia, the Kremlin will have assured its victory in the battle for the world . . . The Western World will be forced to surrender without the firing of a shot . . . We ourselves may be starved for essential raw materials and crushed without a single warlike act."[35]

Nowhere was this a more vital concern than in Southeast Asia. The Second World War in the Pacific had been fought for control of the area's resources. It was not just that Britain and America still wanted access to Malayan rubber and Indonesian tin. If Japan was to be restored economically, it would need them too. The problem became even more urgent after the fall of China to the Communists. Access to Chinese resources, especially in Manchuria, had been vital for the Japanese economy. Now they were no longer available. In the immediate aftermath of the war, when Allied policy focused on the partial deindustrialization of Japan, this did not seem so crucial an issue. But the start of the Cold War in Europe changed the American perspective. In 1947, George Kennan argued for the urgent rehabilitation of the Japanese economy, which was suffering from "the loss of its markets and raw material resources in Soviet-dominated portions of the mainland, with highly unstable conditions prevailing in China, in Indonesia, in Indochina, and in India."[36] The stabilization of Southeast Asia took on a new importance. In 1949, the State Department proposed a "Marshall Plan" for the area, which would "create democratic governments, restore viable economies, and check Soviet expansion." In one master stroke, the United States could both "advance the dignity of man" and keep "vital raw materials" out of Communist control.[37]

When the loss of China in 1949 was rapidly followed by the near loss of South Korea in 1950, it began to look as if the countries of East Asia might fall like a line of dominoes. A new theory was born that called for drawing a line in the sand against any further Communist advances in the region. Vietnam had never been important for its raw materials, but it was seen as the gateway to Southeast Asia. When Japan had started advancing down the coast of Indochina in 1940–1941, it had raised alarm bells in Washington and London not because of the loss of Indochina but because of the threat to Malaya and the Dutch East Indies. The same logic applied after 1950. Richard Nixon expressed American fears in stark terms:

> Why is the United States spending hundreds of millions of dollars supporting the forces of the French Union in the fight against communism? If Indochina falls, Thailand is put in an almost impossible position. The same is true of Malaya with its rubber and tin. The same is true of Indonesia. If this whole part of south-east Asia goes under Communist domination or Communist influence, Japan, who trades and must trade

with this area in order to exist, must inevitably be oriented towards the Communist regime.[38]

Despite American financial assistance, French attempts to regain control of Vietnam faltered in the face of determined opposition by the Viet Minh. In 1954, France gave up the unequal struggle and accepted the loss of the northern part of the country so that it could establish a friendly regime in the south and withdraw. For the United States, the 1954 border between the two Vietnams along the 17th parallel, although originally intended to be no more than a provisional division of the country, became the line beyond which communism must not be allowed to advance for fear of toppling the Southeast Asian dominoes.

During the Second World War, the United States had opposed France's attempt to reclaim Indochina and had advocated a policy of decolonization. American unofficial advisers had initially helped Ho Chi Minh's bid for independence in 1945. The rising Communist threat in the Far East soon made the United States reconsider its position. Decolonization should be supported only as long as it led to the establishment of noncommunist regimes. The Dutch were encouraged to leave Indonesia in the late 1940s because Sukarno was not seen as a threat to Western interests and because continued Dutch attempts to put down the pro-independence movement risked radicalizing the population. The British and French were encouraged to stay in Malaya and Indochina to contain the threat of Communist takeovers. As the stability of South Vietnam after 1954 was threatened by the Viet Cong, the United States found itself in the uncomfortable position of taking over the French role in Indochina, which it had at one time deplored. This only made it easier for Soviet leaders to denounce America as living proof of Lenin's equation of capitalism and imperialism.

Many have criticized the domino theory in the light of history, but at the time few wanted to take the risk. In any case, an argument can be made that the Vietnam War, even if unsuccessful militarily, and devastatingly destructive in Indochina, provided a firebreak that allowed the rest of Southeast Asia to be secured by pro-Western leaders. The Communist insurgency in Malaya was finally tamed in 1960. But Indonesia, which had looked reasonably stable at the time of independence in 1949, started to become a source of nervousness in Western capitals. Sukarno abandoned the original constitution in 1959 in favor of "Guided Democracy" in alliance with the Indonesian Communist Party. He turned the country toward alliance with China and in 1963 denounced the newly independent Malaysia as a neocolonial plot to encircle Indonesia, leading to intermittent hostilities between the two countries over several years. Finally Sukarno was deposed in 1967 by General Suharto, a pro-Western, pro-business ruler who ran Indonesia efficiently but with scant regard for human rights and with increasing corruption, until 1998. Together with the consolidation of the equally pro-Western (and equally corrupt) Marcos regime in the Philippines, Southeast Asia no longer appeared at risk, and it scarcely mattered from a geopolitical standpoint when South Vietnam eventually fell to the North in 1975. This certainly was the view of Lee Kuan Yew, the prime minister of Singapore, who argued in his memoirs that "Although American intervention failed in Vietnam, it bought time for the rest of Southeast Asia . . . America's action enabled noncommunist Southeast Asia to put their own houses in order."[39] The price to America of the Vietnam War was not just blood and money but also the moral cost of propping up regimes that bore little resemblance to American ideals of liberal democracy and whose main virtue was their anticommunism. But then, how different was this compromise to the awkward Anglo-American alliance with Stalin's Russia during the Second World War (which had prompted Winston Churchill to remark that if Hitler invaded hell he would be happy to speak favorably of the devil)?

The Soviet raw materials threat during the Cold War turned out to be less serious than originally feared. Apart from Korea and Vietnam, the only country whose resources were withdrawn from the Western economy as a result of a Communist takeover was Cuba. Since Cuba was a major supplier of nickel, a mineral for which America was entirely dependent on imports, this was precisely the kind of geopolitical blow about which Nixon had warned in 1958. Yet the loss of Cuban nickel imports did little to damage the American economy (nor did the loss of Cuban sugar imports do much to reduce the growth of American waistlines). Moreover, Cuba did not become the first of a series of Latin American dominoes to topple, in spite of the best efforts of Fidel Castro and Che Guevara.

The lack of Communist success in the third world can be attributed to a number of factors. One element was that Soviet economic self-sufficiency meant that the area was of less importance to Moscow than to Washington. The United States was simply willing to play harder to keep the area inside the global economy than the Soviet Union was to keep it out. Equally important was the fact that, whatever the attractions of anticapitalist ideologies, the central instinctive concern of the rulers of the ex-colonies was to keep their countries independent. The idea of falling under Soviet domination, having just escaped British or French domination, held little appeal even to left-leaning governments. In response to the growing superpower competition for third-world allegiance, the leaders of Yugoslavia, Egypt, Ghana, India, and Indonesia formed the Non-Aligned Movement in 1961. The overall political leaning of the member countries was undoubtedly toward the left, but few, if any, wanted to put themselves in the position of Cuba, whose revolution merely resulted in the transformation of the country from an American dependency into a Soviet one.

The Cuban switch of allegiance revealed another problem confronting the Kremlin. Like most third-world countries, Cuba depended on exports of raw materials. But a largely self-sufficient Russia was a poorer economic partner for such countries than the industrialized West. Fortunately, Russia was able to make use of Cuba's sugar, but it had no use for nickel, of which Cuba had the world's second-largest reserves, because Russia was itself the possessor of the world's largest reserves. The rarity of the prize of a communist country not contiguous with the Soviet Union (and therefore not policeable by Soviet tanks) meant that Russia was willing to trade with Cuba on terms that bore no relation to economic reality and meant, in effect, the extraction of a large reverse tribute by its Latin American satellite. Russia bought Cuban sugar (which it needed) and nickel (which it did not) at prices above the prevailing world market, and sold Cuba oil at below-market prices. This was an attractive arrangement for Castro, who was able to subsidize the Cuban experiment with socialism and indulge in an adventurous foreign policy beyond the means of a modest island state. But it was scarcely a plausible model for expanding the Soviet empire throughout the third world, since such generosity on a large scale would quickly bankrupt the Soviet state. In effect, Russia was learning the same lessons as Britain and France: Empires were easily affordable in the nineteenth century when, in the words of Hilaire Belloc, "Whatever happens, we have got / The Maxim gun, and they have not." In the late twentieth century this was no longer the case, and empires could be maintained only at so great an expense, whether in crushing opposition or buying support, that they were in most cases no longer worth the candle.

Yet even if they were reluctant to accept the bearlike embrace of the Soviet Union, the leaders of the third world were deeply affected by theories emanating from the socialist world that were inimical to the old economic order. According to this view, the Western powers had created their empires in order only to exploit the raw materials they needed for their prosperity. If the ex-colonies were to prosper, they should reject the role of raw-materials producers and foster their own industrialization. The industrialized countries were wealthier than their ex-colonies only because they had understood early on that manufacturing was a more successful route to power and riches than agriculture. Their products would always sell at a premium. History showed that commodity prices not only were unstable but also that they tended to decline relative to the prices of manufactured goods. This meant that raw-materials producers were not only more susceptible to economic swings than industrialized countries but also that the terms of trade were inexorably moving against them in the long term, forcing them to produce ever more commodities in exchange for the same quantity of manufactured imports. From a Marxist perspective, this unequal exchange was explained by the corrupt deal the Western capitalists had made with their domestic proletariats—buying off their revolutionary fervor with higher wages and welfare spending, while continuing to make profits on the ever-cheaper resources from the third world. The continuation of such lopsided north-south trading relationships after independence was merely a form of neocolonialism.

The events of the interwar years seemed to confirm this diagnosis. The Great Depression had devastated the economies of developing countries as the prices of their raw-materials exports collapsed. It was easy to argue that they would have done better to have followed the example of the Soviet Union under Stalin, which had withdrawn from contact with the West and driven forward its industrialization through its own endeavors. As early as 1929, a Russian trade delegate had described Stalin's economic policy as "an endeavor to advance as far as possible from the position of a colony. I would define the object of Soviet trade as 'decolonization.'"[40] For Marxists, the bonus of ex-colonies following the Soviet economic paradigm was that if breakup of the European empires led to the withdrawal by developing countries from international trade, the capitalist West could be starved just as effectively as if they had joined the Soviet bloc. In 1958, the Rockefeller Brothers Fund worried that "if Asia, Middle Eastern and African nationalism, exploited by the Soviet bloc, becomes a destructive force, European supplies of oil and other essential raw materials may be jeopardized."[41] A more recent work on third-world economic nationalism observed:

If Nkrumah of Ghana was correct when he said in 1965 that neo-colonialism is the last stage of imperialism, and if imperialism is the highest stage of capitalism (Lenin), then there can be little doubt in the minds of some that . . . a genuine self-reliant nationalism would have profound consequences for the countries in the North. The ensuing reduction in the external flow of nourishment to the established welfare states would be bound to threaten the stability of society and politics there. It could possibly elevate the contradictions of capitalism to the point of terminal crisis in the West.[42]

The accusation of the neo-Marxists and "dependency" theorists was that the industrialized countries would do all that they could to prevent the industrialization of the third world so that they could continue to profit from its raw materials. Although it was possible to see how history could be interpreted in this fashion, the accusation was inaccurate. Quite apart from the fact that the desire for economic development could not ethically be denied, there were sound reasons for the West to accept and promote it. It had been an element of American internationalist policy since Woodrow Wilson that "prosperity in one part of the world ministers to prosperity everywhere."[43] The self-defeating economic nationalism of the 1930s and '40s made the point more urgent. "The lesson that must be learned is that prosperous neighbors are the best neighbors," argued Harry Dexter White in proposing the Bretton Woods arrangements in 1944.[44] With the outbreak of the Cold War, competition with the Soviet Union also urged the need for growth-producing policies for the third world. As Averell Harriman put it in 1954, economic aid to developing countries was essential in the interests of "maintaining an upward trend of economic, social and political development . . . as a bulwark against Communist penetration."[45]

The objection to the new theories of "import substitution" in American eyes was not so much the developing countries' protection of domestic industry but the aversion to commodity exports.

After all, the United States had risen to prosperity by combining industrial protectionism and raw materials exports, financed to a large degree by foreign capital. Henry Clay, who as well as being the champion of American industry was the owner of a substantial agricultural estate growing cash crops, had argued a century earlier that tariffs on manufactured imports were not only compatible with agricultural exports, but would actually help them because the additional domestic consumption from the industrial cities would sustain prices: "If we do not create some new market, if we persevere in the existing pursuits of agriculture, the inevitable consequences must be, to augment greatly the quantity of our produce [for export], and to lessen its value in the foreign market."[46] Other ex-colonies such as Canada and Australia had also become wealthy by combining raw-materials exports and the protection of domestic industry. There was no reason why the developing countries should not do the same.

These principles—the diffusion of high standards of living, the expansion of world trade, and the understanding that less-developed countries needed to protect their industries—were written into the General Agreement on Tariffs and Trade, which has a good claim to be considered the founding document of Western postwar economic policy.* The underlying premise of the agreement was that "trade and economic endeavor should be conducted with a view to raising standards of living, ensuring full employment and a large and steadily growing volume of real income and effective demand, developing the full use of the resources of the world and expanding the production and exchange of goods." At the same time, specific exceptions to the underlying principle of free trade were made for less-developed countries (LDCs). The rules allowed them to maintain tariff and other

* The other main pillar of the postwar economic order, Bretton Woods, was established with considerably greater fanfare but had a far shorter life span. In practice, its monetary arrangements operated only from 1958 to 1971. By contrast, GATT, which got off to a slow start, increased in importance over the decades and was transformed into the World Trade Organization in 1995.

trade barriers to protect nascent industries (Article 17) and did not require them to reciprocate concessions made by developed countries (Article 36).

The negative effects of import-substitution policies on world trade were strongest when they occurred in tandem with another manifestation of economic nationalism: the resentment of foreign ownership of vital resources. The first signs of the potency of this issue came in 1917 when the revolutionary Mexican government nationalized the country's mineral resources. This led to years of disputes with the American and British oil companies that continued to own the country's oil wells even if in theory they no longer owned the oil. Finally in 1938, the Mexican government nationalized the entire oil industry. The primary result of this dispute was a sharp reduction in output due to lack of investment and aging wells. In 1920, Mexican oil production of 23 million tons per year had been the second-largest in the world. By 1940, this had fallen to under 6 million tons, and the country had been overtaken by the more foreign-investment-friendly Venezuela, whose production had risen from almost nothing to 28.5 million tons over the same period.[47] After the Second World War, Mexican economic policy focused on internal development through import substitution. Without foreign capital, oil production increased so slowly that it failed to keep up even with domestic demand, and in 1957 Mexico became a net oil importer. The result of postcolonial economic nationalism, therefore, was that Mexico's oil resources disappeared from the global economy almost as completely as if the country had joined the communist bloc.

It was undoubtedly with this history in mind that an American government study of raw-materials policy in 1952 held up the example of Venezuela as a lesson to third-world governments pursuing shortsighted policies of economic self-sufficiency:

An almost classic example of economic cooperation between two free world nations, to the benefit of both, is afforded by Venezuela and the United States. By developing her rich materials resources, mainly with the aid of private investment and technical know-how supplied by the United States, Venezuela has achieved in a short span of years an almost unparalleled record of economic and social development.[48]

The Mexican example was extreme. More typically, economic nationalism led not to the abandonment of exports but to pressure for a revision of terms to the advantage of the host country. This was scarcely surprising given the very favorable terms that had been agreed to when the oil was no more than a prospector's gamble. In 1932, the shah of Iran, whose income was suffering from the worldwide fall in oil prices, demanded and obtained a fixed royalty per barrel in addition to an increase in his share of the profits from 16 percent to 20 percent. In 1943, Venezuela put forward the even more radical idea of a fifty-fifty profit split. Anxious not to repeat the Mexican debacle, the oil companies agreed—encouraged by the American and British governments, which did not want disruption to wartime supplies. The fifty-fifty principle made its way to the Middle East in the late 1940s thanks to a Venezuelan delegation that was keen to spread the gospel of natural-resources fairness (and, not incidentally, to increase the cost of doing business in an area where huge recent finds in Kuwait and Saudi Arabia were flooding the market with cheap oil). In 1950, Aramco, the American-led consortium that controlled Saudi Arabia's oil, agreed to the split (with the Saudi share subtly expressed as a tax, so that Aramco's increased costs could be offset by a reduction in its US taxes). The Saudi-Aramco arrangement proved contagious, with Kuwait and Iraq following suit.

It was not always so smooth. Saudi Arabia and Kuwait were sparsely populated desert kingdoms whose rulers were happy to make deals with the Western governments that had helped them into being. By contrast, Iran had historically been, like China, a venerable imperial power in its own right. It felt the humiliations of Western hegemony deeply, even though it had never formally been colonized. A fifty-fifty profit split might possibly have soothed

passions if it had been agreed to on a timely basis, but by 1951 opposition to British dominance was running so high that the expul-
sion of the Anglo-Iranian Oil Company* from Iran and the
nationalization of its assets became the common cause of Iranian
politics. In October, the company was forced out at gunpoint,
and in response Britain organized a boycott of Iranian oil. The
feared world shortage did not materialize because of the extremely
rapid increase of production in Saudi Arabia and Kuwait. But Iran
looked increasingly unstable as it plunged into economic chaos
without its main source of income. The country's nationalist prime
minister Mohammed Mossadegh was not a communist, but his
position was threatened by the Tudeh, the main Iranian Communist party. To the north, Russia lurked, ready to take advantage of
the situation. It had had its eye on Iran since the nineteenth century,
and Stalin's nonaggression agreement with Hitler in 1940 had
staked out the country as part of Russia's plans for the future.
During the war, it had occupied the northern part of the country,
and it had been forced to withdraw only in 1946 by strong American and British pressure.

The United States had hitherto accepted that Iran was part of
the British sphere of influence, but the British position in the
country had become so untenable that the United States was
forced to intervene—initially as an honest broker, subsequently as
a power broker. At the beginning of the crisis, Washington had
argued against British plans to use force for the same reason that
it had previously opposed the Dutch use of force in Indonesia:
that it would further radicalize the country. However, the rising
threat of anarchy and communism in Iran made it think otherwise. Allen Dulles, the head of the CIA, saw another chain of
dominoes at risk if the Russians got control of the country: "Not
only would the free world be deprived of the enormous assets represented by Iranian oil production and reserves . . . Worse still . . .

* The Anglo-Persian Oil Company was renamed Anglo-Iranian in 1935 after
the shah requested that Iran be used as the formal name of his country.

if Iran succumbed to the Communists there was little doubt that in short order the other areas of the Middle East, with some 60 percent of the world's oil reserves, would fall into Communist control."[49]

In August 1953, the CIA backed a coup d'état that ousted Mossadegh and reinstalled the young shah as an absolute monarch. There was no question of restoring Anglo-Iranian's position in the country since local opinion remained adamant on the question of nationalization. However, a new Anglo-American consortium was put into place to run the industry under contract from the newly formed National Iranian Oil Company on the basis of a fifty-fifty profit split. For the next twenty-five years, the shah became a bastion of Western influence in the Gulf— although that did not make him any less of a hawk on the question of obtaining the highest possible income from his country's mineral resources.

The events in Iran illustrate several aspects of the early postwar era that explain why the West continued to enjoy access to raw materials even after the collapse of its empires. First, while the United States often encouraged the dissolution of the European empires, it simultaneously assumed the role of protector of Western interests. Iranian oil was of no direct economic concern to America—its output went almost entirely to Britain and other European countries—but the United States still took steps to secure its allies' supply. Second, the greater importance of Iran's resources to an oil-dependent West than to a self-sufficient Soviet Union meant that the United States was the more determined player in this Cold War version of the Great Game. Had it been the Soviet bloc that depended on Iranian oil in 1953, Russia would almost certainly have orchestrated a Communist takeover and sent in the tanks. Finally, the sheer importance of oil revenues for the producing countries meant that the Mexican example of counterproductive resource nationalism was rare. The main interest of raw-materials-producing nations was to increase their revenues rather than to divert or shut off supply. It could be argued that it was fortunate that oil reserves were concentrated in a few areas. The countries in these geologically privileged regions were more likely to depend on their oil income.

But sometimes not even the need for revenues could be counted on to keep supplies flowing. The crux of the postwar order came in the 1970s. Several trends coalesced to make this the most dangerous decade of the Cold War for Western interests. Stalin had largely ignored Arab nationalism, and the Russian press initially referred to Nasser as a "lackey of British imperialism." However, under Khrushchev, Soviet tactics changed. The Middle East was seen as the soft underbelly of the West, and Russian penetration might undermine the West's ability to control the region. In 1955, the Soviets concluded an arms deal with Egypt, and the following year Russia proved its pro-Arab credentials by threatening to use nuclear weapons against Britain and France when they sent troops to retake control of the Suez Canal in the wake of its nationalization. American policy during the Suez crisis was almost entirely ineffective, hoping to wean Nasser from Russia by sacrificing British power in the region. In the end it achieved the latter without gaining the former. Russian influence in the Arab world continued to grow. Iraq joined Egypt in the Soviet camp in 1958, followed by Algeria, Syria, South Yemen, and Libya during the 1960s and early '70s.

Rising Soviet influence was made more dangerous by rising Soviet military power. The US advantage in nuclear weapons was progressively closed, so that whereas in 1962 Kennedy could still face down Khrushchev in the Cuban missile crisis, by the late 1960s the two powers were evenly matched. Equally important was the growth of the Soviet navy. Starting with the appointment of Sergey Gorshkov as admiral of the fleet in 1955, Russia's naval forces underwent continuous expansion, especially its submarine fleet. This was an unexpected development for what was traditionally a land-based power, and like the growth of the German navy in the early twentieth century, it was equally unsettling for the established sea-based order. The entry of Syria into the Soviet sphere of influence gave Russia the naval base in the Mediterranean that it had sought for more than a century. By the mid-1970s, the Soviet navy outnumbered the American and was so powerful that, in the opinion of Admiral Elmo Zumwalt, the chief of American naval operations, "The odds are that we would have lost a war with the Soviet Union if we had had to fight it any year since 1970; the navy dropped to about a 35 percent probability of victory."[50]

The growth of Soviet influence in the Middle East was greatly facilitated by the Arab-Israeli conflict. Stalin had supported the independence of Israel in 1948, but in 1956 Khrushchev seized the opportunity offered by the Israeli attack on Egypt to cement Soviet ties with the Arab states by opposing Zionism. Russia now became the arms supplier to Israel's hostile neighbors and in 1969 added a military presence in Egypt to its naval base in Syria. At the same time, American and European support for Israel made the Western position in the region far harder to sustain. It turned out that the Arab-Israeli conflict, although unconnected with the question of postcolonial raw-materials supply, was more dangerous to Western economic interests than either communism or third-world economic nationalism. It was the Zionist thorn in the side of Arab nationalism that turned the West's fears of being shut off from vital resources into reality.

Ever since the closing of the Suez Canal in 1956, Arabs had discussed using the oil weapon in their struggle against the state of Israel. In 1967, the opportunity offered itself. On June 6, the day after the outbreak of the Six-Day War, Arab oil ministers called for an embargo on oil sales to the three main Western supporters of Israel: the United States, the United Kingdom, and Germany. Oil supply from the Middle East fell by half, to around 1.5 million barrels per day, and the simultaneous closing of the Suez Canal meant that what was left had to take the long route around the Cape of Good Hope. The oil weapon proved ineffective because the United States still had spare capacity that it could switch on at times of need through the operations of the Texas

Railroad Commission, which since the 1930s had ensured that the Texas oil fields produced less than their full potential so that prices could be stabilized. Other countries, such as Venezuela and Iran, also increased their production. By July, it was apparent that the embargo had failed.

By the early 1970s, however, the situation was different. Surplus American capacity, which had been around four million barrels per day in the early 1960s, had virtually disappeared as a result of the inexorable increase in consumption and the peaking of American production. In 1971, the Texas Railroad Commission allowed 100 percent production for the first time. Free-world oil demand had risen from nineteen million barrels per day in 1960 to forty-four million barrels per day in 1972, and almost all the extra supply came from the Middle East. Saudi Arabia was about to inherit the mantle of the Texas Railroad Commission as the world's swing producer, but in the early 1970s the country was producing at full capacity. In October 1973, the fourth Arab-Israeli war broke out. This time the prospects for the oil weapon were far better.

In mid-October, the Arab oil ministers agreed to increase prices immediately by 70 percent and to progressively cut back that supply by 5 percent per month until their political demands were met. By December, Arab oil output had been reduced by five million barrels per day. This time there was no American surge capacity, and increases elsewhere offset little more than 10 percent of the shortfall. The combined effect of oil shortages and prices that soared to four times their precrisis level was to plunge much of the world into the worst economic crisis since the Second World War. American power and influence were unable to prevent the embargo. Talk of military intervention was countered by Arab threats of preemptive sabotage. Both the United States and Russia reinforced their naval presences in the eastern Mediterranean, but the Russian fleet boasted ninety-eight ships to America's sixty-five. In 1975, a US congressional study discussed the possibility of taking over the Middle Eastern oil fields in the event of a total OPEC embargo but worried that if the Soviet Union decided to intervene it could strangle the West through a submarine blockade.[51] It did not look as if Pax Americana was able to offer meaningful protection of Western interests, and the postwar alliance started to show signs of strain. As the embargo took its toll, a number of countries shifted their foreign policies in a direction more congenial to the Arab point of view, and others started to discuss bilateral trade deals in a return to the *sauve qui peut* mentality of the 1930s.

After the war, the United States was able to recoup some of its losses by bringing Egypt into the Western sphere of influence and negotiating the Camp David Accords in 1978. But the limits of American power in the area were again revealed the following year, first by the fall of the shah of Iran, the most reliably pro-Western ruler in the Gulf, and then by the Soviet invasion of Afghanistan. This time there was no question of a repeat of the 1953 coup to overthrow an anti-Western Iranian regime. Nor could the Russians be pressured into withdrawing from Afghanistan as they had been pressured into withdrawing from northern Iran in 1946. The best that could be done, other than covert support for Afghan resistance, was to declare publicly that America would act forcefully to prevent any foreign power from threatening the oil supplies of the Gulf. The "Carter Doctrine" helped draw a line in the sand, but it could not reverse the setbacks of 1978–1979. The Iranian revolution had immediate effects on oil production, and the world soon faced a second oil shock almost as severe as the first.

Yet the oil crises of the 1970s, however painful in the short term, were not as disastrous as originally feared. The 1973 oil embargo failed for two reasons. Because the Arab oil producers did not control transport, their oil weapon had no ability to distinguish between friend and foe. This made it impossible to reward countries that moved toward the Arab position while continuing to punish those that did not. More important, the objectives of the exporters were to some extent confused: They wished to change

Western policy toward Israel, but they also wanted to increase their revenues by raising prices. Once they had achieved the latter, the coalition started to fracture. Instead of complete Israeli withdrawal from the areas conquered in 1967, as originally demanded, the Saudis, crucial to the success of the embargo, declared themselves satisfied by withdrawal from the west side of the Suez Canal and by the promise of further negotiations under American auspices. In March 1974, the embargo came to an end.

The second oil crisis, of 1979–1980, while demonstrating once again the dangerous unreliability of Middle Eastern supplies, also showed that the West could learn to live with unfriendly suppliers. Iran under Ayatollah Khomeini still needed its oil revenues. So did Libya under Ghadaffi, Iraq under Saddam Hussein, and later Venezuela under Hugo Chávez. Nationalization of oil resources, the center of earlier disputes with Mexico and Iran, also turned out to be less threatening than originally thought. During the 1970s, nationalization became the norm in OPEC, but the oil continued to flow—if perhaps at a somewhat lower rate owing to the lack of foreign investment and technology.

Paradoxically, in many ways the oil crises of the 1970s worked to further rather than hinder the Western vision of the postwar world. One of its first victims was the idea of the dependency theorists that only by rejecting the role of raw-materials producers could developing countries prosper. Now it seemed that the opposite was true: The producers of raw materials could prosper at the expense of industrialized countries. The "terms of trade" argument had stated that commodity prices must decline over the long term compared to the prices of manufactured goods. They were now countered by a rival theory that went back to David Ricardo: that the profits of economic growth from industrialization would end up flowing mainly to the owners of finite resources, such as land. This pessimistic line of thought, together with Thomas Malthus's theory that population growth would always end up counteracting any increase in food production, gave economics the reputation of being a fundamentally "dismal science." In the

1970s, Ricardo's argument seemed all the more relevant, given that the oil crises came hot on the heels of the publication of *The Limits to Growth* by the Club of Rome, which argued that the world was running out of resources. Raw-materials producers, far from being the impoverished brethren of the world order, were becoming a privileged elite.

Perhaps most important was the effect of rising oil prices on international trade. The higher cost of oil imports could be balanced in the medium term only by increased exports of other goods. The indirect result of the oil crises, therefore, was to increase the volume of world trade. Between 1970 and 1980, total trade as a percentage of GDP doubled in the United States, rose by around 40 percent in Germany, France, and Japan, and by close to 30 percent in the United Kingdom—whereas in the 1960s, trade had merely kept pace with economic growth. In the longer term, the rising price of oil put pressure on oil-importing LDCs to look beyond import substitution and to reenter the world market. The attempt merely to recycle petrodollars to the oil-consuming LDCs through the international banking system was a stopgap measure that could end only in a debt crisis.

In the Far East, the process of trade liberalization had started even before the oil crisis. Malaysia and Thailand were among the few developing countries that remained open to trade throughout the postwar period. Japan joined GATT in 1955 and abolished currency controls in 1964. In practice it was returning to the strategy of economic growth through integration with the world economy, which it had pursued since the late nineteenth century, before the ill-fated attempt at self-sufficiency in the 1930s and '40s. It was joined in the 1960s by South Korea and Taiwan in following an export-oriented growth strategy combined with the protection of nascent industries. The events of the 1970s encouraged them to redouble their efforts to export. The most striking Asian addition to the ranks of the trade liberalizers was China after 1978. In Latin America, by contrast, the process took far longer. Only the autocratic Pinochet regime was able to force through liberalization in the 1970s. In the rest of the continent, it took the failure of successive economic policies, including borrowing to cover current account deficits in the late 1970s, and import restrictions after the resultant debt crisis in 1982, to force the pace of change. Between 1985 and 1990, Mexico, Argentina, Brazil, and a number of other countries started to open their doors. India, saddled with the back-to-the-spinning-wheel philosophy of Gandhi in addition to the anticolonial economic dogma of the Congress Party, took even longer to change direction.

The most important new participant in the global trading system in the 1970s was the Soviet Union. Its reentry into the world market marked the beginning of the end of the Cold War.

An underlying self-sufficiency and an aversion to international trade were the two main reasons communist Russia had been unlikely to take part in the kind of struggle for resources and markets that had propelled the two world wars. But beyond that was the fact that insofar as the Soviet Union did trade with the outside world, it never managed to advance beyond the position of an exporter of raw materials. Such a position was unacceptable to communist thinkers. It was associated with economic backwardness, as well as demonstrating dependence on the advanced capitalist world. As Anastas Mikoyan declared at the 28th Party Congress in 1939, "In the period when we were still backward and poor, when we did not have our own developed machine-building industry and we had to build industry at any cost, we were forced to export abroad a great deal of raw materials and foodstuffs, which we needed ourselves."[52]

In theory, the development of industry should have enabled the Soviet Union to become a competitive producer of manufactured goods. But except for some military equipment, this was never the case. In 1964, Khrushchev bemoaned the inferior quality of Soviet goods: "If the workers, engineers and employees manufacture excellent goods while working for the capitalists, then must we, the workers, engineers and technologists in the

Socialist countries, work less well, producing goods of lower quality?"[53] Yet in a system that refused to accept that production needed to respond to demand through the mechanism of prices, Khrushchev's plans for high-quality manufacturing were to remain unfulfilled. Much of Soviet output was based on the reverse engineering of Western products. In the 1970s, the dissident Alexander Zinoviev lampooned the shortcomings of Soviet industry: "On top of all that, there's abroad. If only it didn't exist! Then we'd be home and dry. But they're eternally dreaming up something new over there. And we have to compete with them. To show our superiority. No sooner have you pinched one little machine from them than it's time to pinch the next one. By the time we've got it into production, the bastard's obsolete."[54]

The result was that by the late 1960s, Russia once again felt that it needed to import Western technology in order to catch up industrially. And once again it had to find raw materials with which to trade. In theory this should not have been a problem. Russia still had the same agricultural and mineral resources that it possessed in tsarist days. But grain production, for so long the backbone of Russian export earnings, was suffering from fundamental flaws in communist policy. In the early 1930s, collectivization led to chaos and famine. Subsequently, Stalin's fixation with Lysenko's theories diverted Russian agriculture from advances in genetically based seed selection until the late 1950s. As long as the consumption of the general population was kept low, as it was under the semifeudal conditions of imperial Russia or under the harsh five-year plans of Stalin, there was enough grain to feed the population and to generate an exportable surplus. But after Stalin's death, policy changed. Total repression could be sustained for only so long. It was now time to enjoy some of the gains so hard won under the dictator and to demonstrate the intrinsic superiority of communism by raising living standards. Food prices were frozen at low levels while wages were allowed to rise.

Consumption increased, but production failed to keep up. By the early 1970s, the Soviet Union had turned from a food exporter into an importer. In 1972, grain imports came to fifteen million tons, compared to exports of around nine million tons in the heyday of pre-1914 tsarist Russia.

The situation was saved by the other traditional Russian exportable resource: oil. The Soviet Union's reentry into the global market coincided with the oil boom. Between 1970 and 1980, Soviet revenues from oil exports rose from $2 billion to $17 billion. The problem was that these oil revenues should have paid for foreign technology to revitalize industry. Instead they were spent on food imports, which rose from $500 million to $15 billion over the same period. However, booming oil exports turned out to be only a temporary solution to the underlying problem. Between 1981 and 1985, world oil prices fell by more than 50 percent, decreasing Russia's export earnings. But demand for food imports continued to rise, as was inevitable when prices for bread had been frozen in the mid-1950s, and for meat and milk in 1962. By 1990, a year's supply of meat cost no more than a pair of boots. Instead of freeing prices to decrease local demand and stimulate production, the Politburo chose to borrow abroad to cover an ever-growing budget deficit. In 1970, the Soviet Union had been debt free, but by 1990, it owed $75 billion to the West. By this stage, food subsidies amounted to 10 percent of national income and 20 percent of the state budget.[55] In 1987, Gorbachev proposed increasing food prices, but he backed off in the face of protests by industrial workers. It was lost on no one in the Politburo with a sense of history that the 1917 revolution had been sparked by food riots.

By 1980, Soviet foreign trade had grown to 20 percent of GDP— higher than pre–World War I levels. But the reentry of Russia into the world economy exposed the shortcomings and contradictions of the Soviet economic system. In Marx's scheme of history, communism was supposed to lead to a harmonious society enjoying the highest possible standard of living. The failure of the Soviet

Union to produce such a society meant that its existence was justified by its military might and by the subsidization of a standard
of living that the economy was increasingly incapable of producing. Supporting these two pillars of the system eventually cost
the Soviet state more than half its total budget. As long as Russia
remained an autarky, such expenses might have been sustainable.
But when it could no longer pay for them without recourse to the
capitalist world it despised, the cracks in the system were exposed
and the edifice collapsed.

THE END OF PAX AMERICANA?

China's peaceful development has broken away from the traditional pattern where a rising power was bound to seek hegemony.

—CHINESE WHITE PAPER, 2011

The Cold War was never formally declared and therefore never formally ended. It petered out without fanfare amid a series of eye-catching events from the fall of the Berlin Wall in 1989 to the failure of the August coup against Gorbachev in 1991. The peaceful triumph of "people power" in countries where popular protest had previously been suppressed by tanks was a cause for celebration on both sides of the defunct iron curtain. So too was the disappearance of a world order based on a perilous balance of terror.

Yet the Cold War, for all its horrors, had preserved a kind of peace for decades. Both sides of the ideological divide thought of their opponents as dangerous militarists (while they themselves were peaceable), but nonetheless they had not directly come to blows.

Throughout the Cold War, Soviet propaganda referred to the communist bloc either as the "democratic nations" (without, apparently, a sense of irony) or more frequently as the "peace-loving nations" (following Lenin's doctrine of the inevitability of war between capitalist states). But in reality the heretical Soviet economist Eugen Varga had been right. The West no longer competed for resources and markets at the point of a gun. Partly because it had learned the bitter lesson of two world wars, and partly because the Cold War forced it to unite, the West was content to prosper under Pax Americana. The unspoken bargain was that the United States would exercise a near monopoly of military force. However, it would use its force not to gain exclusive economic advantages but as an impartial protector of Western interests. Under the American umbrella, the noncommunist world flourished. It was no longer necessary for Germany and Japan to demand empires in order to enjoy their place in the sun. The other ex-imperial countries of Europe found that they too could prosper without their colonial appendages.

There had always been a tension between the theory of how the postwar order was supposed to work and how it worked in practice. Originally there was supposed to be cooperation among the members of the Security Council, who together would police the world. In practice, the ideological impasse of the Cold War had rendered the Security Council next to useless, and peace had instead been maintained by the rival hegemonies of the two superpowers operating within their separate spheres of interest. It had been, in many ways, a Pax Americana et Sovietica.

As the hostilities of the Cold War faded in the late 1980s under Gorbachev's policies of internal reform and rapprochement with the West, it started to seem that the original intention of the United Nations might have a new lease on life. The test came on August 1, 1990, when Iraq unexpectedly invaded Kuwait. This crisis provided justifications for intervention founded on both the original vision of a postwar order policed by the United Nations and the de facto postwar order based on Pax Americana. The invasion of one member of the United Nations by another was a clear contravention of Article 2 of its charter and justified international intervention under Articles 40–47. At the same time, the threat to the security of global oil supplies justified American intervention on the basis of the Carter Doctrine and its Reagan Corollary.* George H. W. Bush perceived, wisely, that the new openness of the Soviet Union to cooperation with the West, combined with its by now terminal economic weakness, provided an opportunity to square the circle. The two principles of preserving international security could for once be united. America would not have to act simply as the protector of Western interests but could take up the role originally envisaged in 1945 as the leading member of the Security Council of the United Nations.

On September 9, 1990, Bush and Gorbachev met in Helsinki, in what is sometimes described as the first post–Cold War summit. Gorbachev agreed to support a UN resolution authorizing economic sanctions against Iraq, while hinting that Russia needed American loans as an unspoken quid pro quo. In the event, the Soviet Union's negotiating position was so weakened at that point, and its life expectancy so short, that America was able to obtain its cooperation without financial lubrication.

One thing is for sure: Had the Cold War been in full flower, Saddam might have gotten away with his adventurism. The United Nations would have been hamstrung by the Soviet Union's protection of one of its longtime allies. Nor would unilateral American action have looked very prudent if Russia had chosen to respond with the threat of countervailing military force, as it had during earlier Middle Eastern crises.

Even though the Gulf War was undertaken by a broad coalition of countries operating under a United Nations mandate, the true balance of power was clear. The coalition consisted largely of NATO members and Gulf states, with a smattering of countries

* The Carter Doctrine of January 1980 stated that America would respond with force to any outside threat to the security of oil supplies in the Persian Gulf. It was explicitly directed at the Soviet Union after its invasion of Afghanistan. In October 1981, in response to the Iran-Iraq War, Ronald Reagan extended the doctrine to guarantee the security of Saudi Arabia from hostile forces within the Gulf.

from elsewhere. Neither the USSR nor China participated, the most notable presence from the old communist world being a number of erstwhile Soviet satellites from Eastern Europe happy to demonstrate their newfound independence. The United States not only put together the coalition but also provided nearly three-quarters of the troops and more than 90 percent of the firepower. It could easily have undertaken the operation on its own, with perhaps the participation of its one crucial ally, Saudi Arabia, which provided the necessary ground bases as well as the next-largest contingent in the alliance.

After the war, it was possible to interpret events as the birth of a "new world order"—a revitalization of the dreams of the founders of the United Nations that had been put into abeyance by the Cold War. However, it was also possible to interpret them as the arrival of a true Pax Americana, untrammeled by the military and ideological competition of a rival superpower.

In public, American officials talked of the former, but there was a streak of opinion that advocated the latter. In March 1992, *The New York Times* obtained a draft of a Pentagon policy paper stating that, in the wake of the demise of the Soviet Union, America should prevent any power rising to a position where it could challenge the United States. Instead it should aim at "convincing potential competitors that they need not aspire to a greater role or pursue a more aggressive posture to protect their legitimate interests." The newspaper commented that "with its focus on this concept of benevolent domination by one power, the Pentagon document articulates the clearest rejection to date of collective internationalism, the strategy that emerged from World War II when the five victorious powers sought to form a United Nations that could mediate disputes and police outbreaks of violence."[1] Amid the ensuing outcry, the implications of the Pentagon paper were rejected by the White House, leading to a substantial re-wording to put greater emphasis on cooperation and multilateralism. Instead of seeking to deter "potential competitors from even aspiring to a larger regional or global role," the final policy paper talked of "turning old enmities into new cooperative relationships." The ideal should be to bring "a democratic Russia . . . into the defense community of democratic nations."[2]

The debate brought up a number of unresolved issues surrounding the postwar order. Since 1945, the United States had enjoyed a position of virtually unquestioned supremacy within the West. But its supremacy was never officially stated and was exercised with the cooperation of its allies. Any attempt to make American hegemony overt might undo the unspoken consensus that made it possible. One of the notable features of America's rise to dominance was that it had not provoked a countervailing alliance of other powers, as had the earlier Spanish, French, and German attempts at hegemony. This was in part because America's power was exercised to protect its allies rather than in its own narrow self-interest; but it was also in part because the alliance was a response to the Soviet threat. What would happen to the alliance now that this threat no longer existed?

A second unanswered question was whether the original postwar plan for peace under the United Nations could actually work. For the first forty-five years of its life, it had been stillborn. The only time it had appeared to operate as intended had been in the Korean War. But this was an aberration based on a mistaken ploy by the Soviet Union of boycotting the crucial meeting of the Security Council. The Gulf War had appeared to show that the United Nations could operate as originally intended (in other words, without automatic vetoes from rival superpowers), but this might have been simply because Russia was temporarily too weak to take a stand. It was not at all clear how easy it would be to incorporate Russia into "the defense community of democratic nations."

Yet if Russia, or any other country, decided not to cooperate fully in this "new world order," the more emollient final Defense Strategy paper sounded almost as severe as the unreconstructed original draft. The United States should take action to "preclude any hostile power from dominating a region critical to our interests . . . These regions include Europe, East Asia, the Middle East/Persian Gulf, and Latin America. Consolidated, nondemocratic control of the resources of such a critical region could generate a significant threat to our security."[3]

In practice, the facts of American ascendancy outweighed attempts to harness it to the service of multilateral institutions. In the 1990s, the American economy seemed to gain a new lease on life. Although in the "old economy" of traditional manufacturing its position was far less dominant than in the immediate postwar period, in the "new economy" of information technology its advance seemed unstoppable. Silicon Valley appeared to hold a near monopoly of advances in this field, especially in putting them into commercial practice. The stock market boomed, the dollar strengthened, and other industrialized nations struggled to keep up. Among the hardest hit were America's closest economic rivals, the countries of the now former USSR and Japan, whose economies had been the second- and third-largest in the world in the 1980s.

Confronted by the combination of slowing economic growth and the growing need to borrow from the West, the rulers of the Soviet Union had lost confidence in their old model. The attempt to revive the economy by policies of glasnost (openness) and perestroika (reform) had achieved few if any results. When the regime collapsed in 1991, there was an attempt to move rapidly from central planning to free-market capitalism. But the idea that doing so would increase output was based on a misunderstanding of how the economy had previously worked. Without the underpinning of constant coercion by a totalitarian state, the economy simply imploded, contracting by close to 40 percent between 1990 and 1993. As a former Soviet official put it, "We used to work in a centrally controlled system where they told you what to produce. Now they've stopped telling us what to produce, so we don't produce anything."[4] While the Soviet Union had still been the world's second-largest economy in 1990, by 1995 the Russian Federation ranked only tenth.*

Events in Japan were far less dramatic, but they also confounded the assumptions of the 1980s. As with Russia, the foundations of the Japanese economy were exposed as weaker than had been thought. In Japan's case, excessive reliance on easy credit and capital investment led to an unsustainable boom that went into reverse in the early 1990s. Output did not fall dramatically, as in Russia, but it did not grow either. Whereas pundits on both sides of the Pacific had spent the 1980s discussing the rising economic power of Japan and its potential threat to American dominance, by the beginning of the twenty-first century such ideas had been forgotten. In 1990, Japan's economic output was 43 percent of America's, an astonishing achievement for a country whose economy had been less than one-tenth the size of America's in 1960. By 2005, however, its relative output had fallen back to 31 percent.

American dominance was also manifest in the military balance of power. As the Soviet Union disintegrated, so too did Soviet military might (although its nuclear arsenal remained intact). The Russian navy, which had grown from modest beginnings in the immediate postwar period to challenge American naval supremacy by the 1970s, was deprived of funding and went into decline, with many of its ships being scrapped or simply rusting away. It had never looked to challenge the United States in aircraft carriers but had concentrated on missile-bearing surface ships and its nuclear submarine fleet, which was designed to threaten US carrier groups and intercept NATO convoys in the event of war. By 2006, Russia had only 26 operational submarines, compared to 170 in 1991. With the Russian threat diminishing, the US Navy looked even more dominant. Its eleven carrier groups

---

* This calculation is based on IMF figures at purchasing-power parity. On a nominal basis, Russia had fallen as low as fourteenth in 1995, behind South Korea and the Netherlands.

based on the *Nimitz*-class carrier could hold substantially more planes than all the rest of the world's carriers combined. The tonnage of the rest of its surface fleet also exceeded that of the next six navies (three of which in any case belonged to US allies). Moreover, the United States held an unquestionable lead in the most advanced weapons systems, such as smart munitions and stealth technology. This weight of numbers and firepower vastly exceeded the level of dominance achieved by the Royal Navy in its heyday. As the US Navy liked to proclaim, the *Nimitz*-class carriers represent "4.5 acres of sovereign and mobile American territory" able to project American power anywhere in the world on short notice.

From an economic perspective too, the post–Cold War world looked like a universalized version of the order that had operated in the West since 1945. The conversion of the Soviet bloc countries to free-market economies was far from painless, but nonetheless it appeared to be irreversible. It put the seal on what appeared to be an inexorable trend away from central planning and economic self-sufficiency. The progress toward worldwide free trade took a step forward in 1995 with the transformation of the General Agreement on Tariffs and Trade, which had existed in a strange institutional limbo as an intergovernmental agreement rather than a formal institution, into the World Trade Organization (WTO). The 23 countries that had taken part in the original GATT talks in 1947 had swelled to 102 by the time of the Tokyo round of negotiations in the 1970s, and to 159 by 2001. Free trade was by no means absolute at the end of the century. As Ronald Findlay and Kevin O'Rourke point out in their history of world trade, two-thirds of the world still lived in countries with higher tariff barriers than in 1914.[5] Moreover, oil, crucial to the world economy but heavily government controlled, was outside its compass. However, there were increasingly few who argued against the idea that integration into the world economy was the best way to promote prosperity.

Perhaps it was not surprising that some thought the ideological battles that had raged throughout the century were coming to an end. In 1992, Francis Fukuyama published *The End of History*, in which he argued that since there was no longer any serious alternative to Western liberal democracy as the best way to govern society, it could be said that history (as he defined it) was coming to an end. Fukuyama focused on the conflict between liberal democracy and autocracy, but the same argument could have been made about the rivalry between free trade and autarky. The belief in economic self-sufficiency had at one time been held, for different reasons, by much, if not most, of the world. The "imperial" version had been a leading strain of thought among the Great Powers from the late nineteenth century to the Second World War. The communist and "anticolonial" versions had been prevalent throughout much of the rest of the world from the 1920s to the 1970s. By the end of the century, however, relics of the belief in autarky were increasingly found only in dark corners of the world such as North Korea and Burma.

Yet it was not quite so simple. The very processes that had brought about the demise of communism and the rise of free trade contained within them the seeds of a threat to this seemingly peaceful and prosperous world order. A large number of countries were now entering what had previously been essentially a Western club. It was not clear that all of them would fully accept the rules as they had been understood hitherto.

It was soon apparent that there were significant differences among states. The countries of Eastern Europe accepted the rules of the club completely and immediately. They applied to join the WTO, the EU, and NATO as soon as they possibly could. Their reaction was scarcely surprising since communism had been imposed on them from outside and had never enjoyed much popular support. Poland and Hungary had managed to join GATT in 1967 and 1973 while they were still communist states in an early demonstration of latent economic heresy.

Russia was a different matter. Its immediate policy when it emerged from the collapse of the Soviet Union was to become more "Western." It applied for WTO membership in 1993, and joined the Partnership for Peace, set up to promote peaceful cooperation between NATO and other European states in 1994. In practice, however, its relations with the West remained at best fitful, and since 2000 increasingly hostile. Admission to the WTO took eighteen years, partly because oil and gas, Russia's main exports, were not covered by WTO regulations, giving it little incentive to press the issue. Thoughts about incorporating the country into the "defense community of democratic nations" turned out to be illusory. Increasingly, the collapse of communism was seen by much of the population not as a liberation but as a surrender, and the expansion of NATO as a hostile act. In 2005, Vladimir Putin described the breakup of the Soviet Union as the "greatest geopolitical disaster of the last century." Russian foreign policy has been increasingly directed toward halting and, where possible, reversing this dissolution, partly through Russian-centered political and economic organizations in the ex-Soviet states, such as the customs union that Russia hopes to extend throughout the area, and sometimes by force, as in Chechnya, Georgia, and Ukraine. Russia is now more integrated into the global economic system than at any stage in its history, with foreign trade representing over 40 percent of GDP, compared to 15 percent before 1914, but this has not made it part of the Western world order. Like America in the 1940s, it holds an energy weapon. But history has shown that these weapons do not always work as anticipated, and because Russia is far more dependent on foreign trade than prewar America (whose foreign trade amounted to only 5 percent of GDP), it cannot use its energy weapon with total impunity.

Another major new entrant into the global trading system, although not ex-communist, was India. During the Cold War, India's insular and statist economy was described as the "Licence Raj." Its foreign policy, while firmly nonaligned in principle, had in practice been closer to the Soviet Union than to the West. The end of the Cold War brought about changes that, although not so immediately spectacular as in the ex–Soviet Union, were equally significant in the long term. Under the supervision of the reformist finance minister Manmohan Singh after 1991, the country's economy was deregulated and opened up to the outside world. The country's subsequent increased growth rate, when combined with its vast population and its strategic position in the Indian Ocean, meant that India was bound to become a power to be reckoned with in the long term. By 1998, it had joined the nuclear club, and in 2012 its military budget of $46 billion was the eighth-largest in the world, while in terms of purchasing-power parity it was third. Since the end of the Cold War, India's relations with the West, and in particular with the United States, have improved markedly. But the country cannot be described as a confirmed part of a Western global order, and the long-term implications of its rise remain unclear.

The most important reason for India's strategic shift toward the United States is the rise of China. And it is China's path since its rejection of communist economic orthodoxy in the late 1970s that has most profoundly transformed the global order.

Following the 1949 revolution, China had become a close ally of the Soviet Union, following a policy of "leaning to one side" in the global struggle between communism and capitalism. Economically, too, it had followed the Soviet strategy of forced industrialization focusing on heavy industry, using funds extracted from the dominant agricultural sector. In China's case, the process was somewhat less self-contained than in 1930s Russia simply because the earlier industrial development of the Soviet Union gave China access to funding from a more advanced communist ally. Industrial output rose rapidly, but at the cost of agricultural stagnation and the increasing difficulty of feeding the growing urban population.

After 1958, there was a change in direction. This was the start of a period of Chinese isolation not only from the capitalist West, which had already been the case in the 1950s, but also from the rest of the communist bloc and the third world. In 1960, Mao turned against Soviet influence in China, leading to the breaking off of trade and withdrawal of Soviet advisers. During the 1960s, Chinese propaganda rejected the Soviet policy of coexistence with the West as a betrayal of true revolutionary Marxism and characterized the USSR as a hegemonic power little better than the United States. Tensions between the two communist giants worsened continuously, culminating in a border conflict in 1969. Relations with the third world had been cordial after China participated in the Bandung Conference of 1955, which established the basis of what would later become the Non-Aligned Movement. In the 1960s, however, Chinese advocacy of the principles of mutual respect and nonintervention was replaced by support for Maoist revolutionary movements worldwide, leading to a souring of relations with all but the most radical third-world governments.

Economically, too, China turned in on itself. In 1958, Mao decided to force the pace of change in both agriculture and industry simultaneously, through mass collectivization. The idea was to drive forward modernization through a policy of "self-reliance." The result of the Great Leap Forward, as with Stalin's collectivization of Soviet agriculture thirty years earlier, was mass starvation. When saner economic policies were restored in the early 1960s by the more moderate members of the regime, the focus on self-reliance remained. Mao withdrew to write and ponder the revolution. The result was the Cultural Revolution, unleashed in 1966 as an attack on moderate elements in the country and within the party. Economic progress was once again halted. With these adverse headwinds, it was scarcely surprising that during the 1960s, China's trade stagnated. The country's dependence on the outside world was further diminished by the discovery of substantial quantities of oil. By the end of the decade, China was approaching a state of autarky, even if never quite so absolute a one as in Soviet Russia under Stalin. In 1972, China's trade with the outside world was similar to Taiwan's, even though its population was fifty times larger.

The 1970s witnessed a strategic rethink. The border war with the Soviet Union convinced Mao that Russia was a greater menace than America. In Washington, a parallel thought process suggested that a Sino-American rapprochement would put the Soviet Union on the back foot and ease America's disentanglement from Vietnam. For China, the resumption of relations with the United States was a prelude not only to its return to the United Nations (including membership on the Security Council) but also to trade with the outside world. By the time of Mao's death in 1976, China's trade had more than doubled, albeit from a small base. And whereas in 1955 three-quarters of trade had been conducted with the Soviet bloc, by 1975 more than 80 percent was with the noncommunist world.

The process of opening up to the outside world was the subject of an agonizing debate within the Communist Party. In 1974, an article in the *People's Daily* argued that the new pattern of trade was perfectly compatible with communist orthodoxy. "By advocating the principle of maintaining independence . . . we never mean that we advocate a policy of exclusion . . . We have consistently held that it is necessary to vigorously develop commerce and trade and carry out economic and technical exchanges with various countries."[6] But there were plenty within the party who felt that contact with the capitalist world contravened the communist ideal of self-sufficiency and was bound to end up with the recolonization of the country, turning it into a subservient producer of raw materials. In April 1976, an article in the *Red Flag* reiterated the old socialist shibboleths:

> We import everything that we can produce without restriction, export everything that is badly needed in the country without restriction, buy what is advanced from others, produce what is backward ourselves, and even give to others the sovereign right to open up mineral resources. Then, as time passed, would we not turn our country into a market where the imperialist countries dump their goods, a raw material base, a repair and assembly workshop, and an investment center?[7]

Until Mao's death in September 1976, and after, the issue of integrating China with the world remained undecided. The radical Gang of Four, who advocated a return to the Cultural Revolution, were arrested before they could seize power. Mao's immediate successor, Hua Guofeng, was an advocate of Soviet-style industrial planning. It took until he was replaced by Deng Xiaoping in December 1978 for China's path to become clear. Deng was a veteran of the Long March and had been a rising member of the party elite in the 1950s. He had become an advocate of economic reform after the catastrophic failure of the Great Leap Forward (which he had initially supported), and for this he had been excluded from power for long periods. As recently as February 1976, he had once again been banished from the central organs of the party during the power struggles surrounding Mao's death. Now, at the advanced age of seventy-four, he finally got hold of the reins of government, and the process of economic reform could begin in earnest.

The first stage was to liberalize agriculture, lifting the constricting hand of collectivization and encouraging the "household responsibility system." Farmers were given their own plots of land, and while they still had to allocate a percentage of their production to the government, the surplus could be sold on the free market. The result was a rapid increase in agricultural production, with output growing by over 8 percent per year. In the 1980s, China became a net food exporter, in contrast with prior periods when it had struggled, and sometimes failed, to feed itself. Equally important was the sharp rise in agricultural productivity, enabling more food to be produced with less labor, a process that released excess manpower for the industrial revolution that was starting to take place in the cities.

Industry was encouraged by a process similar to that in agriculture. Enterprises were still nominally state owned, but the percentage of their production that had to be sold at fixed prices was reduced, allowing them to sell the rest for a profit that they were allowed to keep. Companies that were in effect private started up, initially operating under the guise of local collectives until a change in the constitution in 1988 recognized private enterprise as a valid form of organization. A new class of entrepreneurs emerged, as dynamic as any in East Asia. Not surprisingly, the private sector started to increase its market share at the expense of state-run enterprises. The Shanghai stock market, closed by Mao after the revolution, reopened in 1990. After the mid-1980s, failing state-run enterprises were gradually sold off. By the mid-1990s, the private sector overtook the state sector.

Perhaps most important of all was the opening up of the country. In 1980, "special economic zones" were set up in Shenzhen and three other cities. They were granted tax incentives, private property rights were protected, and foreign investment was encouraged. They were expected to focus on export-based industries. Four years later, fourteen coastal cities including Shanghai were given similar concessions. The process has since been gradually extended to many other parts of China, so that now there are few areas of the country that remain outside the reach of the international economy.

Deng characterized the new economic system as "socialism with Chinese characteristics." However, in reality it had nothing to do with socialism at all and was a version of the Japanese growth model that had been adopted progressively by a number of other East Asian countries. This model had always focused on integration into the world economy and had emphasized exports of manufactured and semimanufactured goods in order to pay for raw materials imports. Japan's economic growth rate, impressive since the late nineteenth century, had received an additional boost after the war by very high levels of savings and investment at the expense of domestic consumption. China's new economic system was based on this export-led growth model, although it varied from Japan's in a number of ways. Dependence on foreign investment and exports was considerably higher than in Japan, while domestic consumption was lower. Nonetheless, the system is better described as a Japanese growth model with Chinese characteristics than as socialism with Chinese characteristics. The obvious economic features of socialism, such as state-owned enterprises, remained present, but more as a relic of the past than as an engine of progress. The exception was in strategic sectors such as banking and energy, where the state retained a dominant role.

The results of Deng's economic liberalization were truly impressive. Economic growth over the following twenty years averaged 10 percent per year. By the time of his death in early 1997, the country's GDP had more than quintupled in real terms. The performance of exports, the main driver of this growth, was even more remarkable, increasing by eighteen times over the same period.

In some ways the greatest of Deng's achievements may have been managing the process of liberalization in a way that largely avoided both economic and political pitfalls. Reforms were introduced gradually, on a small scale, and then allowed to develop from the bottom up. At the same time, the firm hand of government was always maintained. This policy avoided the problems experienced by the Soviet Union and its satellites a decade later when they attempted to move to a market economy almost overnight while simultaneously weakening central political control. Politically the process was not without its traumas, particularly in 1989 when hopes that economic freedom would be matched by political freedom were suppressed by tanks. The Tiananmen Square massacre came close to derailing the project of economic reform, partly because of Western economic sanctions and partly because of the reaction against the reform process within the Communist Party itself. It was not until 1992 that Deng managed to reassert his authority and reaffirm the commitment to economic liberalization. Deng's final achievement was to put an end to the cult of the single great leader who would govern until his death and leave behind him a destabilizing power struggle with an uncertain outcome. By semiretiring early and establishing an orderly process of succession, Deng made it far more likely that his reforms would endure.

And endure they did. Ten years after his death in 1997, the Chinese economy had grown a further two and a half times. Performance was again driven largely by exports, which grew by nearly seven times over the same period. In 1980, despite its enormous population, China had been only the world's ninth-largest economy. By 2000, it had risen to sixth. Ten years later it was second, overtaking France, Britain, Germany, and finally Japan.

China's rise posed a number of questions. Instead of focusing on self-sufficiency or on the export of raw materials, China had transformed itself into an industrial powerhouse that depended on the import of raw materials and the export of manufactured goods. In this way, its position had become similar to that of Britain, Germany, and Japan, whose desire to secure raw materials and markets had led to two world wars. The conflicts of the first half of the century had been resolved by the acceptance by the industrialized West of unchallenged American leadership and military dominance. But would China be willing to accept American tutelage and protection?

The question was an obvious one because China, unlike the Asian Tigers, had not grown up under the American umbrella. Since 1949, it had been a committed adherent of a rival ideology and had fought the United States directly in Korea, indirectly in Vietnam, and rhetorically throughout the world. It was one thing for the countries of Eastern Europe to become committed members of the Western alliance when the Soviet bloc collapsed at the end of the 1980s. But these countries had had communism imposed on them at the point of a gun, and it never felt like a true part of their national identities. They rapidly adopted not only Western-style capitalism but also Western-style democracy. This was far from the case in China. Even more than Russia, it remained committed to its communist past even as it abandoned communism's economic principles. Far from moving to democracy, it remained determined to maintain the rule of the party. No statues of Mao were toppled in Beijing in the way that Lenin and Stalin were deposed from their pedestals in Moscow and

St. Petersburg. If a nominally democratic Russian Federation had a hard time deciding if it would join or oppose the West, it was unlikely that a still communist China would find it any easier.

Yet answering this question was more urgent because of the country's sheer size. Other East Asian Tigers, such as South Korea, Taiwan, or even Japan, had populations that were a fraction of America's. Quite apart from their desire for American protection against a Communist threat, their appetite for raw materials was unlikely to stretch global supplies to the extent of bringing them into excessive competition with other industrial nations. This was not the case with China. Its population was the largest in the world, and although it was well endowed with many natural resources, by the twenty-first century the pace of its development was starting to put severe pressure on the supply of a number of important commodities. The country ceased to be self-sufficient in oil after 1993, and is now the second-largest importer in the world. Around 2005, its growing appetite started to push up international prices. China is the world's largest producer of iron ore and the third-largest producer of copper, but the pace of its growth has been such that its imports of both commodities grew rapidly after 2000 and started affecting international prices after 2004–2005. Food production kept pace with consumption until around 2000, but China is now a significant net food importer and has effectively abandoned the goal of remaining self-sufficient.

In public, Chinese officials have never hesitated to reiterate the party line that the country's newfound economic power would not threaten world peace in any way. For many years they propagated the concept of China's "peaceful rise." In 2005, as economists were already starting to forecast the day when China's economy would become as large as America's, the word "rise," even with the adjective "peaceful" in front of it, started to seem too provocative, and the wording was changed to "peaceful development." That year, the China State Council published *China's Peaceful Development Road*, which put the principle clearly: "China will unswervingly follow the road of peaceful development . . . devoting itself to building a harmonious world by sustained peace and common prosperity . . . China did not seek hegemony in the past, nor does it now, and will not do so in the future when it gets stronger. China's development will never pose a threat to anyone."[8] To back this up, China could quite rightly point out that so far the country's extraordinary economic advance had occurred without causing any threat or disruption to the world order.

And yet it was not quite so straightforward as such mellifluous assertions made it appear. The guiding principle of Chinese relations with the outside world since 1978 has been Deng's dictum of "hide your strength, bide your time." This principle implicitly raises the question of whether official statements are merely a temporary tactic until the country becomes strong enough to assert itself. China has always made it clear that while it does not seek hegemony itself, neither should any other country. In the 1970s, China put forward an alternative tripartite subdivision of the planet. In its view, the "Three Worlds" were composed not of capitalist, communist, and third world but of the two hegemons, their allies, and the third world. By advancing this scheme, China subtly promoted the Soviet Union from the second to the first world, while demoting itself from the second to the third. This exercise served two purposes. It put an end to the idea that China should "lean to one side" in the conflict between capitalism and communism (and by implication justified China's relations with the United States). And it simultaneously allowed China to attack both superpowers from the position of one of the unprivileged. This strategy proved fertile, and China has never ceased to condemn the concept of hegemony. China therefore portrays itself as a nonthreatening power while at the same time being a challenger to the status quo. In 2002, for instance, the soon to be named president Hu Jintao was able to find a new justification for China's rising strength. "As China develops," he said, "we will simply have more resources to oppose hegemonism and power politics."[9] Given that since 1991 there was only one country that could be described as a hegemon, there was no doubt at which country Hu's comments were directed.

In theory, China's advocacy of harmonious cooperation rather than hegemony should make it a staunch member of the United Nations and other international bodies. Yet it has often resisted attempts to assume more international responsibility. Some Chinese officials have denounced the very idea of "responsibility" as a Western trap designed to shackle the country. According to an article published in the journal of the International Department of the Chinese Communist Party in November 2011, "The very concept of 'great power responsibility' is flawed as all it does is serve the global hegemon by compromising the sovereignty of other states, holding these states accountable to so-called 'universal' values that were invented by an exclusive group of dominant states."[10]

Underneath the declarations of party officials lies a wide spectrum of Chinese opinion that rejects the current global order. At one end there are sophisticated attempts, such as Zhao Tingyang's 2005 book *The Tianxia System*, to propagate an alternative "Chinese" global morality in which timeless Chinese values of peace and order are contrasted to a Western history of international anarchy and violence.[11] At the other end of the spectrum are the rising voices of extreme nationalists with an aching desire to avenge China's "century of humiliation" from the Opium War of 1840 until the Communist victory in 1949. These voices rise up and demand retaliation for any perceived attack on the country. To some extent they have been encouraged by the government which, since Tiananmen Square, has fostered a more nationalist education system, with the result that, as Peter Gries observes in *China's New Nationalism*, "ironically, the 'fourth generation' appears to find the new victimization narrative of Chinese suffering at the hands of Western imperialists appealing precisely because they, unlike older Chinese, have never been directly victimized."[12] The China scholar David Shambaugh describes seven different schools of Chinese opinion, from "Nativists" (unreconstructed

Maoists and extreme nationalists), through "Realists" (particularly prevalent in the military) who argue that the United States is fundamentally hostile and that China should stand up for itself, all the way to "Globalists" who believe in participation in the existing order. As he says, "The center of gravity on the spectrum does not lie in the middle or toward the Globalist end of the spectrum; rather, it resides down toward the left end, anchored on the Realists but with a strong pull from the Nativists."[13]

In other words, China's position in relation to the existing global order is a good deal more ambivalent than official statements imply. Insofar as that order has been a de facto Pax Americana, China's position is one of outright rejection. Even its support for a United Nations–led order is uncertain, given that a strong strand of Chinese thought considers that attempts to encourage China to be a responsible "team player" in existing international bodies are simply a covert method of bringing it to heel.

The discrepancy between words and deeds is apparent in military spending. China started its economic reform with a "peace dividend." Under Mao, China had typically spent around 7 percent of GDP on its military, rising to 10 percent in the late 1960s as tensions with the Soviet Union were added to those with the United States. Rapprochement with America in the 1970s meant that China could afford to reduce this heavy economic burden somewhat, but when Deng came to power, military spending still amounted to around 6 percent of GDP. Deng decided that a reduction in the defense budget would be one of the ways to propel economic growth. By the early 1990s, military spending had fallen to around 2 percent of GDP. In this period, China had, in effect, quietly taken another leaf from the Japanese postwar economic miracle and enjoyed the economic benefits of the American military umbrella—without, however, admitting that it was doing so and while continuing to inveigh publicly against hegemonism.

A rethink started in the early 1990s. As long as the Soviet Union existed, it was seen in Beijing as the biggest threat to world peace, and the United States as a relatively benign, or at least less threatening, hegemon. The collapse of the Soviet Union removed the threat that had fostered Sino-American rapprochement. At the same time, adverse American reaction to Tiananmen Square was a prelude to what was perceived as a triumphalist post–Cold War determination to remake the world in America's image. The Gulf War provided an alarming display of American prowess in advanced military technology, which appeared to render traditional massed land-based armies, such as China had hitherto relied on, almost powerless.

As a result, the Chinese abandoned the almost two-decades-old policy of minimal investment in defense. Between 1970 and 1990, military spending had grown by only 1.8 percent per year, considerably less than the rate of inflation. Over the following two decades, it grew by 15.5 percent per year. Before 1990, China had enjoyed a "peace dividend"—a boost to economic growth from falling military spending. After 1990, it was able to enjoy the opposite—a boost to military spending from rapid economic growth. Even with 15.5 percent annual increases in the defense budget, China still spends only around 2 percent of GDP on its military.[14] By 2012, China had easily the second-largest military budget in the world, calculated by the Stockholm International Peace Research Institute (SIPRI) at $166 billion, or $250 billion in purchasing-power-parity terms. To put this in perspective, it was greater than the combined defense budgets of all the other countries of East Asia including Japan, greater than the combined military budgets of China's two giant land neighbors, Russia and India (and, for that matter, greater than the combined defense budgets of Britain, France, and Germany). China's military budget is less than one-third of America's, but only a part of American military spending is focused on East Asia.

Given that China was not facing any major military threats like those of the Cold War, the only logical aim of a military buildup on such a scale had to be geostrategic—to counter the dominance of American power and to put teeth into the country's otherwise toothless antihegemonism rhetoric. It certainly did not look like the act of a country that was willing to accept living under the American military umbrella like other members of the industrialized world.

A crux in Sino-American military relations came during the Taiwanese elections in 1996, when the Taiwanese turned away from the Nationalist Party, which since 1949 had virtually monopolized political power and had always advocated reunification with the mainland (on Nationalist terms), in favor of a party that argued for independence. An intimidatory Chinese barrage of rockets close to the island was countered by the arrival two American carrier fleets to deter any thoughts of invasion.

This reminder of China's powerlessness to achieve one of its most sacrosanct national objectives in the face of American military dominance was a watershed. A military modernization program was undertaken with the ultimate objective of denying the United States access to the China seas. Like the Soviet naval buildup after the 1950s, the approach was asymmetric, focusing on submarines and missiles rather than on attempting to rival American dominance in aircraft carriers. In 1999, the Chinese navy introduced the ultraquiet *Song*-class diesel-electric submarine armed with hard-to-evade wake-homing torpedoes. In 2006, one of these submarines shocked the American navy by surfacing undetected within the protective screen of the carrier *Kitty Hawk*. Even more eye-catching was the development of a land-based maneuverable ballistic missile, known as the Dong-Feng ("East Wind") DF21D, designed specifically to destroy moving aircraft carriers within a radius of over one thousand miles of the Chinese coast. The connection of Chinese military planning to the 1996 Taiwan Straits Crisis is shown in the memories of a US Army attaché in Beijing at the time. "The first time a senior Chinese military officer of the General Staff Department mentioned ballistic missiles attacking aircraft carriers was after our two carriers showed up, and he put his arm around me and said we're going to sink your carriers with ballistic missiles, and we had a long conversation about it."[15]

If the Chinese military buildup was intended only to prevent American meddling in the matter of Taiwan, it might have only local significance. However, its strategic implications are far wider than that. Taiwan is important to China not just because its return would symbolize the definitive end of the "century of humiliation" when the province was lost to Japan. Taiwan sits in the middle of a chain of small islands from Japan in the north to the Philippines in the south. Together they block China's access to the Pacific. Taiwan's return to the mainland would open a crucial breach in this wall. To Japan, however, the issue is seen in the reverse:

> Taiwan serves as a critical component of Japan's sea-lane. If Taiwan were integrated into China, the South China Sea would become China's sea, bringing the sea lane to the Middle East and Southeast Asian countries under strong Chinese influence. If the East China Sea were brought under Chinese influence . . . the Korean Peninsula will fall under the sphere of Chinese influence. Moreover, China will probably use Taiwan as a stepping-stone and make its way into the Pacific . . . Taiwan is Japan's "lifeline."[16]

Many strategists feel that the United States has no good answer to land-based antiship missiles and that its vaunted carrier force risks being made redundant by a new wave of military technology, just as the battleship was made redundant by the advent of aircraft carriers in the 1920s and '30s. They worry that Chinese antiaccess and area-denial strategies (A2/AD in military parlance) are already starting the make the China seas too dangerous for the US Navy to control. In 2010, James Kraska wrote a darkly foreboding piece recounting "How the United States Lost the Naval War of 2015" when a surprise Chinese ballistic missile attack destroyed the USS *George Washington* in the East China Sea.[17]

The western Pacific is full of countries that depend on trade and whose vital sea-lane security has been provided by the US Navy. Japan, in particular, was reconciled to the postwar order by giving up its quest for empire in exchange for American protection. If this protection is threatened by a Chinese military buildup that reflects the country's refusal to accept Pax Americana, the underlying premises of the postwar order may start to unravel.

In fact there is evidence that they are already unraveling. Japan has elected a conservative prime minister who is intent on altering the country's pacifist postwar constitution and has started to upgrade its military forces. Japan's actions are part of a general trend in the neighborhood. The countries around the western Pacific from the Koreas to Australia are involved in a quiet but accelerating naval arms race. In 2010, Toshi Yoshihara and James Holmes, of the U.S. Naval War College, observed that

> a naval arms race is gathering pace in the Asia-Pacific. It will be unlike the competition that gripped Europe over a century ago, when the great powers sought to outdo each other in the number and tonnage of warships. Today, a major component of this maritime rivalry is taking place in the murky world of undersea warfare where, instead of the big-gun battleships that became the hallmark of the arms buildup prior to World War I, nations over the next decade will put to sea small, seemingly unassuming submarines.[18]

Submarines and antisubmarine warfare are the major elements in this new arms race because the principal concern of the trading states of East Asia is the protection of their sea lines of communication and, possibly (although this is unspoken), the ability to blockade potential enemies. Since the article was written, the race is starting to become visible on the surface as well, with the launch of China's first aircraft carrier and of two Japanese helicopter carriers that in the eyes of many are small aircraft carriers in all but name.

In 2007, the historian Paul Kennedy wrote an article for *The New York Times* in which he pointed out that the Asian focus on expanding naval power contrasted with a near-complete European apathy on the subject, and asked rhetorically: "What do naval strategic planners in the one continent assume about the future of the world that the planners in the second continent do not?"[19]

The objective of naval power, now as in the nineteenth century, is not only to protect sea lines of communication but also to gain access to strategic raw materials. The China seas are home to a series of uninhabited islands that are the fulcrums of increasingly acrimonious disputes between China and its neighbors. In the East China Sea, both Japan and China lay claim to the Senkaku (in Japanese) or Diaoyu (in Chinese) Islands. In the South China Sea, there is an even more convoluted set of claims to the Spratly and Paracel Islands, which in different points involves China, Taiwan, the Philippines, Vietnam, Malaysia, Indonesia, and Brunei. At stake in both these seas is control of fishing rights, which have taken on a growing importance as China becomes more deficient in domestic food production for an increasingly wealthy population that is moving to a more protein-rich diet. Even more important are the prospective oil and natural gas reserves under both seas—crucial strategic prizes for countries that depend heavily on imported fuel. In addition the South China Sea, now claimed almost in its entirety by China, is, as the writer Robert Kaplan notes, where global sea routes coalesce, with more than half of the world's annual merchant tonnage traversing it. Over the past years there have been a series of incidents in the two seas involving fishing vessels, coast guards, naval vessels, and military aircraft. Kaplan calls the South China Sea "Asia's Cauldron"—a description that could equally fit the East China Sea, where the situation is only one error away from military conflict.[20]

The answer to Paul Kennedy's rhetorical question about different attitudes to naval power is that it is impossible to translate these Asian disputes into a European context. The idea of the countries bordering the North Sea building up their navies so that they can contest control of oil reserves is inconceivable. The lessons of the world wars have been far too deeply instilled in the Old Continent. Not so in the Far East, where it seems that the rise of a great power that rejects American military dominance is already causing the region to revert to a pre-1914 mind-set, even while the US Navy still appears to rule the waves.

China's attitude toward raw materials within its land borders has also alarmed its neighbors. It controls around 90 percent of the worldwide production of rare earths—obscure metals vital for advanced electronics. In the 1990s, China put almost all foreign producers out of business by undercutting them. After 2009, it cut back on exports so as to advantage local manufacturing. Worse, it appears to have used a sharp reduction in export quotas in 2011 to put pressure on Japan over their island disputes. Such actions go to the heart of the postwar economic settlement in which all countries would be assured access to vital raw materials without political interference. The rules of GATT (and subsequently the WTO) have always prohibited artificial restrictions on exports as well as imports. In 2012, Japan, together with the United States, the European Union, and a number of other countries, took the rare earth issue to the WTO, which ruled against China at the end of October 2013.

A similar attitude is manifest toward the least rare mineral of earth: water. China's assertion of sovereignty over Tibet has allowed it to control the source of many of the most important river systems in East and South Asia, including the Mekong, the Irtysh, the Brahmaputra, and the Irawaddy, which provide crucial water supplies to Vietnam, Kazahkstan, Bangladesh, India, and Burma. China is one of three countries that have failed to sign the 1997 UN Convention on International Watercourses, which protects the rights of downstream water users, and its plans to dam, and possibly divert, these rivers has been causing anxiety and even outrage among its neighbors.[21]

If China's neighbors are anxious about their water supplies,

China itself is equally anxious about its dependence on imported raw materials. It is not just in the China seas that Beijing is seeking to get control of crucial resources. For many years China was willing simply to translate almost the entirety of its growing trade surplus into foreign-exchange reserves. But since the mid-2000s, it has been using an increasing percentage of its surpluses to make investments in overseas resources. In 2012, it invested nearly $80 billion, compared to less than $10 billion in 2005, becoming the third-largest overseas investor in the world. The principal focus has been on energy ($320 billion currently invested) and mining ($110 billion).[22] However, it has also made the news by buying up vast tracts of land in Africa and South America for food production.

Yet in practice, China faces a number of currently insuperable obstacles in its objective of assuaging its anxiety by getting control of foreign sources of supply. The country has made what seem to be very large investments in overseas production, but they pale compared to its imports. In 2012, oil production from fields in which Chinese companies had an equity stake covered less than one-third of the country's import requirements,[23] and this figure is likely to decline given the rate of growth of imports, even on optimistic assumptions about further increases in production.[24] One of China's problems is that, as a latecomer to the table, it has found that most of the world's potential oil and mineral resources are already locked up. Much of the oil reserves are firmly in the hands of state-owned companies that are reluctant to dilute their control. Even where resources are open to foreign investment, the forces of economic nationalism still operate. Host nations are made more wary by the fact that China's strategic investments are invariably made by state-owned companies. The United States blocked China National Offshore Oil Corporation's planned acquisition of the American oil company Unocal in 2005, encouraging a merger with another American firm instead. In 2008, Chinalco (Aluminum Corporation of China) managed to obtain a 9 percent stake in the British-Australian Rio Tinto, one of the world's three largest mining companies, but plans to double its stake ran afoul of Australian concerns about China gaining control of vital mineral resources.

But even if it were able to acquire control of greater quantities of raw materials, China's geostrategic anxieties would not go away. Only around 12 percent of its oil imports come overland (from Russia and Kazakhstan); the rest have to go by sea. This leaves the country with what Hu Jintao identified as the "Malacca Dilemma" in November 2003. Hu was referring to the Malacca Straits through which almost all of China's trade with the Middle East, Africa, and Europe has to pass. Hu noted that "certain powers have all along encroached on and tried to control navigation through the strait."[25] The reference to the United States (and before it to Great Britain) was oblique but clear. China, in other words, is vulnerable to the shutting off of its sea trade by a strategic rival. In order to get around the Malacca Dilemma, the Beijing government has been proposing oil pipelines from China to the Indian Ocean through Myanmar and through Pakistan. However, most analysts doubt that this will relieve the problem, even when and if they are completed, because the oil will still have to be transported from the Persian Gulf to the pipeline terminals over seas that China does not control, and because fixed pipelines are more vulnerable to attack than mobile tankers.[26]

Of course, in reality, China has no more of a "dilemma" than Japan, Taiwan, or South Korea, all of which depend on the Malacca Straits for their trade. The rulers of these countries do not lose sleep about the problem, for the simple reason that they are pleased, rather than worried, that the US Navy is in a position to control such a vital sea-lane. That the Malacca Straits pose a dilemma for China is a reflection of the dangers inherent in a return to a pre-1914 mind-set.

Many commentators have noted the parallels between China's position today and that of Germany in the decades before the First World War. The issue has even been included in a twelve-part television series in China that looked at the rise and fall of empires over the past centuries.[27] The question is usually portrayed as one of the tensions between an established and a rising power—in the nineteenth century between Great Britain and Germany, now between America and China. Will the established power attempt to hem in its challenger, and will this lead to an explosion as the challenger attempts to claim a place in the world order commensurate with its economic strength? According to John Mearsheimer, such conflicts are inevitable simply because military power is the surest means of assuring self-preservation, and all great powers inevitably attempt to create regional hegemonies to protect themselves: "A wealthy China would not be a status quo power but an aggressive state determined to achieve regional hegemony. This is not because a rich China would have wicked motives, but because the best way for any state to maximize its prospects for survival is to become the hegemon in its region of the world."[28]*

It is easy to see how this picture fits with the rise of Imperial Germany and its aim to establish a predominant position in Europe. But the parallels are more multidimensional than this. China's emphasis on its "peaceful rise," for instance, can be compared to Bismarck's careful diplomacy after 1870, aiming to consolidate Germany's position while making as few enemies as possible (barring the irreconcilable France, of course). The country's more assertive stance since 2009 seems to parallel the more aggressive international policies adopted by William II and his chancellors after the 1890s once Germany's economic rise had brought it to the point of overtaking Britain. The result in both cases was to scare neighboring countries, including those as far afield as India,

---

* In an updated 2014 edition of his book, Mearsheimer discusses developments in the thirteen years since it was first published, which seem to confirm his analysis. Mearsheimer looks at the idea that economic interdependence makes war prohibitively expensive, but argues that such considerations must inevitably take a back seat to the inherent drive of Great Powers for hegemonic status.

into forming alliances against what they saw as a dangerous and aggressive nation.

Strategically, Imperial Germany, like China today, found that it was a latecomer to the competition for global resources. It had to make do with acquisitions in Africa that seemed mere crumbs compared to the colonial empires of Britain, France, or even Portugal, which had the unfair advantage of historical precedence. The percentage of its imports that it could source from its overseas possessions was small compared to its needs. In the meantime, Germany, again like China traditionally a land power, now found it needed a navy to protect its international trade that could otherwise be throttled by the existing maritime superpower. Moreover, its geographic position was hemmed in by offshore islands controlled by its potential enemies. The only way to ensure control of the sea-lanes on which it depended was to build up a powerful naval presence able to threaten Britain's local maritime dominance and deny it access to the seas around Germany's shores.

Germany's naval strategy was only a partial success. It managed to deny Britain access to the Baltic, but Britain simply compensated by exploiting Germany's equivalent of the Malacca Dilemma—its reliance on the North Sea passage between Scotland and Norway, which the British could blockade from their naval base at Scapa Flow in the Orkney Islands. American strategists now suggest that in a future conflict, the United States follow a similar strategy rather than rely on a hazardous "air-sea battle" designed to knock out Chinese land-based missile capabilities at the start of a conflict.[29] Douglas Peifer of the Air War College in Montgomery, Alabama, argues that

> the United States need not fret too much over its pending loss of command of the China Seas: given geographical, political, and technological realities, it can maintain its command of the Indian and Pacific Oceans while all China can do is deny

access to a limited maritime sphere ringed by choke points, competitor powers, and American military power . . . Much like Britain could choke off German trade and commerce in both world wars without contesting the North Sea, so the United States can impose a distant blockade on China should China choose use of force against U.S. interests in East Asia.[30]

Military strategists are paid to plan for all types of confrontations, even if they are not particularly likely. The US Navy had plans for taking on the Royal Navy (and vice versa) well into the interwar period when such a conflict was a very remote possibility. However, the sheer volume of publicly available articles from official and semiofficial sources positing a Sino-American military confrontation is worrying. It suggests that even if such a conflict is still unlikely, and even if the global geopolitical and military balance still suggests an overwhelming American predominance, the world is already reverting to a dangerous multipolar way of thinking.

Some commentators have noted that as in the early twentieth century, a rising tide of mutual suspicion makes it harder for both sides to avoid hostility. There is a tendency to discount conciliatory official statements, even though they reflect significant strands of opinion within each country. Peter Gries points out that the existence of a large body of official and popular opinion that treats the other side as a threat tends to drown out more moderate voices and risks becoming a self-fulfilling prophecy: "Indulging in fits of self-righteous anger . . . America bashers in China and China bashers in the United States seem oblivious to the impact that their polemics have on their foreign counterparts. While blaming others may be emotionally gratifying, it is dangerous, because excessive criticism can create an escalating pattern of abuse, in which criticism begets criticism."[31]

It is not as if other voices do not exist. There is a strong strand of opinion among well-informed observers that China's rise need not lead to conflict. Alastair Johnston argues that as a major participant in and beneficiary of the global economy, China is forced to become a status quo power:

> It strains logic to say, as many in the policy and pundit world do, that China is dissatisfied with the international "rules of the game" when these same individuals also say that Chinese leaders base their legitimacy on economic growth. Chinese leaders recognize that this economic growth—hence their legitimacy—comes from integration into the global capitalist institutions, not isolation from them or attempts to alter them fundamentally.[32]

John Ikenberry strikes a similar note:

> The most farsighted Chinese leaders understand that globalization has changed the game and that China accordingly needs strong, prosperous partners around the world. From the United States' perspective, a healthy Chinese economy is vital to the United States and the rest of the world. Technology and the global economic revolution have created a logic of economic relations that is different from the past—making the political and institutional logic of the current order all the more powerful.[33]

Ikenberry, like most commentators, accepts that the "unipolar" moment of American dominance will pass, but there is no reason to fear a return of a multipolar world when the forces of interdependence centered on multilateral organizations can keep the peace. All that is necessary is to still the self-destructive voices of competitive nationalism.

The trouble with these arguments is that they are based on the same premise as those of the liberal free traders of the nineteenth century. The amicable ties of commerce were supposed to replace the futile military competition of earlier centuries. By making econ-omies interdependent, trade would make war so costly that it would cease to be a practical tool of statecraft. Yet in 1914, the countries of Europe went to war in spite of the bonds of trade that united them. And in many ways it was the insecurities created by their increasing dependence on trade that drove them to fight each other.

This book has come a full circle. We seem to be back to the late nineteenth century with its combination of peace and prosperity, punctured only by a growing sense of geopolitical uncertainty. What it there to suggest that this time is different?

The peace of the post-1945 era was arguably based on at least eight different elements. What are they, and how far are they still alive and well?

1. The lessons of history. There is no doubt that memories of the horrors of the two world wars have acted as a significant disin-centive to conflict. Nowhere is this truer than in Europe, where the European Union is regularly justified as a way out of the carnage of the first half of the twentieth century. How-ever, one of the main lessons of history is that history lessons are eventually forgotten. This holds as true of geopolitics as of finance. It is too much to hope that this particular underpin-ning of peace will last forever. Moreover, what is true of Eu-rope does not seem to apply in the Far East. It took two world wars for Europeans to be convinced of the futility of war and for France and Germany to make a profound and lasting peace. In the Far East, the "Second" World War was in reality only the first. This may explain why the hatreds generated by the conflict have not yet been resolved, and why Japan, whose wartime objectives were in some ways more similar to Impe-rial Germany's than to Hitler's, is reluctant to apologize with what its victims perceive as sufficient sincerity. Even within Europe, the lessons of history appear to be read differently in

the East. Russia, in spite of suffering more than any other country in two wars, seems psychically closer to interwar than to postwar Germany. In this mind-set, the collapse of the Soviet empire, like that of Imperial Germany, was due to defeatist politicians at home rather than military defeat. Vladimir Putin's reading of history appears to be that its verdict should be overturned.

2. The Cold War. Ironically, the enduring hostility between Western capitalism and Soviet communism proved to be one of the most effective buttresses of peace—albeit an unquiet peace. It divided the world into two camps, only one of which participated in the global economy, and it encouraged the Western capitalist nations to cooperate and to accept American supremacy. It goes without saying that this incongruous but effective pillar of peace no longer exists. It is always possible that the intense Soviet-American hostility of the Cold War could be replaced by an equally intense Sino-American hostility. But such a standoff would be substantively different from the Cold War in that it would not be buttressed by the indifference of one side to securing access to international resources.

3. The United Nations. The continued existence of the United Nations is not in doubt, but its value as a preserver of the peace is questionable. It is certainly an improvement on the informal conference system of the pre-1914 era and on the League of Nations of the interwar period—it meets regularly and countries do not refuse to participate. However, it can be effective only on the basis of consensus among the major powers, and it is not clear that any such consensus would prevail in a multipolar world. During the Cold War, the Security Council was hobbled by the veto power of the superpowers, and the same tendency to gridlock is apparent now that the momentary appearance of consensus at the end of the Cold War is a thing of the past.

4. Pax Americana. Uncontested American supremacy was a crucial element in the peaceful functioning of the noncommunist world during the Cold War. But now that capitalism (euphemistically described as "socialism with Chinese characteristics") has been adopted by a rising power that rejects the idea of Pax Americana entirely, its future is uncertain. Perhaps it is possible to envisage the peaceful replacement of Pax Americana by a Pax Sino-Americana, in which the United States accommodates a rising China in the same way that Britain accommodated a rising America at the end of the nineteenth century—by allowing China to have regional hegemony in East Asia, while America retains its predominant position elsewhere in the world. However, this possibility runs afoul of two objections. Britain cooperated with the United States because of greater threats to its security from elsewhere. There is no evidence that a two-power division of the world could run smoothly without such an incentive to cooperate rather than compete. Moreover, there is little to suggest that a Pax Sinica would be an acceptable substitute for Pax Americana in East Asia, given that the new hegemon has so far shown itself to be far from benign, displaying a tendency to bully its potential clients over such things as offshore oil resources, water supplies, and access to rare earths. Most East Asian countries are vocal in their desire for the United States to remain in the region.

5. Free trade. If states are not to return to self-destructive competition for resources, free trade remains a sine qua non of peace. Pax Americana would never have worked if the United States had remained protectionist. So far free trade seems to be pretty resilient, having survived the Great Recession in better shape than many initially expected. Compared to the nineteenth century, free trade has the advantage of being embedded in international organizations and agreements, in particular the WTO. However, it is worth noting that free trade is far from

absolute in the modern world and that further progress appears to have slowed to stall speed. Agriculture and energy remain subject to extensive government restrictions. The European Commission has recently noted an ominous drift toward potentially trade-restrictive measures among emerging economies.[34] Perhaps the biggest threat to free trade could paradoxically turn out to be the globalization that the West did so much to foster. The inevitable result of this process was the incorporation into the global economy of billions of low-paid workers from the third world, which has led to a protracted squeeze, first on working-class and subsequently on middle-class incomes in developed countries. So far this process has not translated into more than sporadic calls for protection, but what the future holds is unclear.

6. Financial interdependence. The outbreak of war in 1914 triggered the largest and most global financial crisis to that date. The crisis might have brought the war to an end even before it truly started, but governments ignored it and rapidly found ways to place their economies on a war footing. Over the following one hundred years, global financial interdependence has increased sharply. Levels of credit as a percentage of GDP have grown, as has the percentage of debt held by foreign creditors and the velocity of financial trading. The outbreak of war among major powers would undoubtedly trigger a financial crisis on a scale and speed that would make 1914 look archaic. The questions are: Would the threat of financial meltdown prevent war from occurring? And if it did occur, would governments be able to adjust their financial systems to a war footing once again? The jury is obviously out on both questions, but on the second there is some reason to suspect that the limits of government intervention have not yet been reached. The 2008 financial crisis threatened the global financial system with collapse. It was resolved by government intervention, both fiscal and monetary, on a hitherto unimagined peacetime scale. Yet

in many ways the level of government intervention did not come close to the wartime controls imposed in 1914–1918 or in 1939–1945.

7. Decolonization. The breakup of the European empires, even though it has often created its own sources of conflict, has contributed to the postwar peace among the Great Powers by breaking up economic blocs and reducing the causes of friction and envy that helped spur wars. Even if the economic pressures of a competitive multipolar world were to push toward a return of colonialism, it is hard to imagine any return to the formal empire building of the nineteenth century. The difficulties encountered by the United States in Iraq and Afghanistan are an indication that what seemed so easy in the nineteenth century is no longer so. Even more indirect forms of economic colonization are hard to establish firmly, given the hypersensitivity of third-world countries to "neocolonialism" in any shape or form. Some African voices are already leveling the *n*-word accusation at China.

8. Nuclear weapons. Free trade encourages states to believe that they can obtain the resources necessary for their survival without resort to force or empire building. However, it requires the backup of an enforcement mechanism. The problem goes back to the observation by the League of Nations in 1921 that the war had shown that economic interdependence was potentially harmful unless "a super-State organization could guarantee the continuity [of free trade] even through a period of economic crisis, and if it could also exclude the possibility of war."[35] Given the inherent limitations of the United Nations and the uncertainty over the future of Pax Americana, it appears that the role of global enforcer may be left to nuclear weapons. There is little doubt that the balance of nuclear terror helped ensure that the simmering tensions of the Cold War never boiled over. However, nuclear arsenals are at best an

uncomfortable method of maintaining peace. And in a context where Pax Americana had been replaced by a multipolar balance of power, they would have to operate largely unaided in a world that had rediscovered the perils of unbridled competition for resources. The idea of a return to the competitive multipolar world of the early twentieth century is not a pleasing one, and the idea of Kaiser Wilhelm and Tsar Nicholas armed with nuclear weapons does not make the notion any more attractive.

Given this at best mixed report card for the props of postwar peace, what is the outlook? Current trends are not at all encouraging. During the time it took to research and write this book, levels of tension in the Far East and in Europe have risen from barely perceptible to headline news. Are there any possible solutions for the problems that this book outlines, or are we destined to enter a period of ever increasing geopolitical instability?

More than ten years ago, books like Michael Klare's *Resource Wars* argued convincingly that the looming global competition for energy supplies was a threat to world peace.[36] Today, the use of fracking technology to release untapped reserves of oil and gas has changed this narrative. Indeed, it is said that America's return to energy independence is also changing the geopolitical outlook. It will not only ease pressures on global supplies of oil and gas but will also mean that there is less reason for the United States to get involved in the dangerous competition for oil from the Middle East or the ex-Soviet states in Central Asia. American gas exports may also be able to offset Europe's dangerous dependence on Russian gas.

Underlying this line of argument is a twenty-first-century revival of the theory, so prevalent in the 1930s, that self-sufficiency is a route to peace. The problem, of course, is that America was self-sufficient in oil in the 1930s, but this did not in any way save the world from war. All that happened was that the comforting feeling of economic autonomy reinforced American isolationism—

with disastrous consequences for the maintenance of global peace. The economic insecurity of have-not countries such as Germany and Japan was in no way relieved by America's energy independence, nor was it mitigated by the fact that there was a global oversupply of commodities. The fact remains that it is inconceivable, short of an unanticipated scientific and technological revolution, that the whole world would suddenly become self-sufficient in energy, let alone in other resources. In these circumstances, economic security for one country is possible only at the expense of others—with the dangerous results that this book has narrated.

Fortunately, it seems unlikely that a new American isolationism will gain much traction, even though opinion polls show that the American public is increasingly wary of foreign entanglements. Quite apart from powerful memories of the consequences of American isolationism between the wars, the country has too much at stake throughout the world to retreat from it. The United States will, in all likelihood, stay center stage in world affairs.

The question remains whether there is any strategy that can prevent the world from descending into competitive multipolarity. America's current approach involves reinforcing its regional alliances so as to contain the revisionist powers' expansionism, while hoping to cajole them into accepting the existing world order. While the maintenance of existing alliances is certainly essential in order to avoid further fragmentation, the problem with a strategy of containment is that it reinforces Russia's and China's sense of encirclement and encourages them to create a powerful opposing bloc.

To avoid such an outcome, containment should be balanced by continuing attempts to encourage the revisionist powers to join expanded versions of the existing Western security arrangements. This was the principle that governed relations with Russia in the 1990s, when the aim was to bring Russia "into the defense community of democratic nations." Such ideas have fallen by the wayside in the light of recent events, but they should not be abandoned as a long-term goal. The situation in the Far East is more fluid and, in many ways, more complex. Regional security has never been formalized into a NATO-like structure. However, the creation of an Asian security system that includes China as well as the United States may be the best hope of peace. The Australian writer Hugh White has proposed a "Concert of Asia" that would include the United States, China, Japan, and India, modeled on the Concert of Europe that helped keep the peace (albeit with only temporary success, as noted in the first chapter) in the nineteenth century.[37]

Since any broadly based Asian security system would require the reconciliation of regional enemies, a second method of encouraging peaceful coexistence would be to take a leaf from the means by which Europe overcame the historic antagonisms of its greatest powers. The conflict between France and Germany was based on, as much as anything else, a competition for coal and iron ore. The decision to share these crucial resources was the beginning of their reconciliation. The same principle could be applied to the China Seas, where competition for potential energy reserves lies at the center of the conflict between China and Japan over the Diaoyu/Senkaku islands. Such an idea is not far-fetched, given that an agreement in principle to share these resources was negotiated in 2008, before the subsequent escalation in tension. As in postwar Europe, the United States is well placed to encourage such an arrangement since it has no interest in the resources themselves.

An Asian-American security system that incorporates a country as powerful as China would represent a dilution of Pax Americana, but it would not eliminate it. Of course, such an arrangement would not fulfill China's dream of a United States–free western Pacific, and would therefore fall short of completely reversing the country's "century of humiliation" by reestablishing its historic position as the dominant power in East Asia. But in a globalized world, such dreams are an unaffordable luxury. The history of the twentieth century shows that a system of competing regional power blocs is a recipe for disaster. If the world is to avoid a return to competitive multipolarity, it is crucial that the United States retains its global presence.

After the Second World War, the Western countries showed they had learned from the blood-stained history of the first half of the century by setting aside their historical differences and prospering under an American umbrella. Stalin refused to believe this was possible: the capitalist countries would never accept Pax Americana. In his view, onetime great powers such as Germany and Japan were "languishing in misery under the jackboot of American imperialism." To think they would not "try to get on their feet again, will not try to smash the US regime . . . is to believe in miracles." By a terrible irony of history, Stalin's reasoning, completely wrong in the case of postwar Germany and Japan, can be applied only too well to post–Cold War Russia and China.

Russian history relates that its greatest moment of power was squandered by defeatist politicians, and that the West took advantage of a moment of weakness to strip it of its geopolitical patrimony. Chinese history relates that the golden age of European empires was a moment of unprecedented humiliation for China and unprecedented glory for Europeans. Such national experiences run deep. It is understandable that the two countries wish to resume what they see as their rightful places in the world. What is worrying, however, is that the Russian view of history does not appear to have comprehended that its moment of world power was not some global nirvana but an era fraught with danger when world war was avoided in part because of Russia's economic isolation, which no longer exists. At the same time, the Chinese view of history does not appear to have comprehended that, thanks to the rivalries that led them to carve up the world, the apogee of the European empires was a moment not of glory but of hubris followed by inescapable nemesis. Quite different lessons need to be drawn if history is not to repeat itself.

NOTES

Introduction

1. The period from 1945 to 2000 was not devoid of bloodshed, with a total death toll calculated at around 12 million in wars between states. Out of this total, 4.5 million were in the Korean War, the closest approximation to a Great Power war in the period.
2. Richard Cobden speaking in Manchester on January 15, 1846. *Speeches on Questions of Public Policy* (London: Routledge, 1995), 1:363.
3. Angus Maddison estimates world exports as 1 percent of GDP in 1820 and 8.7 percent in 1913 in *Monitoring the World Economy, 1820–1992* (Paris: OECD, 1996), p. 233. Total world trade, defined as the sum of exports and imports, is by definition double those figures, since overall world trade has to be in balance. Throughout the book, figures on foreign trade always indicate the sum of imports and exports.
4. Quoted in Warren F. Kimball, "Lend-Lease and the Open Door: The Temptation of British Opulence, 1937–1942," *Political Science Quarterly* 86, no. 2 (1971): 235.
5. Thomas L. Friedman, *The World Is Flat: A Brief History of the Twenty-first Century* (New York: Farrar, Straus and Giroux, 2005), p. 421.

1. The First Era of Globalization

1. Quoted in Michael Howard, *War and the Liberal Conscience* (New York: Columbia University Press), p. 43.
2. Ibid., p. 37.
3. Ibid., p. 43.

4. Quoted in Harold James, *The End of Globalization: Lessons from the Great Depression* (Cambridge, MA: Harvard University Press, 2001), p. 13.

5. Quoted in Paul Bairoch and Susan Burke, "European Trade Policy, 1815–1914," in *Cambridge Economic History of Europe* (New York: Cambridge University Press, 1989), 8:29.

6. Cobden, *Speeches*, 1:363.

7. Ronald Findlay and Kevin H. O'Rourke, *Power and Plenty: Trade, War, and the World Economy in the Second Millennium* (Princeton, NJ: Princeton University Press, 2007), pp. 378–83.

8. Paul Bairoch, "International Industrialization Levels from 1750 to 1980," *Journal of European Economic History* 11, no. 2 (1982): 269–333.

9. Lord Milner, *The Nation and the Empire* (London: Constable, 1913), p. xxxiii.

10. John B. Parrish, "Iron and Steel in the Balance of World Power," *Journal of Political Economy* 64, no. 5 (1956): 374.

11. Friedrich List, *The National System of Political Economy* (New York: Longmans, Green, 1909), p. 70.

12. Ibid., p. 323.

13. The *Times*, December 1, 1877, quoted in Ross J. S. Hoffmann, *Great Britain and the German Trade Rivalry, 1875–1914* (Philadelphia: University of Pennsylvania Press, 1933), p. 23.

14. Michael Hudson, *Trade, Development and Foreign Debt* (London: Pluto Press, 1993), p. 177.

15. Henry Clay addressing the Senate in February 1832, in Robert C. Byrd, comp., *The Senate 1789–1989, Classic Speeches 1830–1993* (Washington, DC: GPO, 1994), 3:91.

16. Jonathan Steinberg, *Bismarck: A Life* (New York: Oxford University Press, 2011), p. 331.

17. Quoted in Ernest N. Paolino, *The Foundations of American Empire: William Henry Seward and U.S. Foreign Policy* (Ithaca, NY: Cornell University Press, 1973), pp. 27, 29.

18. Quoted in Thomas Packenham, *The Scramble for Africa, 1876–1912* (New York: Random House, 1991), p. 358.

19. List, *National System of Political Economy*, p. 8.

20. Quoted in Paolino, *Foundations of American Empire*, p. 27.

21. Quoted in D. K. Fieldhouse, *Economics and Empire, 1830–1914* (Ithaca, NY: Cornell University Press, 1973), p. 22.

22. Ibid., p. 23.

23. Ibid.

24. General Friedrich von Bernhardi, *Germany and the Next War* (London: Edward Arnold, 1912), p. 82.

25. Benjamin Kidd, *The Control of the Tropics* (New York: Macmillan, 1898), pp. 4–5.

26. Ibid., p. 2.

27. Ibid., pp. 28–29.

28. Quoted in Kenneth E. Boulding and Tapan Mukerjee, eds., *Economic Imperialism* (Ann Arbor: University of Michigan Press, 1972), p. 120.

29. H. J. Mackinder, "The Geographical Pivot of History," *Geographical Journal* 170, no. 4 (1904): 434.

30. A. T. Mahan, *The Interest of America in Sea Power, Present and Future* (Boston: Little, Brown, 1897), pp. 128–29.

31. Christopher M. Clark, *The Sleepwalkers: How Europe Went to War in 1914* (New York: Harper, 2013), p. 149.

32. Jonathan Steinberg, *Yesterday's Deterrent: Tirpitz and the Birth of the German Battle Fleet* (New York: Macmillan, 1965), p. 194.

33. Patrick J. Kelly, *Tirpitz and the Imperial German Navy* (Bloomington: Indiana University Press, 2011), p. 175.

34. Hans Delbrück writing in *Preussische Jahrbücher* in 1912, quoted in Fritz Fischer, *World Power or Decline* (New York: Norton, 1974), p. 68.

35. Paul Kennedy, *The Rise and Fall of the Great Powers* (London: Unwin Hyman, 1988), p. 203.

36. Avner Offer, *The First World War: An Agrarian Interpretation* (New York: Oxford University Press, 1989), p. 218.

37. Royal Commission, *Report of the Royal Commission on the Supply of Food and Raw Materials in Time of War* (London: HMSO, 1905), pp. 35, 44.

38. Niall Ferguson, *The Pity of War* (London: Allen Lane, 1998), p. 92.

39. John A. Hobson, "The Ethics of Internationalism," *International Journal of Ethics* 17, no. 1 (1906): 23.

40. J. A. Hobson, *Imperialism: A Study* (Ann Arbor: University of Michigan Press, 1905), pp. 77–78.

41. Ibid., p. 32.

42. Bairoch, "European Trade Policy, 1815–1914," p. 127.

43. Herbert Feis, *Europe: The World's Banker, 1870–1914* (New Haven, CT: Yale University Press, 1930), pp. 23, 51, 74.

44. Norman Angell, *The Great Illusion* (New York: Putnam, 1910), pp. 28, 52.

45. Quoted in Georges Haupt, *Socialism and the Great War: The Collapse of the Second International* (Oxford: Clarendon Press, 1972), pp. 150–51.

46. Joseph Schumpeter, *Imperialism and Social Classes* (New York: A. M. Kelly, 1951).

47. Frédéric Bastiat, *The Fallacies of Protection* (New York: Cassell, 1909), pp. 107–08.

48. Mahan, *Some Neglected Aspects of War*, 1907, quoted in Offer, *First World War*, p. 237.

49. Paul Rohrbach, *Die Bagdadbahn*, 1903, quoted in Edward Mead Earle, *Turkey, the Great Powers, and the Bagdad Railway* (New York: Macmillan, 1923), p. 128.

50. Charles Sarolea, *The Anglo-German Problem*, 1912, quoted ibid., p. 131.

51. This argument is made very powerfully in Clark, *Sleepwalkers*.

52. Sean McMeekin, *The Russian Origins of the First World War* (Cambridge, MA: Harvard University Press, 2011), p. 31.

53. Ibid., pp. 30–31.

54. Quoted in Fischer, *World Power or Decline*, p. 60.

55. Ferguson, *The Pity of War*, p. 171.

56. Ibid., p. 163.

57. Ibid., p. 168.

58. Clark, *Sleepwalkers*, p. 546.

2. Economic Warfare, 1914–1918

1. Ivan Stanislovich Bloch, *Is War Now Impossible?* (London: Grant Richards, 1899), p. xlv.

2. Richard Roberts, *Saving the City: The Great Financial Crisis of 1914* (New York: Oxford University Press, 2013), p. 21.

3. Ferguson, *The Pity of War*, p. 188.

4. Hobson, *Imperialism*, p. 51.

5. Roberts, *Saving the City*, p. 228.

6. Bloch, *Is War Now Impossible?*, pp. xxxviii, 308.

7. Ibid., p. 251.

8. Nicholas A. Lambert, *Planning Armageddon: British Economic Warfare in the First World War* (Cambridge, MA: Harvard University Press, 2012), p. 163.

9. Quoted in Offer, *First World War*, p. 298.

10. Lambert, *Planning Armageddon.*

11. Louis Guichard, *The Naval Blockade, 1914–1918* (London: Philip Allan, 1930), p. 266.

12. Albrecht Ritschel, "Germany's Economy at War, 1914–1918 and Beyond," in Peter Broadberry and Mark Harrison, eds., *The Economics of World War I* (New York: Cambridge University Press, 2005), p. 50. Figures in constant prices.

13. Lance E. Davis and Stanley L. Engerman, *Naval Blockades in Peace and War: An Economic History Since 1750* (New York: Cambridge University Press, 2006), p. 204.

14. Peter Overlack, "The Function of Commerce Warfare in Anglo-German Conflict to 1914," *Journal of Strategic Studies* 20, no. 4 (1997): 102.

15. Quoted in Offer, *First World War*, p. 283.

16. Quoted in Abraham Berglund, "The Iron-Ore Problem of Lorraine," *Quarterly Journal of Economics* 33, no. 3 (1919): 552–53.

17. Parrish, "Iron and Steel in the Balance of World Power," *Journal of Political Economy* 64, no. 5 (1956): 374.

18. Quoted in Lucien Gallois, "Alsace-Lorraine and Europe," *Geographical Review* 6, no. 2 (1918): 113–14.

19. Broadberry and Harrison, *The Economics of World War I*, pp. 50, 183.

20. Friedrich Naumann, *Central Europe* (New York: Knopf, 1917), pp. 194–95.

21. Quoted in Ralph Haswell Lutz, *The Causes of the German Collapse in 1918* (Stanford, CA: Stanford University Press, 1934), p. 42.

22. Quoted in H. E. Goemans, *War and Punishment: The Causes of War Termination and the First World War* (Princeton: Princeton University Press, 2000), p. 290.

23. Quoted in Offer, *First World War*, p. 74.

24. Quoted in Goemans, *War and Punishment*, p. 257.

25. Quoted in Offer, *First World War*, p. 76.

3. The Failure of Economic Isolationism

1. *Papers Relating to the Foreign Relations of the United States, 1918, Supplement 1: The World War* (Washington, DC: GPO, 1933), 1:406.

2. Colonel Edward House, telegram to President Woodrow Wilson seeking approval for an interpretation of Wilson's Fourteen Points, October 29, 1918, ibid.: 413.

3. Norman Angell, *The Fruits of Victory: A Sequel to "The Great Illusion"* (New York: Century Co., 1921), p. 70.

4. Quoted in John Holladay Lantané, *From Isolation to Leadership: A Review of American Foreign Policy* (Garden City, NY: Doubleday, 1918), p. 193.

5. Corrado Gini, *Report on the Problem of Raw Materials and Foodstuffs* (Geneva: League of Nations, 1921), pp. 39–40.

6. Angell, *Fruits of Victory*, p. 102.

7. *American Economist,* January 25, 1918, quoted in Arno J. Mayer, *Politics and Diplomacy of Peacemaking: Containment and Counterrevolution at Versailles, 1918–1919* (New York: Knopf, 1967), p. 122.

8. Quoted in Ian M. Drummond, *British Economic Policy and the Empire, 1919–1939* (London: Allen & Unwin, 1972), pp. 144–45.

9. Ibid., p. 146.

10. Ibid., p. 162.

11. Leonard Woolf, *Economic Imperialism* (London: Swarthmore Press, 1920), pp. 30–31.

12. Lord Arnold, under-secretary of state for the colonies, in Cabinet, February 25, 1924, quoted in Drummond, *British Economic Policy*, p. 177.

13. Quoted in General Franz Ritter von Epp, "The Question of Colonies: The German Standpoint," *Journal of the Royal African Society* 36 (1937): 25.

14. *Millard's Review* 7, no. 6 (1919): 194.

15. K. K. Kawakami, *The Real Japanese Question* (New York: Macmillan, 1921), pp. 229–30, 235–36.

16. Quoted in Helmer Key, *The New Colonial Policy* (London: Methuen, 1927), pp. 104–105.

17. Ibid., p. 111.

18. Clemenceau addressing the National Assembly, December 29, 1918, quoted in Thomas J. Knock, *To End All Wars: Woodrow Wilson and the Quest for a New World Order* (Princeton: Princeton University Press, 1995), p. 198.

19. W. M. Jordan, *Great Britain, France, and the German Problem, 1918–1939* (New York: Oxford University Press, 1943), pp. 38–39.

20. John Maynard Keynes, *The Economic Consequences of the Peace* (New York: Harcourt, Brace, 1920), p. 14.

21. Ibid., p. 217.

22. 71 Cong., Rec. May 5, 1930.

23. David L. Glickman, "The British Imperial System," *The Quarterly Journal of Economics*, vol. 16, no. 3 (May 1947): 447.

24. John Maynard Keynes, "National Self-Sufficiency," *Yale Review* 22, no. 4 (1933): 758.

25. Quoted in David M. Kennedy, *Freedom from Fear: The American People in Depression and War, 1929–1945* (New York: Oxford University Press, 2004), p. 157.

26. Naumann, *Central Europe*, p. 147.

27. Quoted in Antonin Basch, *The New Economic Warfare* (New York: Columbia University Press, 1941), p. 6.

28. Quoted in Lizzie Collingham, *The Taste of War: World War II and the Battle for Food* (New York: Penguin, 2012), p. 49.

29. *La Beffa delle Ricchezze: Il problema delle materie prime spiegato ai giovani* (Rome, [1936–1937?]), pp. 12, 26, 31.

30. Ernesto Massi, *La partecipazione delle colonie alla produzione delle materie prime* (Milan: Istituto Coloniale Fascista, 1937), p. 91.

31. Corrado Gini, "Problems of the International Distribution of Population and Raw Materials," *Annals of the American Academy of Political and Social Science* 189, no. 1 (1937): 212.

32. Adam Tooze, *The Wages of Destruction: The Making and Breaking of the Nazi Economy* (New York: Viking, 2007), p. 709.

33. Hjalmar Schacht, "Germany's Colonial Demands," *Foreign Affairs* 15, no. 2, (1937): 227–28.

34. Normal Angell, *This Have and Have-Not Business: Political Fantasy and Economic Fact* (London: Hamish Hamilton, 1936), pp. 14–15.

35. League of Nations, *Raw Material Problems and Policies* (Geneva, 1946), p. 66.

36. Labour Party, Advisory Committee, *The Demand for Colonial Territories and Equality of Economic Opportunity* (London: Labour Party, 1936), p. 17.

37. Angell, *This Have and Have-Not Business*, p. 133.

38. Anton Mohr, *The Oil War* (London: M. Hopkinson, 1926), p. 198.

39. Frank H. Simonds and Brooks Emeny, *The Price of Peace: The Challenge of Economic Nationalism* (New York: Harper, 1935), pp. 342–43.

40. Memorandum by Hull, January 22, 1936, quoted in Arthur W. Schatz, "The Anglo-American Trade Agreement and Cordell Hull's Search for Peace, 1936–1938," *Journal of American History* 57, no. 1 (1970): 91.

41. Quoted in Benjamin M. Rowland, ed., *Balance of Power or Hegemony: The Interwar Monetary System* (New York: New York University Press, 1976), p. 203.
42. Schatz, "Anglo-American Trade Agreement," p. 98.
43. Adolf Hitler, *Mein Kampf* (Boston: Houghton Mifflin, 1939), pp. 122, 118–19.
44. Quoted in Office of the United States Chief Counsel for the Prosecution of Axis Criminality, *Nazi Conspiracy and Aggression* (Washington, DC, 1947), p. 380.
45. Ibid., p. 391.
46. Quoted in Catherine Porter, "Mineral Deficiency Versus Self-Sufficiency in Japan," *Far Eastern Survey* 5, no. 2 (1936): 9.
47. Quoted in Joyce C. Lebra, ed., *Japan's Greater East Asia Co-Prosperity Sphere in World War II* (New York: Oxford University Press, 1975), pp. 74–77.
48. Eliot Janeway, "The Americans and the New Pacific," February 1939, quoted in Jonathan Marshall, *To Have and Have Not: Southeast Asian Raw Materials and the Origins of the Pacific War* (Berkeley: University of California Press, 1995), p. xi.
49. Quoted ibid., p. 3.
50. Stanley Hornbeck, State Department memorandum, June 1940, quoted ibid., p. xi.
51. Quoted in James William Morley, ed., *The Fateful Choice: Japan's Advance into Southeast Asia, 1939–1941* (New York: Columbia University Press, 1980), p. 242.

4. Economic Warfare, 1939–1945

1. Adolf Hitler, *Hitler's Table Talk, 1941–44* (London: Weidenfeld & Nicolson, 1973), p. 53.
2. Ibid., p. 43.
3. Ibid., p. 53.
4. Paul Einzig, *Economic Problems of the Next War* (London: Macmillan, 1939), p. 15.
5. Ibid., p. 103.
6. Tooze, *Wages of Destruction*, p. 321.
7. Karl G. Larew, "The Royal Navy in the Battle of Britain," *The Historian* 54, no. 2 (1992): 243–54.

8. W. W. Medlicott, *The Economic Blockade*, Vol. 2 (London: HMSO, 1959), p. 651.

9. Tooze, *Wages of Destruction*, p. 420.

10. Timothy Snyder, *Bloodlands: Europe Between Hitler and Stalin* (New York: Basic Books, 2010), p. 163.

11. Karl Dönitz, *Memoirs—Ten Years and Twenty Days* (Annapolis, MD: Naval Institute Press, 2012), p. 341.

12. W. K. Hancock, ed., *Statistical Digest of the War* (London: HMSO, 1951), p. 174.

13. D. J. Payton-Smith, *Oil: A Study in War-time Policy and Administration* (London: HMSO, 1971), p. 401.

14. Hancock, *Statistical Digest of the War*, pp. 87–88.

15. Dönitz, *Memoirs*, p. 333.

16. Lieut-General von Metzsch, "New Tendencies of Development in Warfare," in Norman Angell et al., *What Would Be the Character of a New War?* (London: Victor Gollancz, 1933), p. 40.

17. Quoted in Ronald Schaffer, *Wings of Judgment: American Bombing in World War II* (New York: Oxford University Press, 1985), p. 22.

18. Winston Churchill, July 8, 1940, quoted in Max Hastings, *Bomber Command* (New York: Dial Press, 1979), p. 116.

19. Quoted in Peter W. Becker, "The Role of Synthetic Fuel in World War II Germany," *Air University Review*, July–August 1981.

20. Medlicott, *The Economic Blockade*, p. 640.

21. Suzuki at the Imperial Conference, November 1, 1941, quoted in Nabutaka Ike, *Japan's Decision for War* (Stanford, CA: Stanford University Press, 1967), p. 202.

22. Davis and Engerman, *Naval Blockades in Peace and War*, p. 379.

23. United States Strategic Bombing Survey, *Summary Report (Pacific War)* (Washington, DC: GPO, 1946), p. 19.

24. Ibid., p. 21.

5. Pax Americana and the Second Era of Globalization

1. Robert A. Divine, *Second Chance: The Triumph of Internationalism in America During World War II* (New York: Atheneum, 1967), pp. 43–44.

2. Henry R. Luce, "The American Century," *Life* (February 17, 1941): 64.

3. Quoted in Stephen Howarth, *To Shining Sea: A History of the United States Navy, 1775–1991* (Norman: University of Oklahoma Press, 1999), p. 383.
4. Wendell L. Willkie, *One World* (New York: Simon & Schuster, 1943), pp. 198, 201.
5. William Y. Elliot, ed., *The Political Economy of American Foreign Policy: Its Concepts, Strategy and Limits* (New York: Henry Holt, 1955), pp. 210–11.
6. Quoted in Christopher Layne, *Peace of Illusions: American Grand Strategy from 1940 to the Present* (Ithaca, NY: Cornell University Press, 2006), pp. 44, 42.
7. Quoted in Kimball, "Lend-Lease and the Open Door," p. 235.
8. J. B. Condliffe, *The Reconstruction of World Trade* (New York: Norton, 1940), p. 57.
9. Herbert Hoover and Hugh Gibson, *The Problems of Lasting Peace* (Garden City, NY: Doubleday, Doran, 1942), p. 225.
10. Quoted in Kimball, "Lend-Lease and the Open Door," p. 249.
11. Quoted in Alec Cairncross, "A British Perspective on Bretton Woods," in Orin Kirshner, ed., *The Bretton Woods–GATT System: Retrospect and Prospect After Fifty Years* (Armonk, NY: M. E. Sharpe, 1996), pp. 71–72.
12. Robert Skidelsky, *John Maynard Keynes: Fighting for Freedom, 1937–1946* (New York: Viking, 2000), p. 128.
13. Ambassador John G. Winant to Cordell Hull, August 11, 1944, in *Papers Relating to the Foreign Relations of the United States* (Washington, DC: GPO, 1967), 2:68–69.
14. Quoted in I. M. Destler, *American Trade Politics: System Under Stress* (Washington, DC: Institute for International Economics, 2005), p. 16.
15. Quoted in Cairncross, "A British Perspective," p. 79.
16. Willkie, *One World*, p. 204.
17. Quoted in Wm. Roger Louis, *Imperialism at Bay: The United States and the Decolonization of the British Empire, 1941–1945* (New York: Oxford University Press, 1977), p. 277.
18. Quoted in Herbert Feis, "The Future of British Imperial Preferences," *Foreign Affairs*, vol. 24, no. 4 (July 1946): 663.
19. S. Milward, *The Reconstruction of Western Europe, 1945–51* (Berkeley: University of California Press, 1984), pp. 131–35.

20. Michael Shaller, *The American Occupation of Japan: The Origins of the Cold War in Asia* (New York: Oxford University Press, 1985), p. 25.

21. Ibid., p. 35.

22. W. Averell Harriman, "Leadership in World Affairs," *Foreign Affairs* 32, no. 4 (1954): 525.

23. Alec Cairncross, *The Price of War: British Policy on German Reparations, 1941–1949* (New York: Blackwell, 1986), p. 219. The figures include food and other aid in the postwar period as well as Marshall Plan aid.

24. Schuman Declaration, May 9, 1950, European Union website, http:// europa.eu/about-eu/basic-information/symbols/europe-day/schuman -declaration/.

25. Quoted in Euan Graham, *Japan's Sea Lane Security, 1940–2004: A Matter of Life and Death?* (New York: Routledge, 2006), p. 93.

26. Andrew Hrykaj, "Challenging the United States: French Foreign Policy 1944–1948" (master's thesis, Concordia University, Montreal, 2000).

27. Bruce Franklin, ed., *The Essential Stalin: Major Theoretical Writings, 1905–52* (Garden City, NY: Anchor Books, 1972), p. 338.

28. William Curti Wohlforth, *The Elusive Balance: Power and Perception during the Cold War* (Ithaca, NY: Cornell University Press, 1993), p. 83.

29. Franklin, *Essential Stalin*, pp. 469–73.

30. Quoted in Leon M. Herman, "The Promise of Economic Self-Sufficiency Under Soviet Socialism," in Vladimir G. Treml and Robert Farrell, eds., *The Development of the Soviet Economy* (New York: Praeger, 1968), p. 223.

31. D. D. Mishustin, *Foreign Trade and the Industrialization of the USSR* (Moscow, 1938), quoted in Herman, "Promise of Economic Self-Sufficiency," p. 225.

32. *Political Economy* (Moscow, 1954), quoted in Herman, "Promise of Economic Self-Sufficiency," p. 228.

33. Willard L. Thorp, "American Policy and the Soviet Economic Offensive," *Foreign Affairs* 35, no. 2 (1957): 278.

34. Philip Hanson, *The Rise and Fall of the Soviet Economy* (New York: Longman, 2003), p. 121.

35. Alfred E. Eckes Jr., *The United States and the Global Struggle for Minerals* (Austin: University of Texas Press, 1979), p. 231.

36. Schaller, *American Occupation of Japan*, p. 106.

37. Ibid., p. 144.
38. Gabriel Kolko, *Vietnam: Anatomy of a War, 1940–1975* (London: Allen & Unwin, 1986), p. 76.
39. Lee Kuan Yew, *From Third World to First* (New York: Harper, 2000), p. 467. Quoted in Robert Kaplan, *Asia's Cauldron: The South China Sea and the End of a Stable Pacific* (New York: Random House, 2014), p. 106.
40. Henryk Szlajfer, *Economic Nationalism and Globalization: Lessons from Latin America and Central Europe* (Boston: Brill, 2012), p. 32.
41. Harry Magdoff, *The Age of Imperialism: The Economics of U.S. Foreign Policy* (New York: Monthly Review Press, 1969), p. 53.
42. Peter J. Burnell, *Economic Nationalism in the Third World* (Boulder, CO: Westview, 1986), pp. 265–66.
43. Woodrow Wilson, message to Congress, May 20, 1919, quoted in Michael Krenn, *U.S. Policy Toward Economic Nationalism in Latin America, 1917–1929* (Wilmington, DE: SR Books, 1990), p. 13.
44. Quoted in Alfred E. Eckes Jr., "Open Door Expansionism Reconsidered: The World War II Experience," *Journal of American History* 59, no. 4 (1973): 918.
45. Harriman, "Leadership in World Affairs," p. 531.
46. Hudson, *Trade, Development and Foreign Debt*, p. 156.
47. Mohr, *The Oil War*, pp. 183, 190, and E. M. Friedwald, *Oil and the War* (London: William Heinemann, 1941), p. 13.
48. President's Materials Policy Commission, *Resources for Freedom: A Report to the President* (Washington, DC: GPO, 1952), 2:99.
49. Daniel Yergin, *The Prize: The Epic Quest for Oil, Money, and Power* (New York: Free Press, 2008), p. 450.
50. Howarth, *To Shining Sea*, p. 531.
51. U.S. Congress, Committee on International Relations, Special Situations Subcommittee on Investigations, *Oil Fields as Military Objectives: A Feasability Study* (Washington, DC: GPO, 1975).
52. Herman, "Promise of Economic Self-Sufficiency," p. 227.
53. Khrushchev in *Pravda*, April 2, 1964, quoted ibid., pp. 228–29.
54. Quoted in Hanson, *Rise and Fall of the Soviet Economy*, p. 124.
55. "Why Is It So Difficult to Replace a Failed Economic System: The Former USSR," in John M. Antle and Daniel A. Sumner, eds., *Selected Papers of D. Gale Johnson* (Chicago: University of Chicago Press, 1996).

6. The End of Pax Americana?

1. Patrick E. Tyler, "U.S. Strategy Calls for Insuring No Rivals Develop," *New York Times*, March 8, 1992.
2. Dick Cheney, *Defense Strategy for the 1990s: The Regional Defense Strategy* (Washington, DC: Office of the Secretary of Defense, January 1993), p. 7.
3. Ibid., p. 4.
4. Quoted in Mark Harrison, "Coercion, Compliance, and the Collapse of the Soviet Economy," *Economic History Review* 55, no. 3 (2002): 414.
5. Ronald Findlay and Kevin H. O'Rourke, *Power and Plenty: Trade, War, and the World Economy in the Second Millennium* (Princeton: Princeton University Press, 2007), p. 500.
6. Quoted in Alexander Eckstein, *China's Economic Revolution* (New York: Cambridge University Press, 1977), p. 241.
7. Quoted ibid., p. 242.
8. Quoted in Benjamin I. Page and Tao Xie, *Living with the Dragon: How the American Public Views the Rise of China* (New York, Columbia University Press, 2010), p. 41.
9. Quoted in Andrew J. Nathan and Bruce Gilley, *China's New Rulers: The Secret Files*, 2nd rev. ed. (New York: New York Review Books, 2003), p. 235.
10. Quoted in David Shambaugh, *China Goes Global: The Partial Power* (New York: Oxford University Press, 2013), p. 129.
11. Zhao Tingyang, *Tianxia Tixi: Shijie Zhidu Zhexue Daolun* (Nanjing: Jiangsu Jiaoyu Chubanshe, 2005). The book is discussed in William A. Callahan, "Tianxia, Empire, and the World: Chinese Visions of World Order for the Twenty-first Century," in William A. Callahan and Elena Barabantseva, eds., *China Orders the World* (Washington, DC: Woodrow Wilson Center Press, 2011).
12. Peter Hays Gries, *China's New Nationalism: Pride, Politics, and Diplomacy* (Berkeley: University of California Press, 2004), p. 5.
13. Shambaugh, *China Goes Global*, p. 43.
14. These figures are based on estimates by SIPRI (Stockholm International Peace Research Institute), rather than official Chinese figures, which exclude a number of military items from the defense budget.

15. Quoted in Thomas G. Mahnken, "China's Anti-Access Strategy in Historical and Theoretical Perspective," *Journal of Strategic Studies* 34, no. 3 (2011): 317.

16. Shigeo Hiramatsu, Japanese military analyst, quoted in Richard C. Bush, *The Perils of Proximity: China-Japan Security Relations* (Washington, DC: Brookings Institution Press, 2010), p. 84.

17. James Kraska, "How the United States Lost the Naval War of 2015," *Orbis* (Winter 2010): 35.

18. Toshi Yoshihara and James R. Holmes, "The Next Arms Race," *The Diplomat*, January 2010.

19. Paul Kennedy, "The Rise and Fall of Navies," *New York Times*, October 5, 2007.

20. Kaplan, *Asia's Cauldron*.

21. Elizabeth Economy, testimony before the U.S.-China Economic and Security Review Commission, Washington, DC, January 26, 2012.

22. Derek Scissors, *China's Global Investment Rises: The U.S. Should Focus on Competition* (The Heritage Foundation, January 2013).

23. Where China owns only part of an oil field, this figure assumes that China is entitled to an equivalent portion of the output.

24. John Lee, "China's Geostrategic Search for Oil," *Washington Quarterly* 35, no. 3 (2012): 84.

25. Quoted in Marc Lanteigne, "China's Maritime Security and the 'Malacca Dilemma,'" *Asian Security* 4, no. 2 (2008): 143.

26. Andrew Erickson and Gabriel B. Collins, "China's Oil Security Pipe Dream," *Naval College War Review* 63, no. 2 (2010).

27. David Shambaugh, "Coping with a Conflicted China," *Washington Quarterly* (Winter 2011): 8.

28. John J. Mearsheimer, *The Tragedy of Great Power Politics* (New York: Norton, 2001), p. 402.

29. *Air-Sea Battle: Service Collaboration to Address Anti-Access and Area Denial Challenges* (Washington, DC: U.S. Department of Defense, 2013).

30. Douglas C. Peifer, "Power Projection Versus Distant Blockade: China, the German Analogy, and the New Air-Sea Operational Concept" (Philadelphia: Foreign Policy Research Institute, Winter 2011), pp. 116, 129.

31. Gries, *China's New Nationalism*, p. 140.

32. Alastair Iain Johnston, "Is China a Status-Quo Power?" *International Security* 27, no. 4 (2003): 17.

33. G. John Ikenberry, "The Rise of China and the Future of the West: Can the Liberal System Survive?" *Foreign Affairs* (February 2008).

34. European Commission, Directorate-General for Trade, *Tenth Report on Potentially Trade-Restrictive Measures Identified in the Context of the Financial and Economic Crisis*, May 2013.

35. League of Nations, *Certain Aspects of the Raw Materials Problem*, pp. 39–40.

36. Michael Klare, *Resource Wars: The New Landscape of Global Conflict* (New York: Metropolitan Books, 2001).

37. Hugh White, *The China Choice: Why We Should Share Power* (Oxford: Oxford University Press, 2012).

BIBLIOGRAPHY

Afalo, M. *The Truth About Morocco: An Indictment of the Policy of the British Foreign Office with Regard to the Anglo-French Agreement*. New York: J. Lane, 1904.

Aganbegyan, Abel. *Inside Perestroika: The Future of the Soviet Economy*. New York: Harper, 1989.

Air-Sea Battle: Service Collaboration to Address Anti-Access and Area Denial Challenges. Washington, DC: U.S. Department of Defense, 2013.

Allen, Robert C. "The Rise and Decline of the Soviet Economy." *Canadian Journal of Economics* 34, no. 4 (2001): 859–81.

Anderson, Irvine H. Jr. *The Standard-Vacuum Oil Company and United States East Asian Policy, 1933–1941*. Princeton: Princeton University Press, 1975.

Angell, Norman. *The Fruits of Victory: A Sequel to "The Great Illusion."* New York: Century Co., 1921.

———. *The Great Illusion*. New York: Putnam, 1910.

———. *This Have and Have-Not Business: Political Fantasy and Economic Fact*. London: Hamish Hamilton, 1936.

Angell, Norman, et al. *What Would Be the Character of a New War?* London: Victor Gollancz, 1933.

Antle, John M., and Daniel A. Sumner, eds. *Selected Papers of D. Gale Johnson*. Chicago: University of Chicago Press, 1995.

Arad, Uzi. *The Short-Term Effectiveness of the Arab Oil Embargo*. Tel Aviv: Tel Aviv University, 1978.

Art, Robert J. *America's Grand Strategy and World Politics*. New York: Routledge, 2009.

Bairoch, Paul. "International Industrialization Levels from 1750 to 1980." *Journal of European Economic History* 11, no. 2 (1982): 269–333.

Bairoch, Paul, and Susan Burke. "European Trade Policy, 1815–1914." In *Cambridge Economic History of Europe*, Vol. 8. New York: Cambridge University Press, 1989.

Basch, Antonin. *The New Economic Warfare*. New York: Columbia University Press, 1941.

Bastiat, Frédéric. *The Fallacies of Protection* [*Sophismes Économiques*. 1846]. New York: Cassell, 1909.

Beasley, W. G. *Japanese Imperialism 1894–1945*. New York: Oxford University Press, 1987.

Becker, Peter W. "The Role of Synthetic Fuel in World War II Germany." *Air University Review* (July–August 1981).

La Beffa delle Ricchezze: Il problema delle materie prime spiegato ai giovani. Rome [1936–1937?].

Berglund, Abraham. "The Iron-Ore Problem of Lorraine." *Quarterly Journal of Economics* 33, no. 3 (1919): 531–54.

Bernhardi, General Friedrich von. *Germany and the Next War*. London: Edward Arnold, 1912.

Bidwell, Percy W. *Raw Materials: A Study of American Policy*. New York: Harper, 1958.

Bloch, Ivan Stanislavovich. *Is War Now Impossible?* London: Grant Richards, 1899.

Blouet, Brian W. "The Imperial Vision of Halford Mackinder." *Geographical Journal* 170, no. 4 (2004): 322–29.

Boemeke, Manfred F., Roger Chickering, and Stig Förster, eds. *Anticipating Total War: The German and American Experiences, 1871–1914*. New York: Cambridge University Press, 1999.

Boemeke, Manfred F., Gerald D. Feldman, and Elisabeth Glaser, eds. *The Treaty of Versailles: A Reassessment after 75 Years*. New York: Cambridge University Press, 1998.

Boulding, Kenneth E., and Tapan Mukerjee, eds. *Economic Imperialism: A Book of Readings*. Ann Arbor: University of Michigan Press, 1972.

Brandt, Loren, and Thomas G. Rawski, eds. *China's Great Economic Transformation*. New York: Cambridge University Press, 2008.

Broadberry, Stephen, and Mark Harrison, eds. *The Economics of World War I*. New York: Cambridge University Press, 2005.

Brooks, Karen, and Bruce Gardner. "Russian Agriculture in the Transition to a Market Economy." *Economic Development and Cultural Change* 2, no. 3 (2004): 571–86.

Bruton, Henry J. "A Reconsideration of Import Substitution." *Journal of Economic Literature* 36, no. 2 (1998): 903–36.

Bryce, Robert, ed. *French Foreign and Defense Policy 1918–1940: The Decline and Fall of a Great Power.* London: Routledge, 2005.

Bukharin, Nikolai. *Imperialism and World Economy.* New York: Monthly Review Press, 1929.

Bunker, Stephen G., and Paul S. Ciccantell. *Globalization and the Race for Resources.* Baltimore: Johns Hopkins University Press, 2005.

Burin, Frederic S. "The Communist Doctrine of the Inevitability of War." *American Political Science Review* 57, no. 2 (1963).

Burn, Duncan. *The Steel Industry 1939–1959: A Study in Competition and Planning.* Cambridge: Cambridge University Press, 1961.

Burnell, Peter J. *Economic Nationalism in the Third World.* Boulder, CO: Westview, 1986.

Bush, Richard C. *The Perils of Proximity: China-Japan Security Relations.* Washington, DC: Brookings Institution Press, 2010.

Bush, Richard C., and Michael E. O'Hanlon. *A War Like No Other: The Truth About China's Challenge to America.* Hoboken, NJ: John Wiley, 2007.

Byrd, Robert C., comp. *The Senate 1789–1989.* Vol. 3, *Classic Speeches 1830–1993.* Washington, DC: U.S. Senate Historical Office, 1995.

Cafruny, Alan W. *Ruling the Waves: The Political Economy of International Shipping.* Berkeley: University of California Press, 1987.

Cairncross, Alec. *The Price of War: British Policy on German Reparations, 1941–1949.* New York: Blackwell, 1986.

Callahan, William A. "Chinese Visions of World Order: Post-Hegemonic or a New Hegemony?" *International Studies Review* 10 (2008): 749–61.

Callahan, William A., and Elena Barabantseva, eds., *China Orders the World.* Washington, DC: Woodrow Wilson Center Press, 2011.

Cambridge Economic History of Europe. 8 vols. Cambridge: Cambridge University Press, 1963–1989.

Carr, William. *Arms, Autarky and Aggression.* New York: Norton, 1973.

Chambers, Frank P. *The War Behind the War, 1914–1918: A History of the Political and Civilian Fronts.* London: Faber, 1939.

Cheney, Dick. *Defense Strategy for the 1990s: The Regional Defense Strategy.* Washington, DC: Office of the Secretary of Defense, January 1993.

Chomsky, Noam. *At War with Asia.* New York: Pantheon, 1970.

Choucri, Nazli, Robert C. North, and Susumi Yamakage, eds. *The Challenge of Japan Before World War II and After: A Study of National Growth and Expansion*. New York: Routledge, 1992.

Christensen, Thomas J. "Fostering Stability or Creating a Monster? The Rise of China and U.S. Policy Toward East Asia." *International Security* 31, no. 1 (2006): 81–126.

Claasen, Adam. "Blood and Iron, and *der geist des Atlantiks*: Assessing Hitler's Decision to Invade Norway." *Journal of Strategic Studies* 20, no. 3 (1997): 71–96.

Clark, Christopher M. *The Sleepwalkers: How Europe Went to War in 1914*. New York: Harper, 2013.

Clark, William R. *Petrodollar Warfare: Oil, Iraq and the Future of the Dollar*. Gabriola Island, BC, Canada: New Society Publishers, 2005.

Clyde, Paul Hibbert. "The Open Door." *Pacific Affairs* 3, no. 9 (1930).

Cobden, Richard. *Speeches on Questions of Public Policy*. 2 Vols. London: Routledge, 1995.

Collingham, Lizzie. *The Taste of War: World War II and the Battle for Food*. New York: Penguin, 2012.

Collins, Gabriel B., and William S. McMurray. "No Lamps for the Oil of China?" *Naval War College Review* 61, no. 2 (2008): 79–95.

Committee on International Relations, University of California. *World Resources and Peace*. Berkeley: University of California Press, 1941.

Condliffe, J. B. *The Reconstruction of World Trade*. New York: Norton, 1940.

Consett, Rear Admiral M. W. W. P. *The Triumph of Unarmed Forces (1914–1918)*. London: Williams and Norgate, 1923.

Copeland, D. C. "Economic Interdependence and War: A Theory of Trade Expectations." *International Security* 20, no. 4 (1996): 5–41.

Corn, Tony. "Peaceful Rise Through Unrestricted Warfare: Grand Strategy with Chinese Characteristics." *Small Wars Journal*, 2010.

Crawford, Sir John, and Saburo Okita, eds. *Raw Materials and Pacific Economic Integration*. London: Croom Helm, 1978.

Cromwell, James H. R. *Pax Americana: American Democracy and World Peace*. Chicago: A. Kroch, 1941.

Cromwell, William C. "The Marshall Non-Plan, Congress and the Soviet Union." *Political Research Quarterly* 32, no. 4 (1979): 422–43.

Crowley, James B. *Japan's Quest for Autonomy: National Security and Foreign Policy 1930–1938*. Princeton: Princeton University Press, 1966.

Cunard, Nancy, and George Padmore. *The White Man's Duty: An Analysis of the Colonial Question in the Light of the Atlantic Charter.* London: W. H. Allen, 1942.

Darwin, John. *The Empire Project.* New York: Cambridge University Press, 2009.

Davies, R. W., Mark Harrison, and S. G. Wheatcroft, eds. *The Economic Transformation of the Soviet Union, 1913–1945.* New York: Cambridge University Press, 1994.

Davis, Lance E., and Stanley L. Engerman. *Naval Blockades in Peace and War: An Economic History Since 1750.* New York: Cambridge University Press, 2006.

Day, Richard B. *Leon Trotsky and the Politics of Economic Isolation.* Cambridge: Cambridge University Press, 1973.

Destler, I. M. *American Trade Politics: System Under Stress.* Washington, DC: Institute for International Economics, 2005.

Dickinson, G. Lowes. *War: Its Nature, Cause and Cure.* London: Allen & Unwin, 1923.

Divine, Robert A. *Second Chance: The Triumph of Internationalism in America During World War II.* New York: Atheneum, 1967.

Dockrill, Michael L., and J. Douglas Goold. *Peace Without Promise: Britain and the Peace Conferences, 1919–23.* London: Batsford, 1981.

Dohan, Michael R. "The Economic Origins of Soviet Autarky 1927/28–1934." *Slavic Review* 35, no. 4 (1976): 603–65.

Dönitz, Grand Admiral Karl. *Memoirs—Ten Years and Twenty Days.* Annapolis, MD: Naval Institute Press, 2012.

Dreyer, June Teufel. "Sino-Japanese Rivalry and Its Implications for Developing Nations." *Asian Survey* 46, no. 4 (2006): 538–57.

Drummond, Ian M. *British Economic Policy and the Empire, 1919–1939.* London: Allen & Unwin, 1972.

Earle, Edward Meade. *Turkey, the Great Powers, and the Bagdad Railway.* New York: Macmillan, 1923.

Eckes, Alfred E. Jr. "Open Door Expansionism Reconsidered: The World War II Experience." *Journal of American History* 59, no. 4 (1973): 909–24.

———. *The United States and the Global Struggle for Minerals.* Austin: University of Texas Press, 1979.

Eckstein, Alexander. *China's Economic Revolution.* New York: Cambridge University Press, 1977.

Economy, Elizabeth C., and Michael Levi. *By All Means Possible: How China's Resource Quest Is Changing the World*. New York: Oxford University Press, 2014.

Eggleston, F. W. "Sea Power and Peace in the Pacific." *Pacific Affairs* 8, no. 3 (1935): 352–58.

Einzig, Paul. *Economic Problems of the Next War*. London: Macmillan, 1939.

Eisenman, Joshua, Eric Heginbotham, and Derek Mitchell, eds. *China and the Developing World: Beijing's Strategy for the Twenty-First Century*. Armonk, NY: M. E. Sharpe, 2007.

Elliot, William Y., ed., *The Political Economy of American Foreign Policy*. New York: Henry Holt, 1955.

Emeny, Brooks. *The Strategy of Raw Materials: A Study of America in Peace and War*. New York: Macmillan, 1934.

Engel, Barbara. "Not by Bread Alone: Subsistence Riots in Russia During World War I." *Journal of Modern History* 69, no. 4 (1997): 696–721.

Epp, General Franz Ritter von. "The Question of Colonies: The German Standpoint," *Journal of the Royal African Society* 36 (1937).

Erickson, Andrew S., and Gabriel B. Collins. "China's Oil Security Pipe Dream: The Reality, and Strategic Consequences, of Seaborne Imports." *Naval War College Review* 63, no. 2 (2010): 88–111.

Feis, Herbert. *Europe: the World's Banker, 1870–1914*. New Haven: Yale University Press, 1930.

———."The Future of British Imperial Preferences." *Foreign Affairs* 24, no. 4 (1946).

———. *Seen from E. A.: Three International Episodes*. New York: Knopf, 1947.

———. *The Sinews of Peace*. New York: Harper, 1944.

Feldman, Gerald D., ed. *German Imperialism, 1914–1918*. New York: Wiley, 1972.

Ferguson, Niall. *The Pity of War*. New York: Basic Books, 1999.

Fieldhouse, D. K. *The Colonial Empires: A Comparative Survey from the Eighteenth Century*. New York: Delacorte, 1966.

———. *Economics and Empire, 1830–1914*. Ithaca, NY: Cornell University Press, 1973.

Findlay, Ronald, and Kevin H. O'Rourke. *Power and Plenty: Trade, War, and the World Economy in the Second Millennium*. Princeton: Princeton University Press, 2007.

Fischer, Fritz. *Germany's Aims in the First World War*. New York: Norton, 1967.

————. *World Power or Decline: The Controversy over Germany's Aims in the First World War.* New York: Norton, 1974.

Fisher, A.G.B. *Economic Self-Sufficiency.* Oxford: Clarendon Press, 1939.

Fontaine, Arthur. *French Industry During the War.* New Haven: Yale University Press, 1926.

Foreign Policy Association. *War Tomorrow—Will We Keep Out?* New York: Foreign Policy Association, 1935.

Franklin, Bruce, ed. *The Essential Stalin: Major Theoretical Writings, 1905–52.* Garden City, NY: Anchor Books, 1972.

Freedman, Robert O. *Moscow and the Middle East: Soviet Policy Since the Invasion of Afghanistan.* New York: Cambridge University Press, 1991.

Friedman, George, and Meredith LeBard. *The Coming War with Japan.* New York: St. Martin's Press, 1991.

Friedman, Thomas L. *The World Is Flat: A Brief History of the Twenty-first Century.* New York: Farrar, Straus and Giroux, 2005.

Friedwald, E. M. *Oil and the War.* London: W. Heinemann, 1941.

Gaddis, John Lewis. *The Cold War: A New History.* New York: Penguin, 2005.

————. "Grand Strategies in the Cold War." In *Cambridge History of the Cold War,* Vol. 2, edited by Melvyn P. Leffler and Odd Arne Westad. Cambridge: Cambridge University Press, 2010.

————. *We Now Know: Rethinking Cold War History.* New York: Oxford University Press, 1997.

Gaidar, Yegor. *Collapse of an Empire: Lessons for Modern Russia.* Washington, DC: Brookings Institution Press, 2007.

Gallois, Lucien. "Alsace-Lorraine and Europe." *Geographical Review* 6, no. 2 (1918).

Gardner, Lloyd C. *Economic Aspects of New Deal Diplomacy.* Boston: Beacon Press, 1964.

Garrett, Stephen A. *Ethics and Airpower in World War II: The British Bombing of German Cities.* New York: St. Martin's Press, 1996.

Gatrell, Peter. *Russia's First World War: A Social and Economic History.* Harlow, UK: Pearson Longman, 2005.

Gavin, Francis J. *Gold, Dollars, and Power: The Politics of International Relations, 1958–1971.* Chapel Hill: University of North Carolina Press, 2003.

Gentile, Gian P. *How Effective Is Strategic Bombing? Lessons from World War II to Kosovo.* New York: New York University Press, 2001.

Gerhardt, Major Harrison A. *Strategic and Critical Raw Materials.* West Point, NY: U.S. Military Academy, 1943.

German Institute of Economics. *The European Plans of German Imperialism*. Berlin, 1957.

Gini, Corrado. "Problems on the International Distribution of Population and Raw Materials." *Annals of the American Academy of Political and Social Science* 189, no. 1 (1937): 201–13.

Glickman, David L. "The British Imperial Preference System." *Quarterly Journal of Economics* 61, no. 3 (1947): 439–70.

Goemans, H. E. *War and Punishment: The Causes of War Termination and the First World War*. Princeton: Princeton University Press, 2000.

Gompert, David C. *Sea Power and American Interests in the Western Pacific*. Santa Monica, CA: RAND Corp., 2013.

Gordon, David L., and Royden Dangerfield. *The Hidden Weapon: The Story of Economic Warfare*. New York: Harper, 1947.

Grace, John D. *Russian Oil Supply: Performance and Prospects*. New York: Oxford University Press, 2005.

Graham, Benjamin. *World Commodities and World Currency*. New York: McGraw-Hill, 1944.

Graham, Euan. *Japan's Sea Lane Security, 1940–2004: A Matter of Life and Death?* New York: Routledge, 2006.

Gray, John E., et al. *US Energy Policy and US Foreign Policy in the 1980s*. Cambridge, MA: Ballinger, 1981.

Gries, Peter Hays. *China's New Nationalism: Pride, Politics, and Diplomacy*. Berkeley: University of California Press, 2004.

Guichard, Louis. *The Naval Blockade, 1914–1918*. New York: D. Appleton, 1930.

Hall, Robert Burnett. "American Raw-Material Deficiencies, and Regional Dependence." *Geographical Review* 30, no. 2 (1940): 177–86.

Hamilton, Richard F., and Holger H. Herwig, eds. *The Origins of World War I*. New York: Cambridge University Press, 2003.

Hanighen, Frank C. *The Secret War*. New York: John Day, 1934.

Hanson, Philip. *The Rise and Fall of the Soviet Economy*. New York: Longman, 2003.

Harriman, W. Averell. "Leadership in World Affairs." *Foreign Affairs* 32, no. 4 (1954).

Harrison, Mark. "Coercion, Compliance, and the Collapse of the Soviet Command Economy." *Economic History Review* 55, no. 3 (2002): 397–433.

———, ed. *The Economics of World War II*. New York: Cambridge University Press, 1998.

Hastings, Max. *Bomber Command*. New York: Dial Press, 1979.

Hatch, F. H. *The Iron and Steel Industry of the United Kingdom Under War Conditions*. London: Harrison & Sons, 1919.

Haupt, Georges. *Socialism and the Great War: The Collapse of the Second International*. Oxford: Clarendon Press, 1972.

Henderson, H. D. *Colonies and Raw Materials*. New York: Farrar & Rinehart, 1939.

Herwig, Holger H. "Germany and the 'Short-War' Illusion: Toward a New Interpretation?" *Journal of Military History* 66, no. 3 (2002).

Hitler, Adolf. *Hitler's Second Book*. New York: Enigma Books, 2003.

———. *Hitler's Table Talk, 1941–44*. London: Weidenfeld & Nicolson, 1973.

———. *Mein Kampf*. Boston: Houghton Mifflin, 1939.

Hobson, John A. "The Ethics of Internationalism." *International Journal of Ethics* 17, no. 1 (1906).

———. *Imperialism: A Study*. Ann Arbor: University of Michigan Press, 1965.

———. *The New Protectionism*. New York: Putnam, 1916.

Hoffman, Ross J. S. *Great Britain and the German Trade Rivalry, 1875–1914*. Philadelphia: University of Pennsylvania Press, 1933.

Holmes, James R., and Toshi Yoshihara. "China's Naval Ambitions in the Indian Ocean." *Journal of Strategic Studies* 31, no. 3 (2008): 367–394.

Holzman, Franklyn D. *International Trade Under Commumism: Politics and Economics*. New York: Basic Books, 1976.

Hoover, Herbert, and Hugh Gibson. *The Problems of Lasting Peace*. Garden City, NY: Doubleday, Doran, 1942.

House, Edward Mandell, and Charles Seymour. *What Really Happened at Paris: The Story of the Peace Conference, 1918–1919*. New York: Scribner, 1921.

Howard, Michael. *War and the Liberal Conscience*. New York: Columbia University Press, 2008.

Howarth, Stephen. *To Shining Sea: A History of the United States Navy, 1775–1991*. Norman: University of Oklahoma Press, 1999.

Hrykaj, Andrew. "Challenging the United States: French Foreign Policy 1944–1948," MA thesis, Concordia University, Montreal, 2000.

Hudson, Michael. *Super Imperialism: The Origin and Fundamentals of U.S. World Dominance*. Sterling, VA: Pluto Press, 2003.

———. *Trade, Development and Foreign Debt*. London: Pluto Press, 1993.

Hunt, Barry, and Adrian Preston, eds. *War Aims and Strategic Policy in the Great War, 1914–1918.* Totowa, NJ: Rowman and Littlefield, 1977.

Hurstfield, Joel. *The Control of Raw Materials.* London: HMSO, 1953.

International Energy Agency. *China's Worldwide Quest for Energy Security.* Paris: OECD, 2000.

Jackson, Ian. *The Economic Cold War: America, Britain and East-West Trade, 1948–63.* New York: St. Martin's Press, 2001.

Jacques, Martin. *When China Rules the World: The End of the Western World and the Birth of a New Global Order.* New York: Penguin, 2012.

James, Harold. *The End of Globalization: Lessons from the Great Depression.* Cambridge, MA: Harvard University Press, 2001.

James, Lawrence. *The Rise and Fall of the British Empire.* New York: St. Martin's Press, 1996.

Janeway, Eliot. *The Economics of Crisis: War, Politics, and the Dollar.* New York: Weybright and Talley, 1968.

Jarausch, Konrad H. *The Enigmatic Chancellor: Bethmann Hollweg and the Hubris of Imperial Germany.* New Haven: Yale University Press, 1973.

Johnston, Alastair Iain. "Is China a Status-Quo Power?" *International Security* 27, no. 4 (2003): 5–56.

Joll, James, and Gordon Martell. *The Origins of the First World War.* 3rd ed. Harlow, UK: Pearson Longman, 2006.

Jordan, W. M. *Great Britain, France, and the German Problem, 1918–1938: A Study of Anglo-French Relations in the Making and Maintenance of the Versailles Settlement.* New York: Oxford University Press, 1943.

Judt, Tony. *Postwar: A History of Europe Since 1945.* New York: Penguin, 2005.

Kagan, Robert. *The Return of History and the End of Dreams.* New York: Knopf, 2008.

Kaldor, Mary, Terry Lynn Karl, and Yahia Said, eds. *Oil Wars.* London: Pluto Press, 2007.

Kawakami, K. K. *American-Japanese Relations: An Inside View of Japan's Policies and Purposes.* New York: Fleming Revell, 1912.

———. *The Real Japanese Question.* New York: Macmillan, 1921.

Keegan, John. *A History of Warfare.* New York: Knopf, 1993.

Kelly, Patrick J. *Tirpitz and the Imperial German Navy.* Bloomington: Indiana University Press, 2011.

Kemp, Peter, ed. *History of the Royal Navy.* New York: Putnam, 1969.

Kennedy, David M. *Freedom from Fear: The American People in Depression and War, 1929–1945.* New York: Oxford University Press, 2004.

Kennedy, Greg, ed. *Imperial Defence: The Old World Order 1856–1956.* London: Routledge, 2008.

Kennedy, Paul M. *The Rise and Fall of the Great Powers.* New York: Random House, 1987.

———, ed. *The War Plans of the Great Powers, 1880–1914.* Boston: Allen & Unwin, 1979.

Key, Helmer. *The New Colonial Policy.* London: Methuen, 1927.

Keynes, John Maynard. *The Economic Consequences of the Peace.* New York: Harcourt, Brace, 1920.

———. "National Self-Sufficiency." *Yale Review* 22, no. 4 (1933): 755–69.

Kidd, Benjamin. *The Control of the Tropics.* New York: Macmillan, 1898.

Kimball, Warren F. "Lend-Lease and the Open Door: The Temptation of British Opulence, 1937–1942." *Political Science Quarterly* 86, no. 2 (1971): 232–59.

Kindleberger, Charles P. "Commercial Policy Between the Wars." In *Cambridge Economic History of Europe.* Vol. 8, *The Industrial Economies: The Development of Economic and Social Policies.* Cambridge: Cambridge University Press, 1989.

Kirshner, Orin, ed. *The Bretton Woods–GATT System: Retrospect and Prospect After Fifty Years.* Armonk, NY: M. E. Sharpe, 1996.

Kissinger, Henry C. *A World Restored: Metternich, Castlereagh and the Problems of Peace, 1812–1822.* London: Victor Gollanz, 1974.

Klare, Michael T. *Blood and Oil: The Dangers and Consequences of America's Growing Petroleum Dependency.* New York: Metropolitan Books, 2004.

———. *Resource Wars: The New Landscape of Global Conflict.* New York: Metropolitan Books, 2001.

———. *Rising Powers, Shrinking Planet: The New Geopolitics of Energy.* New York: Metropolitan Books, 2008.

Knock, Thomas J. *To End All Wars: Woodrow Wilson and the Quest for a New World Order.* Princeton: Princeton University Press, 1995.

Koch, H. W., ed. *The Origins of the First World War.* 2nd ed. London: Macmillan, 1984.

Kolko, Gabriel. *Vietnam: Anatomy of a War 1940–1975.* London: Allen & Unwin, 1986.

Konoe, Fumimaro. "Reject the Anglo-American-Centered Peace." *Millard's Review* 7, no. 6 (1919).

Korbonski, Andrzej, and Francis Fukuyama. *The Soviet Union and the Third World*. Ithaca, NY: Cornell University Press, 1987.

Kraska, James. "How the United States Lost the Naval War of 2015." *Orbis* (Winter 2010): 35–46.

Krenn, Michael. *U.S. Policy Toward Economic Nationalism in Latin America, 1917–1929*. Wilmington, DE: SR Books, 1990.

Kuczynski, R. R. *Living-Space and Population Problems*. Oxford: Clarendon Press, 1939.

Kueh, Y. Y. *China's New Industrialization Strategy: Was Chairman Mao Really Necessary?* Northampton, MA: Edward Elgar, 2008.

Kurth, James. "Confronting a Powerful China with Western Characteristics." *Orbis* 56, no. 1 (2012): 39–59.

Labour Party, Advisory Committee. *The Demand for Colonial Territories and Equality of Economic Opportunity*. London: Labour Party, 1936.

Lambert, Nicholas A. *Planning Armageddon: British Economic Warfare in the First World War*. Cambridge, MA: Harvard University Press, 2012.

Lantané, John Holladay. *From Isolation to Leadership: A Review of American Foreign Policy*. Garden City, NY: Doubleday, 1918.

Lanteigne, Marc. "China's Maritime Security and the 'Malacca Dilemma.'" *Asian Security* 4, no. 2 (2008): 143–61.

Larew, Karl G. "The Royal Navy in the Battle of Britain." *The Historian* 54, no. 2 (1992): 243–54.

Layne, Christopher. *The Peace of Illusions: American Grand Strategy from 1940 to the Present*. Ithaca, NY: Cornell University Press, 2006.

League of Nations. *Raw-Material Problems and Policies*. Geneva, 1922.

League of Nations Union. *Bread and Honour*. London, 1938.

Lebra, Joyce C., ed. *Japan's Greater East Asia Co-Prosperity Sphere in World War II*. New York: Oxford University Press, 1975.

Lee, John. "China's Geostrategic Search for Oil." *Washington Quarterly* 35, no. 3 (2012): 75–92.

Leffler, Melvyn P. *The Elusive Quest: America's Pursuit of European Stability, 1919–1933*. Chapel Hill: University of North Carolina Press, 1979.

Leitenberg, Milton. "Deaths and Wars and Conflicts in the 20th Century." Cornell University Peace Studies Program Occasional Paper No. 29. 2006.

Leith, C. K. "The World Iron and Steel Situation in Its Bearing on the French Occupation of the the Ruhr." *Foreign Affairs* 1, no. 4 (1923).

Leith, C. K., J. W. Furness, and Cleona Lewis. *World Minerals and World Peace*. Washington, DC: Brookings Institution, 1943.

Lenin, V. I. *Imperialism, the Highest Stage of Capitalism*. New York: Penguin, 1969.

Leroy-Beaulieu, Paul. *De la colonisation chez les peuples modernes*. Paris, 1874.

Licklider, Roy. "The Power of Oil: The Arab Oil Weapon and the Netherlands, the United Kingdom, Canada, Japan, and the United States." *International Studies Quarterly* 32, no. 2 (1988): 205–26.

Lippmann, Walter. *U.S. Foreign Policy: Shield of the Republic*. Boston: Little, Brown, 1943.

List, Friedrich. *The National System of Political Economy*. New York: Longmans, Green, 1841 and 1909.

Louis, Wm. Roger. *Imperialism at Bay: The United States and the Decolonization of the British Empire, 1941–1945*. New York: Oxford University Press, 1977.

Louw, P. Eric. *Roots of the Pax Americana: Decolonization, Development, Democratization and Trade*. New York: Manchester University Press, 2010.

Luce, Henry R. "The American Century." *Life* (February 17, 1941): 64.

Lutz, Ralph Haswell, ed. *The Causes of the German Collapse in 1918*. Stanford, CA: Stanford University Press, 1934.

Mackinder, H. J. "The Geographical Pivot of History." *Geographical Journal* 23, no. 4 (1904): 421–37.

Magdoff, Harry. *The Age of Imperialism: The Economics of U.S. Foreign Policy*. New York: Monthly Review Press, 1969.

Mahan, A. T. *The Interest of America in Sea Power, Present and Future*. Boston: Little, Brown, 1897.

Mahnken, Thomas G. "China's Anti-Access Strategy in Historical and Theoretical Perspective." *Journal of Strategic Studies* 34, no. 3 (2011): 299–323.

Mandelbaum, Michael. *The Case for Goliath: How America Acts as the World's Government in the Twenty-first Century*. New York: Public Affairs, 2005.

Marshall, Jonathan. *To Have and Have Not: Southeast Asian Raw Materials and the Origin of the Pacific War*. Berkeley: University of California Press, 1995.

Massi, Ernesto. *La partecipazione delle colonie alla produzione delle materie prime*. Milan: Istituto Coloniale Fascista, 1937.

Matsuoka, Hiroshi. "Cold War Perspectives on U.S. Commitment in Vietnam." *Japanese Journal of American Studies* 11 (2000): 49–70.

Mau, Vladimir, and Irina Starodubrovskaya. *The Challenge of Revolution: Contemporary Russia in Historical Perspective*. New York: Oxford University Press, 2001.

Mayer, Arno J. *Politics and Diplomacy of Peacemaking: Containment and Counterrevolution at Versailles, 1918–1919*. New York: Knopf, 1967.

Mazower, Mark. *Governing the World: The History of an Idea*. London: Allen Lane, 2012.

McCauley, Martin. *Russia, America and the Cold War, 1949–1991*. New York: Pearson Longman, 2008.

McMeekin, Sean. *The Russian Origins of the First World War*. Cambridge, MA: Harvard University Press, 2011.

Mearsheimer, John J. *The Tragedy of Great Power Politics*. New York: Norton, 2001.

Medlicott, W. N. *The Economic Blockade*. Vol. 2. London: HMSO, 1952–59.

Mejcher, Helmut. "Oil and British Policy Towards Mesopotamia, 1914–1918." *Middle Eastern Studies* 8, no. 3 (1972): 377–91.

Michel, Serge, and Michel Beuret. *China Safari: On the Trail of China's Expansion in Africa*. New York: Nation Books, 2009.

Middle East Research and Information Project. "A Political Evaluation of the Arab Oil Embargo." *MERIP Reports* 28 (1974): 23–25.

Milner, Lord. *The Nation and the Empire*. London: Constable, 1913.

Milward, A. S. *The Reconstruction of Western Europe, 1945–51*. Berkeley: University of California Press, 1984.

———. *War, Economy, and Society, 1939–1945*. Berkeley: University of California Press, 1977.

Mirski, Sean. "Stranglehold: The Context, Conduct and Consequences of an American Naval Blockade of China." *Journal of Strategic Studies* 36, no. 3 (2013): 385–421.

Mitchell, B. R. *International Historical Statistics, Africa, Asia & Oceania, 1750–2005*. Basingstoke, UK: Palgrave Macmillan, 2007.

———. *International Historical Statistics, Europe, 1750–2005*. Basingstoke, UK: Palgrave Macmillan, 2007.

Mohr, Anton. *The Oil War*. New York: Harcourt, 1926.

Morley, James William, ed. *The Fateful Choice: Japan's Advance into Southeast Asia, 1939–1941*. New York: Columbia University Press, 1980.

Murray, Williamson, and Allan R. Millett, eds. *Military Innovation in the Interwar Period*. New York: Cambridge University Press, 1996.

Nathan, Andrew J., and Bruce Gilley. *China's New Rulers: The Secret Files*. 2nd rev. ed. New York: New York Review Books, 2003.

Naumann, Friedrich. *Central Europe.* New York: Knopf, 1917.

Newbold, J. T. Walton. *Capitalism and the War: The Economic Aims of the Great Powers.* London: National Labour Press, 1918.

O'Connor, Harvey. *World Crisis in Oil.* New York: Monthly Review Press, 1962.

Offer, Avner. *The First World War: An Agrarian Interpretation.* New York: Oxford University Press, 1989.

Office of the United States Chief Counsel for the Prosecution of Axis Criminality. *Nazi Conspiracy and Aggression: Opinion and Judgment.* Washington, DC: GPO, 1947.

Oki, Kazuhisa. "U.S. Food Export Controls Policy: Three Cases from 1973 to 1981." Program on U.S.-Japan Relations, Harvard University, 2008.

Olson, Mancur. *The Economics of the Wartime Shortage: A History of British Food Supplies in the Napoleonic War and in World Wars I and II.* Durham, NC: Duke University Press, 1963.

Osborne, Eric W. *Britain's Economic Blockade of Germany, 1914–1919.* New York: Frank Cass, 2004.

Overlack, Peter. "The Function of Commerce Warfare in Anglo-German Conflict to 1914." *Journal of Strategic Studies,* 20, no. 4 (1997): 94–114.

Overy, R. J. *The Air War, 1939–1945.* Washington, DC: Potomac Books, 2005.

Page, Benjamin I., and Tao Xie. *Living with the Dragon: How the American Public Views the Rise of China.* New York: Columbia University Press, 2010.

Pahl, Walter. *La lutte mondiale pour les matières premières.* Paris: Payot, 1941.

Painter, David S. *Oil and the American Century: The Political Economy of U.S. Foreign Policy, 1941–1954.* Baltimore: Johns Hopkins University Press, 1986.

Pakenham, Thomas. *The Scramble for Africa, 1876–1912.* New York: Random House, 1991.

Pant, Harsh V. "China on the Horizon: India's 'Look East' Policy Gathers Momentum." Philadelphia Foreign Policy Research Institute, Summer 2013.

Paolino, Ernest N. *The Foundations of the American Empire: William Henry Seward and U.S. Foreign Policy.* Ithaca, NY: Cornell University Press, 1973.

Pape, Robert A. *Bombing to Win: Air Power and Coercion in War.* Ithaca, NY: Cornell University Press, 1996.

Papers Relating to the Foreign Relations of the United States. Washington, DC: GPO, 1870– .

Parchami, Ali. *Hegemonic Peace and Empire: The Pax Romana, Britannica and Americana.* New York: Routledge, 2009.

Parrish, John B. "Iron and Steel in the Balance of World Power." *Journal of Political Economy* 64, no. 5 (1956).

Patrick, Stewart. *Best Laid Plans: The Origins of American Multilateralism and the Dawn of the Cold War.* Lanham, MD: Rowman & Littlefield, 2009.

Payton-Smith, D. J. *Oil: A Study in War-time Policy and Administration.* London: HMSO, 1971.

Peifer, Douglas C. "Power Projection Versus Distant Blockade: China, the German Analogy, and the New AirSea Operational Concept." Philadelphia: Foreign Policy Research Institute, Winter 2011.

Platt, D.C.M. *Finance, Trade, and Politics in British Foreign Policy, 1815–1914.* Oxford: Clarendon Press, 1968.

Pollard, Robert A. *Economic Security and the Origins of the Cold War, 1945–1950.* New York: Columbia Unversity Press, 1985.

Porter, Catherine. "Mineral Deficiency Versus Self-Sufficiency in Japan." *Far Eastern Survey* 5, no. 2 (1936): 9–14.

Porter, Robin. *From Mao to Market: China Reconfigured.* New York: Columbia University Press, 2011.

President's Materials Policy Commission. *Resources for Freedom: A Report to the President.* Washington, DC: GPO, 1952.

Preston, Antony. *History of the Royal Navy.* New York: Greenwich House, 1983.

Rachman, Gideon. *Zero-Sum Future: American Power in an Age of Anxiety.* New York: Simon & Schuster, 2011.

Ray, James Lee, and Thomas Webster. "Dependency and Economic Growth in Latin America." *International Studies Quarterly* 22, no. 3 (1978): 409–34.

Rimmer, Douglas. "Have-Not Nations: The Prototype." *Economic Development and Cultural Change* 27, no. 2 (1979):307–25.

Roberts, Richard. *Saving the City: The Great Financial Crisis of 1914.* New York: Oxford University Press, 2013.

Ross, Robert S., Øystein Tunsjø, and Zhang Tuosheng, eds. *US-China-EU Relations: Managing the New World Order.* New York: Routledge, 2010.

Rotberg, Robert I., ed. *China into Africa: Trade, Aid, and Influence.* Washington, DC: Brookings Institution Press, 2008.

Rowland, Benjamin M., ed. *Balance of Power or Hegemony: The Interwar Monetary System*. New York: New York University Press, 1976.

Roy, Denis. "Hegemon on the Horizon? China's Threat to East Asian Security." *International Security* 19, no. 1 (1994).

Royal Commission. *Report of the Royal Commission on Supply of Food and Raw Materials in Time of War*. London: HMSO, 1905.

Rubinstein, Alvin Z. *Moscow's Third World Strategy*. Princeton: Princeton University Press, 1998.

Ryan, David, ed. *The United States and Decolonization*. New York: St. Martin's Press, 2000.

Sacerdote, Cesare. *La guerra e la crisi del carbone in Italia*. Turin: Bocca, 1917.

Salmon, Patrick. *Scandinavia and the Great Powers, 1890–1940*. New York: Cambridge University Press, 1997.

Schacht, Hjalmar. "Germany's Colonial Demands." *Foreign Affairs* 15, no. 2 (1937): 223–34.

Schaffer, Ronald. *Wings of Judgment: American Bombing in World War II*. New York: Oxford University Press, 1985.

Schaller, Michael. *The American Occupation of Japan: The Origins of the Cold War in Asia*. New York: Oxford University Press, 1985.

Schatz, Arthur W. "The Anglo-American Trade Agreement and Cordell Hull's Search for Peace, 1936–1938." *Journal of American History* 57, no. 1 (1970): 85–103.

Schumpeter, Joseph. *Imperialism and Social Classes*. New York: A.M. Kelly, 1951.

Scissors, Derek. *China's Global Investment Rises: The U.S. Should Focus on Competition*. Washington, DC: Heritage Foundation, 2013.

Semmel, Bernard. *The Rise of Free Trade Imperialism*. Cambridge: Cambridge University Press, 1970.

Sethur, Frederick. "The Schuman Plan and Ruhr Coal." *Political Science Quarterly* 67, no. 4 (1952): 503–20.

Shambaugh, David. *Beautiful Imperialist: China Perceives America, 1972–1990*. Princeton: Princeton University Press, 1991.

———. *China Goes Global: The Partial Power*. New York: Oxford University Press, 2013.

———. "China's Military Views the World." *International Security* 24, no. 3 (1999–2000).

Simon, Sheldon W. "Conflict and Diplomacy in the South China Sea: The View from Washington." *Asian Survey* 52, no. 6 (2012): 995–1018.

Simonds, Frank H., and Brooks Emeny. *The Price of Peace: The Challenge of Economic Nationalism*. New York: Harper, 1935.

Skidelsky, Robert. *John Maynard Keynes: Fighting for Freedom, 1937–1946*. New York: Viking, 2000.

Smith, Steven Trent. *Wolf Pack: The American Submarine Strategy That Helped Defeat Japan*. Hoboken, NJ: Wiley, 2003.

Snyder, Timothy. *Bloodlands: Europe Between Hitler and Stalin*. New York: Basic Books, 2010.

Speer, Albert. *Inside the Third Reich*. New York: Macmillan, 1970.

Spykman, Nicholas John. *America's Strategy in World Politics: The United States and the Balance of Power*. New York: Harcourt, 1942.

Starling, Ernest H. "The Food Supply of Germany During the War." *Journal of the Royal Statistical Society* 83, no. 2 (1920): 225–54.

Steinberg, Jonathan. *Bismarck: A Life*. New York: Oxford University Press, 2011.

———. *The Deutsche Bank and Its Gold Transactions During the Second World War*. Munich: C. H. Beck, 1999.

———. *Yesterday's Deterrent: Tirpitz and the Birth of the German Battle Fleet*. New York: Macmillan, 1965.

Sternberg, Fritz. "Japan's Economic Imperialism." *Social Research* 12, no. 3 (1945).

Stevenson, D. *French War Aims Against Germany, 1914–1919*. New York: Clarendon Press, 1982.

Stokes, Doug, and Sam Raphael. *Global Energy Security and American Hegemony*. Baltimore: Johns Hopkins University Press, 2010.

Stokes, Raymond G. "The Oil Industry in Nazi Germany, 1936–1945." *Business History Review* 59, no. 2 (1985): 254–77.

Strachan, Hew. *The First World War*. New York: Oxford University Press, 2001.

Szlajfer, Henryk. *Economic Nationalism and Globalization: Lessons from Latin America and Central Europe*. Boston: Brill, 2012.

Tanzer, Michael. *The Energy Crisis: World Struggle for Power and Wealth*. New York: Monthly Review Press, 1974.

———. *The Race for Resources: Continuing Struggles over Minerals and Fuels*. New York: Monthly Review Press, 1980.

Taylor, Ian. "China's Oil Diplomacy in Africa." *International Affairs* 82, no. 5 (2006): 937–59.

Taylor, Peter J., ed. *Political Geography of the Twentieth Century: A Global Analysis*. New York: John Wiley, 1993.

Thorp, Willard L. "American Policy and the Soviet Economic Offensive." *Foreign Affairs* 35, no. 2 (1957).

Tooze, Adam. *The Wages of Destruction: The Making and Breaking of the Nazi Economy*. New York: Viking, 2007.

Trachtenberg, Marc. "French Foreign Policy in the July 1914 Crisis: A Review Article." H-Diplo/ISSF (November 2010).

———. *Reparation in World Politics*. New York: Columbia University Press, 1980.

Trameyre, Pierre L'Espagnol de la. *The World-Struggle for Oil*. New York: Knopf, 1924.

Treml, Vladimir G., and Robert Farrell, eds. *The Development of the Soviet Economy*. New York: Praeger, 1968.

United Nations. *International Trade Statistics Yearbook*. New York, 1985–.

———. *Yearbook of International Trade Statistics*. New York, 1951–84.

United States Strategic Bombing Survey. *Summary Report (Pacific War)*. Washington, DC: GPO, 1946.

U.S.-China Economic and Security Review Commission. *Hearing: China's Global Quest for Resources and Implications for the United States*. Washington, DC, January 26, 2012.

U.S. Congress, Committee on International Relations, Special Situations Subcommittee on Investigations. *Oil Fields as Military Objectives: A Feasability Study*. Washington, DC: GPO, 1975.

Usher, Roland Greene. *Pan-Germanism, from Its Inception to the Outbreak of the War: A Critical Study*. Boston: Houghton Mifflin, 1914.

Van Evera, Stephen. "The Cult of the Offensive and the Origins of the First World War." *International Security* 9, no. 1 (1984): 58–107.

Vernon, Raymond. *Two Hungry Giants: The United States and Japan in the Quest for Oil and Ores*. Cambridge, MA: Harvard University Press, 1983.

Viner, Jacob. "National Monopolies of Raw Materials." *Foreign Affairs* 4 (July 1926).

Voskuil, Walter H. "Coal and Political Power in Europe." *Economic Geography* 18, no. 3 (1942): 247–58.

Waldron, Arthur. "Political Aspects of Taiwan's Security in a New Asian Environment." Philadelphia: Foreign Policy Research Institute, Summer 2012.

Ward, Robert S. *Asia for the Asiatics? The Techniques of Japanese Occupation*. Chicago: University of Chicago Press, 1945.

Wells, H. G. *In the Fourth Year: Anticipations of a World Peace*. New York: Macmillan, 1918.

Wertheimer, Mildred S. *The Pan-German League, 1890–1914*. New York: Columbia University Press, 1924.

White, Hugh. *The China Choice: Why We Should Share Power*. Oxford: Oxford University Press, 2012.

Willkie, Wendell L. *One World*. New York: Simon & Schuster, 1943.

Wohlforth, William Curti. *The Elusive Balance: Power and Perceptions during the Cold War*. Ithaca, NY: Cornell University Press, 1993.

Woodrow Wilson Foundation. *The Political Economy of American Foreign Policy*. New York: Holt, 1955.

Woolf, Leonard. *Economic Imperialism*. London: Swarthmore Press, 1920.

Wrigley, Chris, ed. *The First World War and the International Economy*. Northampton, MA: Edward Elgar, 2000.

Yasuba, Yasukichi. "Did Japan Ever Suffer from a Shortage of Natural Resources Before World War II?" *Journal of Economic History* 56, no. 3 (1996): 543–60.

Yasuhara, Yoko. "The Myth of Free Trade: The Origins of COCOM 1945–1950." *Japanese Journal of American Studies* 4 (1991).

Yergin, Daniel. *The Prize: The Epic Quest for Oil, Money, and Power*. New York: Free Press, 2008.

Yoshihara, Toshi, and James R. Holmes. "The Next Arms Race." *The Diplomat*, January 2010.

Young, Ralph A. "British Imperial Preference and the American Tariff." *Annals of the American Academy of Political and Social Science* 141, no. 1 (1929).

Zacher, Mark W., ed. *The International Political Economy of Natural Resources*. Brookfield, VT: Edward Elgar, 1993.

Zagorsky, S. O. *State Control of Industry in Russia During the War*. New Haven: Yale University Press, 1928.

Zhang, Shu Guang. *Economic Cold War: America's Embargo Against China and the Sino-Soviet Alliance, 1949–1963*. Stanford, CA: Stanford University Press, 2001.

Zhao, Tingyang. "Rethinking Empire from a Chinese Concept 'All-Under-Heaven' (Tian-xia)." *Social Identities* 12, no. 1 (2006): 29–41.

Zhu, Zhiqun, ed. *The People's Republic of China Today: Internal and External Challenges*. Hackensack, NJ: World Scientific Publishing, 2011.

ACKNOWLEDGMENTS

The germ of this book goes back to reading reports of rapidly rising Chinese overseas investments in raw materials. The motive for these investments was not so much commercial profit as economic security. The reports seemed to me to raise important questions. Since the Second World War, countries had not competed aggressively for control of resources. Why should it be different now? Then, in 2010, Peter Garber, an economist and economic historian at Deutsche Bank, sent me a copy of an article by Hjalmar Schacht, Hitler's minister of economics, that appeared in *Foreign Affairs* in 1937. In it, Schacht made a case for the return of Germany's colonies on the grounds that, in a world without free trade, countries needed to control their sources of raw materials in order to survive. Schacht's arguments gelled with my previous concerns, leading me to think about the vital role in securing the long postwar peace played by the combination of free trade and Pax Americana—a combination taken for granted for many decades, but now perhaps threatened. This line of thought led first to an article in *Cicero*, the German current-affairs magazine, in early 2011, and then to this book.

I would like to thank all those who have helped me during this project. Michael Naumann, editor of *Cicero*, commissioned the original article. Jonathan Galassi and Eric Chinski at Farrar, Straus and Giroux showed their (I hope merited) confidence by their willingness to commission the book. Jonathan Steinberg, Mervyn King, and Peter Garber read all or parts of the manuscript, giving me a great deal of useful advice. The kind contribution of their time has done much to improve the book. Needless to say they are not responsible for its defects. I would also like to thank Richard Roberts for his input on the financial crisis of 1914 and Florian Weidinger for his help with China's overseas investments. Among the many people at Farrar, Straus and Giroux who have helped this book into production, Alex

Star deserves a particular mention. He has been the perfect editor, full of thoughtful suggestions and advice.

I would like to dedicate the book to my immediate and also my wider family, who have been a source of love and support in this as in all my other undertakings.

INDEX